On Guard for Thee:
War, Ethnicity, and the Canadian State, 1939-1945

Edited by

Norman Hillmer
Bohdan Kordan
Lubomyr Luciuk

Canadian Committee for the History of the Second World War
Comité canadien d'Histoire de la Deuxième Guerre mondiale
1988

Canadian Cataloguing in Publication Data

Main entry under title:

On guard for thee : war, ethnicity, and the Canadian state, 1939-1945
ISBN 0-660-12749-0

Includes summaries in French.
Includes bibliographical references.

1. Minorities—Canada—History—Congresses. 2. Minorities—Canada—Governmental policy—Congresses. 3. Canada—Politics and government—1935-1948—Congresses. I. Hillmer, Norman, 1942-   . II. Kordan, Bohdan S. III. Luciuk, Lubomyr Y., 1953-   . IV. Canadian Committee for the History of the Second World War.

D768.15.064   1988   323.1'71   C88-090227-2

© of the collective work, 1988, Minister of Supply and Services; © of the individual articles lies with the respective authors.

ALL RIGHTS RESERVED

No part of this book may be reproduced in any form
without permission in writing from the copyright holders.

ISBN 0-660-12749-0

Printed and bound in Canada by the Department of Supply and Services

©Minister of Supply and Services Canada 1988

Available in Canada through

Associated Bookstores
and other booksellers

or by mail from

Canadian Government Publishing Centre
Supply and Services Canada
Ottawa, Canada   K1A 0S9

Catalogue No. D64-2/1986E
ISBN 0-660-12749-0

Canadian Committee for the History of the Second World War
Comité canadien d'Histoire de la Deuxième Guerre mondiale
1988

Canadian Committee for the History of the Second World War
Comité canadien d'Histoire de la Deuxième Guerre mondiale

President/Président
Norman Hillmer

Vice-President/Vice-présidente
Patricia Roy

Secretary-Treasurer/Secrétaire-trésorier
Marc Milner

Assistant Secretary-Treasurer/Secrétaire-trésorier adjointe
Gloria McKeigan

Board of Directors/Conseil d'administration
Larry Aronsen
David Beatty
Réal Bélanger
James Boutilier
René Durocher
Rénald Fortier
Jean-Pierre Gagnon
Michael Hadley
Mary Halloran
Robert Keyserlingk
Malcolm MacLeod
Ken Osborne
Ruth R. Pierson
Bruno Ramirez
Hon. George F. Stanley
George Urbaniak

In memory of F. J. Hatch

Table of Contents

	Page
Preface	ix
The Second World War as an (Un) National Experience Norman Hillmer	xi
The Rise of a Bureaucracy for Multiculturalism: The Origins of the Nationalities Branch, 1939-1941 N.F. Dreisziger	1
Chauvinism and Canadianism: Canadian Ethnic Groups and the Failure of Wartime Information William R. Young	31
Breaking the Nazi Plot: Canadian Government Attitudes Towards German Canadians, 1939-1945 Robert H. Keyserlingk	53
Ethnicity on Trial: The Italians of Montreal and the Second World War Bruno Ramirez	71
A Prescription for Nationbuilding: Ukrainian Canadians and the Canadian State, 1939-1945 Bohdan S. Kordan and Lubomyr Y. Luciuk	85
The Evacuation of the Japanese Canadians, 1942: A Realist Critique of the Received Version J.L. Granatstein and Gregory A. Johnson	101
"As Far as Conscience Will Allow": Mennonites in Canada During the Second World War David Fransen	131
Fragmented Loyalties: Canadian Jewry, the King Government and the Refugee Dilemma Paula Jean Draper	151
Canada's Response to European Refugees, 1939-1945: The Security Dimension Donald Avery	179

Weird Science: Scientific Refugees and the Montreal
    Laboratory 217
  Robert Bothwell
Commentary
  Howard Palmer 233
  Harold Troper 241
  John English 247
Sommaire des articles 251
Contributors 261
Index 265

Preface

The papers in this collection were originally presented to a symposium entitled *Ethnicity, the State, and War: Canada and its Ethnic Minorities, 1939-1945*, held in the congenial atmosphere of the Donald Gordon Centre at Queen's University, Kingston, Ontario, 25-27 September 1986. Since that meeting some of the papers have been substantially revised by their authors.

We thank Robert Bothwell, John English, and J.L. Granatstein for their help in shaping both the conference and the volume. Gloria McKeigan, the assistant secretary-treasurer of the Canadian Committee for the History of the Second World War, was in effect the conference organizer. Her contribution to this book was no less crucial. Annie Rainville and Loretta Wickens organized the word-processing of the papers; at the publishing end, Gordon Pratt shepherded the volume through from manuscript to final product. Serge Bernier, Jean Pariseau, and Liliane Grantham ensured the acccuracy of the French summaries. Lisa Dillon and Christine Rowe gave administrative support, did proofreading, and a good deal more. Andrea Schlecht prepared the index. The editors are most grateful of all to N.F. Dreisziger, who joined them on the conference's organizing committee, offered editorial suggestions about the papers, and advised on the volume's introduction.

The Kingston conference was made possible through the generous financial support of the Social Sciences and Humanities Research Council of Canada, the Secretary of State for Multiculturalism, and the Department of National Defence.

We dedicate this book to F.J. Hatch, a gentle and generous colleague who was one of the founding members of the Canadian Committee for the History of the Second World War.

NH
BK
LL

Ottawa, Edmonton and Kingston
September 1988

The Second World War as an (Un) National Experience

Norman Hillmer

The twentieth century knows too well the characteristics and consequences of total war — the multiplication of violence; the mobilization of ideology; the destruction of old institutions and the creation of new; the unleashing of technology; the demand for change; innovation in social organization; and unprecedented levels of involvement on the part of ordinary women and men. Public enthusiasms in modern war are inevitably organized, but also spontaneous responses to pressure and patriotism and pride.[1] The British Second World War film, *Mrs. Miniver*, proclaimed: "This is...a war of the people — of all the people — and it must be fought, not only on the battlefield, but in the cities and in the villages, in the factories and on the farms, in the home and in the heart of every man, woman and child who loves freedom!"[2] Employing that cry of a "people's war," the historian Angus Calder writes that from 1940 to 1945 "the people of Britain were protagonists in their own history in a fashion never known before."[3]

The Second World War (and others) are frequently interpreted this way, as powerful "national experiences." The Canadian Committee for the History of the Second World War's most recent conference was directed at precisely that theme. The editor of the conference proceedings, which included studies of Canada, the United States, Great Britain, France, Norway and Yugoslavia, suggested in his introduction that the "1939-1945 War was a collective encounter of epic proportions. It was more than the sum of actions and memories of each participant. It was a shared experience, of national conflict, fought over an international battlefield. Mass involvement was matched by a massive communal commitment."[4]

J.L. Granatstein brings a similar perspective to his analysis of the political life of Canadians in the years 1939-1945, calling the period "Canada's War."[5] A shaky, fearful colonial people became vital, united, outward and forward-looking. At first glance this argument appears unexceptionable — historians have been making the same assertion for a long time — but did the war really contribute to a spirit of unifying, nationalizing, coming together? Professor Granatstein states that the "achievement of the war and the war effort was that Canada entered the peace as a nation," but most of his indices of nationalism and development — increased wealth, government activity, public confidence, and a strong new role in world affairs — are either difficult to measure or imperfect tests of national cohesion.[6] It seems clear that English Canadians were surer of themselves, and believed that their country was more powerful and influential in the world. The French probably shared in this sense of increased capacity, but it is as likely that their *own* strain of nationalism had been accentuated, just as it was in the admittedly more difficult circumstances of 1914-1918.[7] The most that can be said with certainty about French Canada is that there had not been the fragmentation and alienation of the First World War, and that French and English Canadians alike learned to hate a common enemy, first the Nazis and, after the war, the Soviets.

There were other Canadians. The ethnic minorities more than the French were out of the mainstream, and the burden of this volume is that Canada's War was not their war. The loyalty of the "ethnics," a word as awkward, ill-fitting and even insulting as the minority and immigrant experience could be, was in frequent question; all too often they felt deprived of the opportunity to be protagonists in their own history. At the same time that Ottawa stood on guard against the enemy without, the institutions of state and the not always silent majority put up their guard against ethnicity within.

Yet Canada in the Second World War was already a multicultural country. It had always been a nation of immigrants *par excellence*, but the composition of the population had gradually undergone an important transformation, as the sources (in addition to the United States) which fuelled Canadian immigration shifted from Great Britain and Northwest Europe to Eastern and Southern Europe. An increasing proportion of Canadians were from parts of the world that shared few cultural links with the Anglo-French-Celtic stock that dominated the country's demographic makeup. The 1941 Census set out the origins of Canadians as follows:[8]

Racial Origin	Population
British Isles races	**5,715,904**
English	2,968,402
Irish	1,267,702
Scottish	1,403,974
Welsh	74,663
Other	1,163
Other European races	**5,526,964**
French	3,483,038
Albanian	188
Austrian	37,715
Belgian	29,711
Bulgarian	3,260
Czech and Slovak	42,912
Danish	37,439
Finnish	41,683
German	464,682
Greek	11,692
Hungarian	54,598
Icelandic	21,050
Italian	112,625
Jewish	170,241
Lettish	975
Lithuanian	7,789
Luxembourger	489
Netherlands	212,863
Norwegian	100,718
Polish	167,485
Portuguese	763
Roumanian	24,689
Russian	83,708
Spanish	2,954
Swedish	85,396
Ukrainian	305,929
Yugoslavic	21,214
Other	1,158
Asiatic races	**74,064**
Chinese	34,627
Japanese	23,149
Other	16,288
Other races	**189,723**
All races	**11,506,655**

The British and French groups constituted eighty percent of the population during the Second World War — a huge preponderance, but down from 83 percent in 1921 and 88 percent in 1901. From century's beginning the proportion of European races (other than French) increased from 8.53 percent in 1901 to 17.76 in 1941. The numbers of Italians, to take not the most striking example, quadrupled in the decade 1901-1911. "Foreign European stocks," as the *Canada Year Book* phrased it, increased more than four times faster than did those of the various British groups in the important immigration decade of the 1920s. Over the years 1921-1941 the non-British, non-French part of the population grew by 63.9 percent. By the Second World War Germans occupied 4.04 percent of the population; Ukrainians, 2.66 percent; Scandinavians, 2.13 percent; Netherlanders, 1.85 percent; Jews, 1.48 percent; Poles, 1.45 percent; and Italians, 0.98 percent.[9] A "third great factor in Canada's population," trumpeted Winnipeg professor Watson Kirkconnell, "has emerged in the form of some two and a half million inhabitants of European origin who are neither Anglo-Saxon nor French."[10] Kirkconnell exaggerated the numbers — the Census showed 2,043,926 non-French Europeans in 1941[11] — but not the politico-cultural significance of this new force in Canadian life.

Kirkconnell was one of the few who rejoiced. Critics of the "new immigration" abounded in the universities and the public service. They worried about the displacement of "good" Canadians by "strangers," and the consequent flow of the former to the United States; the gathering of the foreign (that is, non-British) in certain parts of the country, the western provinces and urban centres especially; the predominance of young men among most groups of immigrants; the capacity of the land to absorb new immigration; the self-imposed segregation of groups such as Mennonites and Mormons into colonies, "little nations within a nation," where members were "disposed to retain their mother tongue, maintain old customs, harbour ancient prejudices and make little educational progress."[12] The foreign-looking and foreign-sounding, then, were on the rise, concentrated, and unassimilable. "While the bulk of Canadian citizens have been waiting for the assimilation to proceed," wrote a University of Toronto psychology professor, "the foreigner has been thinking of other things, and little Italy, little Austria, little Germany, little Ruthenia have stood in the way of a Canadian people with a common language and a common law."[13]

Arguments along these lines were heard in the economic good times of the 1920s and, more understandably, during the Depression. They were reflected in the public policy of the 1930s and even before: restrictive legislation, deportations and repatriations.[14] Preparing briefings for the Canadian delegation at the Imperial Conference of 1932, another University of Toronto professor, Hubert Kemp, set his face against all immigration, past and future. There was strong evidence, he said, to prove that the intake of the last fifty years had not led to any increase in the Canadian population that would not have taken place naturally: "Had the Canadian government absolutely prohibited immigration as early as 1881, or later in 1907, there is ample reason to believe that the population would still have exceeded ten millions today. It would, however, have been recruited from the native born and their offspring — so many of whom are now scattered through the United States."[15] The unsophisticated generalization that immigration caused emigration was echoed by O.D. Skelton, the most influential public servant of the day, and R.H. Coats, the dominion statistician.[16]

The Kemp outlook readily spilled over into commentaries on Canada's "melting pot problem," which was seen as arising largely from the immigration of non-British groups. Members of parliament, service clubs, newspapers, the Canadian Corps Association and the Native Sons of Canada were among those who desired "to maintain or increase the percentage of Canadian population arising from British stock." If immigration there was to be, the hardy British agriculturalist was the preferred choice.[17] Professor Kemp claimed that the "immigrant who arrives in Canada unable to speak either of the dominant languages of the country, deprived of the support of his old associations, ignorant of the new environment, debarred from the rights of citizenship, (which he could not exercise intelligently if he had them) has lost much of whatever feeling of civic responsibility he may have had in his native country and faces a grave problem of readjustment and assimilation." The natural tendency was to gravitate toward others of the same race, religion and language. In this way racial blocs had been built up on the prairies and, conspicuously, in the larger cities of the east. An inability to speak English or French, illiteracy, a lack of enthusiasm for naturalization, citizenship, or intermarriage — all were rife. "The presence in Canada," Kemp concluded, "of groups so diverse in racial origin, language, religion, political and economic backgrounds, and too often united by no common tie save residence in the same country and the determination to 'get on,' makes itself felt in many ways and is a grave obstacle to the development of national solidarity and a common culture."[18]

Attitudes such as this, anti-immigrant and anti-immigration, were widespread, and they became an essential part of the landscape of Canada's War on the home front. The ethnic boundaries were clearly drawn: the majorities, French and English, and then the minorities — as David Fransen puts it so eloquently in this volume, not two but a multitude of solitudes. It was all the easier to wonder about the loyalty of the identifiably different, especially if their "homeland" was the enemy. The Japanese more than any other group suffered from that unpalatable association. In the United States the Roosevelt administration made the assumption that aliens, foreign nationality groups from enemy *or* friendly countries, automatically represented a security risk. As the president wrote in 1942 to Federal Bureau of Investigation chief J. Edgar Hoover, "Have you pretty well cleaned out the alien waiters in the principal Washington hotels? Altogether too much conversation in the dining rooms!"[19]

This is not to say that as goes the United States so goes Canada. It is to suggest context, to suggest (as Donald Avery writes below) that total war does not encourage fine distinctions. Writing at the end of 1939, in a volume entitled *Canada, Europe, and Hitler*, Watson Kirkconnell tried to assure Canadians that the "third factor" posed no threat to national unity or security. The self-styled "chief authority on the vernacular literatures of the European-Canadians," Kirkconnell surveyed forty periodicals in fourteen languages. The result of this sympathetic endeavour was, he reported, a pattern of quite astonishing unanimity, unity, and loyalty.[20]

Kirkconnell's own evidence, however, was not as convincing. The foreign press, he said, revealed "potent and antagonistic forces at work." There were "active and astute" communists among the Russians, Ukrainians, Finns, and Hungarians; in German, Italian and Ukrainian communities, groups of equally loud opponents of Communism were dedicated to fascist ideals. Canada, Kirkconnell did not doubt, was a base for German and Italian political activities directed from abroad. The second largest German newspaper (the pre-eminent one being Catholic and anti-nazi) was not unique in being "rapturously enthusiastic over Hitler's régime" until the Nazi-Soviet pact, while Italian Canadians and their papers greeted the achievements of the "New Italy" with genuine pride.[21]

Bruno Ramirez demonstrates to readers of this book how the latter phenomenon was bound up with an evolving and genuinely indigenous ethnicity in Canada. But might not authorities at the time have had their doubts? Was it not their *duty* to be concerned, and to regard with skepticism the assurances of loyalty from the German and Italian communities? There is a great deal in this book about the woeful lack of knowledge in and puny resources of the federal government and the RCMP. Even so, Robert Keyserlingk admits that the government educated itself, internally admitted its errors, and, after the scares of 1939-1940 had safely passed, gradually freed the vast majority of internees and lifted the bulk of the restrictions against German and Italian Canadians. As Professor Ramirez makes clear, however, much damage had already been done. And the continuing suspicion and surveillance and the bureaucratic involvement (or, if one prefers, interference) in community life took its toll, helping to create a parcel of national experiences in Canada's War, not a single nationalism.

Only in the case of the Japanese did the government persist in widespread evacuation and internment followed by confiscation of land and deportations. J.L. Granatstein and Gregory Johnson wish to show that there were sufficient military and intelligence concerns to make a case, given the sudden and disastrous turn of events following Pearl Harbor, for the government's decision to evacuate the Japanese-Canadians from the coast. They make it clear, however, that racism and public opinion, two of our collection's major themes, combined to make the Japanese the victims of a society and government that failed to stand up for the ideals for which it claimed to be fighting. The evacuation, they argue, *might* have been justified; later actions against the Japanese Canadian people and their land were not.

At the core of our book is a discussion about the competence and creativity of the government in its wartime dealings with ethnic minorities and refugees. Many of the authors are critical of the suspension of civil liberties, the cruel impact of a fearful and xenophobic public opinion, and the overzealousness and even immorality of many of the government's actions. The bureaucracy and the police, it is generally agreed, were understaffed and ignorant of ethnicity. N. F. Dreisziger applauds those who did care and try to act, but points out that the machinery for involving and accommodating the ethnic peoples simply did not exist. Nor was the creation of the Nationalities Branch of the National War Services Department, with its grandiose staff of two or three, an adequate response to a real need.

The Canadian Committee for the History of the Second World War brought an interdisciplinary group of academics together two years ago to redress an historiographical imbalance, to study aspects of Canada's War — Canada's national experiences — that have remained largely unknown for more than forty years. David Matas wrote recently that "Canada is not a blank slate, a place where we wipe clean the collective consciousness of the people who compose it. We cannot ignore our history. And, except for our aboriginal people, our history is, in part, foreign history. Canada is a multicultural country. We cannot preserve and promote our cultures if we deny the collective memory and consciousness that is part of them."[22] The role of history and historians is to remember and try to understand, not to condemn or condescend. The committee hopes that this volume makes a contribution to that complex process.

Notes

1. See Raymond Aron, *The Century of Total War* (Boston, 1966), *passim*.

2. Quoted in J.L. Granatstein, *Canada's War: The Politics of the Mackenzie King Government, 1939-1945* (Toronto, 1975), vii.

3. Angus Calder, *The People's War: Britain — 1939-1945* (New York, 1969), 17

4. Sidney Aster, ed., *The Second World War as a National Experience* (Ottawa, 1981), 1

5. Granatstein, 424

6. *Ibid.*, 419-22

7. See the opinion polls in *ibid.*, 421, and Margaret Prang, "Nationalism in Canada's First Century," Canadian Historical Association, *Historical Papers 1968*, 115

8. Canada, Dominion Bureau of Statistics, *Eighth Census of Canada, 1941*, vol. IV (Ottawa, 1946), Table 1, "Population by Racial Origin and Sex, for Provinces and Territories, 1941," 2-3.

9. Canada, Dominion Bureau of Statistics, *The Canada Year Book, 1945* (Ottawa, 1945), 103-6

10. Watson Kirkconnell, *Canada, Europe, and Hitler* (Toronto, 1939), 116

11. *The Canada Year Book, 1945*, 104.

12. W.G. Smith, *A Study in Canadian Immigration* (Toronto, 1920), 146-7 and, more generally, 137-49. See also Gerald E. Dirks, *Canada's Refugee Policy: Indifference or Opportunism?* (Montreal, 1977), 50-1, and two articles in *MacLean's Magazine*: W.A. Irwin, "Can We Stem the Exodus," 15 May 1927, 3-4, 34, 36, 38, and A.R.M. Lower, "Can Canada Do Without the Immigrant?" 1 June 1930, 3-4, 70-1

13. Smith, 147

14. Jean R. Burnet, with Howard Palmer, *"Coming Canadians": An Introduction to a History of Canada's Peoples* (Toronto, 1988), 38; Irving Abella and Harold Troper, *None is too Many: Canada and the Jews of Europe 1933-1948* (Toronto, 1982), 5-6

15. Thomas Fisher Rare Book Room, University of Toronto, collection of material relating to the development of immigration policy, H.R. Kemp, "Canadian Immigration Policy," June 1932.

16. *Ibid.*, memorandum of Coats, attached to Coats to H.H. Stevens, 16 March 1932; Ian M. Drummond, *Imperial Economic Policy 1917-1939: Studies in Expansion and Protection* (London, 1974), 93, 96-8

17. Dirks, 52-3

18. Kemp, "Canadian Immigration Policy," June 1932. The American consul general in Montreal wrote: "The ethnical structure of Canada today is distinctly agglomerate, not conglomerate. Little fusion has taken place, and not very much is in immediate prospect." United States National Archives, State Department Records, 842.55/409, memorandum of Wesley Frost, 18 May 1935, 2; see also 1-3.

19. Lorraine M. Lees, "National Security and Ethnicity: Contrasting Views During World War II," *Diplomatic History*, 11, 2 (Spring 1987), 113

20. Kirkconnell, 188, and chapter XI

21. *Ibid.*, 121 ff., 165 ff., 199-200. See also W.R. Young's paper below, 42.

22. David Matas, "Old Country Turmoils," *The Globe and Mail* (Toronto), 24 September 1988

The Rise of a Bureaucracy for Multiculturalism: The Origins of the Nationalities Branch, 1939-1941

N.F. Dreisziger

Historians generally agree that, in September of 1939, Canada was unprepared to fight a war in Europe.[1] This statement is true both of the country's military effectiveness and its political and psychological preparedness for war. On the eve of the Second World War Canada lacked, among other things, the institutional infrastructure needed to organize Canadian society for total war. In particular, the country did not possess the administrative machinery to involve in the war effort the portion of the Canadian population that was neither of British nor of French background.

This deficiency was recognized early during the war by several members of the country's élite and efforts were made to remedy the situation. The most notable result was the establishment of the Nationalities Branch of the Department of National War Services, along with the Advisory Committee on Co-operation in Canadian Citizenship. This administrative apparatus — the Branch in particular — is significant not only from the standpoint of Canada's wartime evolution, but also from the perspective of the country's long-term development. The present-day governmental machinery that deals with the non-British and non-French elements of the population, the multiculturalism sector of the Department of the Secretary of State, is a direct descendant of the wartime Nationalities Branch.

While the Nationalities Branch was the progenitor of today's Multiculturalism Canada, it would be a mistake to equate the Canadian federal government's wartime policies toward "New Canadians" with the multicultural policies that evolved in this country a quarter century later. Few people associated with the creation and work of the Branch were thinking in terms of the preservation and promotion of "heritage cultures," which are the basic aims of today's multicultural policies. Nevertheless, the institutional tie and the similarities between many of the sentiments expressed then and now justify linking the wartime developments to the evolutionary chain that has resulted in the Canadian multiculturalism of recent decades.

While the Canadian government of the late 1930s had done little to prepare the country for involvement in a major European war, it did take steps to meet an international emergency on the domestic front. On March 14, 1938, the government of Prime Minister Mackenzie King set up an interdepartmental committee to prepare emergency legislation. The committee reported to Parliament in July 1939. Its report became the basis of the famous — or infamous — Defence of Canada Regulations, proclaimed by the Canadian government on 3 September under the War Measures Act, enabling the Cabinet to govern the country without reference to Parliament.[2]

The Defence of Canada Regulations (henceforth DOCR) amounted to a wholesale suspension of civil rights in the country. Historian Ramsay Cook summed them up appropriately when he observed that they were "too general in phraseology, too capable of abuse, and ... too free from control by parliament."[3] A further problem that made the regulations unpleasant for large sections of the country's population was the fact that they were being constantly revised. Frequent, in some cases weekly, revisions to the regulations' provisions meant that few people knew exactly how they were to be interpreted; as a result, the rules were applied differently by the various authorities concerned with their enforcement. Most severely affected were recent immigrants to Canada. Under the regulations, those "enemy aliens" considered potentially dangerous to the Canadian state or the Allied war effort were interned, while those not so regarded were paroled. People in the latter category were placed under a strict regime: they were required to report monthly to the local police, and they had certain restrictions placed on their movements. In time, aliens could gain exemption from these requirements on personal application, through the obtaining of the so-called "exemption certificates." In June 1940 the regulations were amended to apply not only to enemy nationals but also to thousands of naturalized immigrants from enemy countries (Germany and Italy — and after December 1941 — still other Axis countries, as well as Japan).

While this severe regime was imposed on many immigrants through Regulation 24 of the DOCR, others were affected by Regulation 21, a measure calling for the "preventative detention" of individuals who were suspected of harbouring anti-state plans or sentiments. In the early years of the war, the immigrants who were thus detained tended to be members of organizations that were considered dangerous to the Canadian war effort, such as the National Socialist Workers' Party in Canada, the German Labour Front, the Canadian Society for German Culture (better known as the *Bund*), and the Communist Party of Canada.[4] Other regulations provided for the closure of buildings used by proscribed organizations and for the closing down of newspapers.

The DOCR, and Regulation 21 in particular, became the subject of controversy from the time of their promulgation to the war's end. Particularly heated were the debates on them in the fall of 1939 and throughout much of 1940. Until the spring of 1940, the regulations were often criticized as being unreasonably restrictive; after the start of Hitler's Western offensive in May, they were deemed by many to be too lenient.[5] The swing in public opinion during the crisis of the spring of 1940 was paralleled by changes in the opinions of even the men who advised the prime minister. This, at least, is what Mackenzie King thought. "It amuses me a little," he stated in his diary on May 24, "how completely some men swing to opposite extremes ... no one was stronger than [O.D.] Skelton [against the DOCR].... Equally, [J.W.] Pickersgill and [Arnold] Heeney, and others around me. Now, Skelton begins to see the need of even going further in some ways than we have thus far gone."[6]

An important part of the debate on the DOCR centered on the provisions concerning enemy aliens. On this issue public opinion was just as divided as it was on the whole question of wartime emergency measures. From the Cabinet War Committee down to the "man in the street," attitudes varied and kept changing throughout the war. Immigrants from enemy countries had their sympathizers and friends in Cabinet (J.G. Gardiner, T.A. Crerar, J.T. Thorson), in the public service (Norman Robertson, Thomas C. Davis, Hugh Keenleyside, H.F. Angus, among others) and among academics and writers (Watson Kirkconnell, George Simpson, Robert England, Murray Gibbon).

However, there were detractors as well, people who favoured the imposition of stringent restrictions on "enemy aliens." Support for such measures was expressed from time to time by a wide variety of Canadian citizens and organizations, ranging from local veterans' clubs, to the RCMP, as well as prominent provincial and federal politicians.[7]

In fact the debate on the treatment of enemy aliens pre-dated the outbreak of war in Europe. It began with the deliberations of an interdepartmental committee established by the government in 1938, the Committee on Enemy Aliens and Enemy Alien Property. This committee generated suggestions for restrictions on aliens in Canada in the event of war; however, the views expressed both inside and outside this body were not at all unanimous. While some people recommended the wholesale internment of enemy nationals in the event of hostilities, others — including enlightened individuals such as Norman Robertson of External Affairs — called for government programmes to promote the integration of immigrants into Canadian society.[8]

After the outbreak of the war, discussions on the treatment of enemy aliens continued in Ottawa. While RCMP representatives on various committees dealing with this issue continued to advocate strict measures against radicals — and, especially, leftists — Robertson advised caution. In his efforts he found an ally in J.F. MacNeill of the Department of Justice. In fact, during the early days of the war, Robertson and MacNeill (along with Inspector Ernest Bevin of the RCMP) sat on a hastily established committee responsible for reviewing the cases of interned aliens.[9] In this capacity they became aware of the hardships that the DOCR imposed on many people. This experience no doubt reinforced Robertson's and MacNeill's sensitivities to the wartime plight of immigrant ethnics.

Robertson's record in this respect is well known.[10] Little, however, has been written on the efforts of MacNeill, which also had an important impact. It appears that, as early as November 1939, MacNeill had become disturbed by the government's excessive reliance on police measures to deal with the immigrant alien population and decided to approach the prime minister. Later that month or early in December, MacNeill spoke about his convictions to Walter J. Turnbull, one of Mackenzie King's aides. A few days later MacNeill followed up his comments with a lengthy memorandum.[11]

MacNeill began by saying that in recent months he had met people who came to Canada from parts of Europe that were under Nazi Germany's rule. He found many of these immigrants apprehensive "as to the treatment which they might receive at the hands of Government officers." These people often lacked any knowledge of English or French, were not familiar "with our system of government" and got their information from their own press. MacNeill continued: "We make very little if any attempt to tell them what we stand for, but the representatives of the various European propaganda mills flood them with all sorts of Nazi, Fascist and Communist propaganda ... in their own language." What was needed, according to MacNeill, was spending:

> a little time and money on making good citizens out of the various races we have in this country.... We ought to see that every citizen is told in language he can understand what we stand for, what we are fighting for and the principles we must hold to if we are to survive the war.... Much has been made of the fact that foreigners in this country read Communist literature.... they read it because it is the reading material most readily available ... and is supplied in profusion.... I suggest that instead of answering this type of propaganda with repressive police measures, we should do so by reasoned argument ... in simple but well written articles published in their own language ... printed and distributed free of charge....

MacNeill, who no doubt wrote his memo with the hope that it would be shown to Mackenzie King, next quoted from one of the prime minister's recent public letters on the war effort, in which King had stressed that Canadians had to unite "in freedom" to win the war. "This message," MacNeill added, "should reach all Canadians in their own language," and he went on that "some one, or perhaps several (persons)," should be hired "to state our case."

Turnbull sent MacNeill's memorandum to Arnold Heeney, principal secretary to the prime minister. Heeney then passed the letter on to King himself. He also suggested that the prime minister might wish to refer the memorandum to the Cabinet Committee on Public Information.[12] King responded after the Christmas holidays. MacNeill's letter was "an excellent one" and "its suggestion should be followed up."[13]

MacNeill had requested two-fold action by the government. One was in the realm of propaganda. In one place in his memorandum, MacNeill asked that pamphlets be published to explain the war to English- and French-speaking Canadians, as well as to those who spoke other

5

European languages. But that was not enough. MacNeill also recommended a bureaucratic solution: that a person or persons be hired to handle relations with the foreign-born residing in Canada.

After many delays, the Canadian government did as MacNeill had suggested. It undertook "information work" among ethnics and established the institutional framework for dealing with them. The propaganda work would be done under the auspices of the Bureau of Public Information (after 1942 the Wartime Information Board) and consisted of such steps as the publication of pamphlets dealing with, or intended for, Canada's foreign-born population. The best known of these was Watson Kirkconnell's pamphlet, *Canadians All*.[14] The creation of a government office to deal with immigrant ethnic groups, the focus of this paper, would become a reality with the establishment of the Nationalities Branch of the Department of National War Services. But the wheels of the Canadian government turned slowly even during the Second World War, and much time — more than a year — passed before the bureaucratic apparatus envisioned by MacNeill began to materialize.

The event that jolted the Canadian government out of its complacency was the opening of the Western Front in Europe in the spring of 1940 and the ensuing crisis in Canada.

When Hitler invaded the Netherlands during the second week of May 1940, the Canadian government was in the midst of discussing the extension of propaganda work among the country's foreign-language population. The subject was being considered by a committee made up of the top two officials of the Bureau of Public Information and representatives of the Department of External Affairs and the prime minister's office.[15] The committee's recommendations were summarized in a memorandum by L.W. Brockington, a counsellor of the Cabinet War Committee who was attached to the prime minister's office. The most important suggestion was no doubt the appeal for the concentration of all propaganda work within a single government department. Other specific recommendations were for the translation of the Mackenzie King's radio addresses into such languages as Polish and Ukrainian, and the giving of government grants to the Canadian Clubs so that they could extend their war information work to foreign-born groups.[16]

It was at this time that the international crisis of the spring of 1940 was unleashed on Canada. While the events in Europe did not constitute an immediate military threat to the country, the reports that German advances in Holland and Belgium were greatly facilitated by the work of fifth columnists were widely believed and caused much hysteria. This outpouring of public concern about enemy agents "within the gates" manifested itself in hundreds of telegrams and letters to the prime minister, demanding every measure from the internment of all Canadian residents of German background to the creation of home defence forces to guard public buildings and strategic installations.

Within a week of the start of the German offensive, the panic in Canada had reached an "hysterical pitch." A "deluge of messages" was flooding the prime minister's office. Vigilante groups were being formed in many Canadian cities. The members of one concerned group wondered if they had authority to shoot on sight any "enemy agents" caught causing damage to utilities. Not surprisingly, by 22 May, Mackenzie King's aides were warning him of "approaching riot conditions" especially in centres of high immigrant (and, in particular, German) concentrations such as Kitchener and Toronto. The hysteria began to subside only during the middle of June.[17]

The panic generated by the Germans' spring military successes in Europe had important consequences. It prompted Mackenzie King's administration to action. Part of the government's measures consisted of public announcements intended to assure the Canadian public that the situation was in hand and that the authorities were able to deal with any emergency. The government also stressed that public hysteria was only helping the cause of the enemy.[18] The other aspect of Ottawa's reaction to the crisis was the passing of the National Resources Mobilization Act and the establishment of the Department of National War Services. One of the functions of the newly created department was to oversee the dissemination of information for the government. The main recommendation of the committee that had been considering the government's handling of information in May 1940 was thus implemented.

In fact, the government's programme of action was put into effect with relative dispatch. The intention to create the new department having been announced by King in the middle of June, the appropriate legislation was put before the new session of Parliament on 12 July and was passed the same day. Also on that day, J.G. Gardiner, the minister of agriculture, was appointed minister of national war services. A few days later he was named to the Cabinet War Committee, giving both him and his new ministry additional political status.[19] A day later, moreover, Gardiner was given authority over the Bureau of Public Information. Gardiner's involvement in these matters would leave an important mark on the course of events during the next several months.

The "panic" of May and June 1940 had further fallout. During the crisis there had been a near-wholesale dismissal of immigrants of German or Italian background — or people with German or Italian sounding names in some cases — from their place of employment in many Canadian cities. They often found it difficult if not impossible to find new employment, and in some cases they were denied relief by local authorities.

The problem was brought to the attention of officials in Ottawa and referred to the Committee on Enemy Aliens and Enemy Alien Property. Norman Robertson, a committee member, prepared a memorandum which listed the dangers resulting from this situation: the exclusion of a class of people from the national economy was wasteful; it had harmful effects on family life and individual health; and it was dangerous even from the point of view of public security.

> This situation [he continued] is rapidly making enemies out of people who should at least have been allies, and is aggravating the Police problem very considerably. People who were good citizens when usefully employed are becoming first class raw material for enemy agents and propagandists when they find themselves out of a job for no fault of their own, with savings dwindling and no relief available....[20]

Robertson's memo was passed on to Minister of Justice Ernest Lapointe by E.H. Coleman, the under secretary of state and custodian of enemy alien property, with sympathetic comments. Lapointe in turn approached Gardiner.[21] Lapointe's letter touched upon a subject that was obviously close to the heart of the minister of national war services. In his reply to the minister of justice, Gardiner poured out his feelings on the subject: "During the last war we did a great deal of damage to the citizenship of our country in the view which we took toward the enlisting of Europeans in our armies. We made those from Europe ... feel that they were not on an equal basis with our own people. There has been a tendency toward the same attitude during this war...." Next, Gardiner expressed the hope that in the government's efforts to create "an entirely different sentiment during this war to that which prevailed during the last," use will be made of his department's Bureau of Public

Information, "as well as another branch which I hope to have established." He then went on to conclude: "I am pleased to note that you think this work ought to be taken up within this department. If that is the wish of the whole Government, I shall be more than pleased to see that a real effort is put forth to create an organization which will be helpful toward making these people feel that we welcome them as loyal citizens of this country."[22]

During the next several weeks the question of dealing with the country's immigrant ethnic population re-surfaced in another context. In the United States a series of radio broadcasts were directed at that country's foreign-speaking population. This circumstance gave rise to suggestions in Ottawa that similar measures should be undertaken in Canada. One of the officials who seems to have agreed was Under Secretary of State for External Affairs O.D. Skelton.

Apparently, Skelton expressed these views in a letter he addressed to Coleman on 11 October. Coleman's reply came ten days later. It did not recommend the radio broadcasts for Canada. Coleman, however, felt that there was a need for a different kind of propaganda directed at the country's foreign-speaking population. Referring to his own experiences in the Canadian West, he suggested that a publicity campaign be started, using the ethnic "press facilities" that were shut down by the government. "We might accomplish a great deal," Coleman argued, "by publishing papers or pamphlets in Finnish, Ukrainian and other languages."

To undertake this work of "patriotic" publicity, Coleman sought the services of Robert England, the former director of the CNR's Immigration Department and the author of various studies on Central and East European settlements in the Canadian West. But England had been hired by the Department of National Defence. Consequently, Coleman thought of approaching Watson Kirkconnell, another former Westerner who was knowledgeable about immigrant groups. Kirkconnell had recently left Winnipeg's Wesley College to take up an appointment at McMaster University in Hamilton. Coleman was planning to discuss this matter with people in the Department of National War Services, "which might assume responsibility for the work."[23]

These views struck a responsive chord in Skelton. In his next letter to Coleman he agreed that radio broadcasts on the American pattern were not suited for Canada. Nevertheless, he expressed keen interest in the plans for a publicity campaign using the press under the control of the Custodian of Enemy Alien Property. "I think there is a real opportunity," Skelton concluded, "for good work here and would be glad to learn how your projects are developing."[24]

By the end of October 1940, then, some of the most influential people in the country had become aware of the problem of the treatment of Canada's immigrant population from enemy or enemy-controlled lands in Europe. They included members of the Cabinet (Gardiner and Lapointe), as well as the country's senior civil servants (Skelton, Coleman, and Robertson). With their interests aroused, and sympathies for the problem at hand expressed, the ground was prepared for action. But the two people who would do the actual building of the bureaucratic infrastructure did not emerge on the Ottawa scene until the second half of 1940. They were the Englishman Tracy Philipps and the Saskatchewan politician and judge, T.C. Davis. Because of the prominent role they would play in subsequent events, it is necessary to introduce them in some detail.

James Erasmus Tracy Philipps came from an old, upper-class family, many of whose members had served Britain and the Empire with distinction as soldiers, scholars or civil servants. Philipps himself had had a most interesting career. He had studied at Oxford and had served in the First World War in Africa, after which he had been in the service of the British government on various diplomatic and intelligence-gathering assignments. He had travelled extensively in Africa, the Middle East and Eastern Europe, and published papers in scientific and anthropological journals. He had an honorary doctorate from the University of Durham and prided himself on his linguistic skills. Philipps spoke French, German and Italian, and claimed knowledge of Turkish as well as thirteen African languages.

More remarkable than his background was Philipps' personality. He was a man of determination, boundless energy, and a great deal of ambition. He gained the admiration of some people while he provoked hostility in others. In May 1940 Philipps' sponsors, the National Council of Education of Canada, had a flyer designed outlining the purpose of his impending Canadian visit as well as his qualifications and background. Its statements reveal a lot about the man who was to become central to the story of Canada's wartime attempts in dealing with her immigrant ethnic population. There can be little doubt that the flyer was drafted by Philipps himself. Its somewhat cumbersome and pretentious prose is full of his high self-esteem and his propensity for unabashed exaggeration. Philipps' "addresses," the flyer proclaimed, will be "supported by a scientific and intimate knowledge, will be welcomed by many people in their efforts to appraise what is happening in Eastern Europe and the Near East." On such questions, the flyer promised, "Tracy Philipps can speak out of rich experience, from a long and scientific study."[25]

Once in Canada, Philipps was handed over to the Association of Canadian Clubs, which became the sponsor for his lectures. Philipps' schedule must have been hectic. He later claimed that in the first year of his Canadian stay he had given 450 speeches.[26] At first, ethnic groups were not singled out as "targets" for his oratory; however, in the early autumn of 1940 it was arranged that he should repeat his tour, this time talking not to English and French Canadians, but to members of certain foreign-language communities. The new tour was initiated by the Department of National War Services and officially sponsored by the various Canadian Clubs. In this way Philipps' expenses were paid (from monies provided to the Canadian Clubs by Ottawa), but he did not become publicly associated with the government.[27]

Two of the ethnic communities that Philipps was directed to focus attention upon were the Ukrainian and the Polish. For his work among these particular immigrants, Philipps was assigned his friend, Vladimir J. Kaye (Kisilevsky). Kaye was well-suited for his assignment. His mother was known for the role she had played in the politics of the Ukrainian minority in Poland, and Kaye himself knew the Canadian West, having lived in Manitoba after he had come to Canada for the first time, in 1924. Later he went to Britain to enroll in the University of London's School of Slavonic and East European Studies. After the outbreak of the war he became a journalist. By early 1940 he had taken on another responsibility: the directorship of what was known in London as the Ukrainian Press Bureau. In the spring of 1940, however, he decided to return to Canada at about the same time as Philipps. Incidentally, when Kaye had married an English girl not long before his departure from England, Philipps was his best man, and the newly-weds were guests at Philipps' country home.[28]

Together, Philipps and Kaye visited various locations, mainly in the Canadian West. While Philipps spoke from the platform, his friend worked behind the scenes talking to members of the audience and gauging their reactions. One of their most important assignments in this period was attendance at the founding convention of the Ukrainian Canadian Committee early in November. Later Philipps claimed that his mission was undertaken at the request of the Department of National War Services, on the suggestion of Ukrainian-Canadian church leaders.[29] At this meeting, a semblance of Ukrainian-Canadian unity was achieved, apparently at the urgings of Philipps.[30]

Philipps' efforts served him well. His value was brought to the attention of a number of people on Parliament Hill. A certain W.C. Barrie reported on Philipps' speeches to J.A. MacKinnon, the minister of trade and commerce, in enthusiastic terms. Barrie used superlatives to describe the speeches: they were "inspiring" and Philipps was a "spell binder." Moreover, according to Barrie, Philipps had achieved Ukrainian-Canadian unity, a fact acknowledged by the Ukrainians themselves.[31] Barrie's letter was shown to various people in Ottawa, including Robertson. At the same time, praise for Philipps reached O.D. Skelton through another source.[32] By the end of 1940, then, Philipps was poised to assume a more important role in the Canadian government's efforts to deal with the problem of immigrant ethnic groups.

Thomas C. Davis was called to Ottawa in July 1940 from the Court of Appeal of Saskatchewan to become an associate deputy minister of the new Department of National War Services. Before becoming a judge, Davis had been the attorney general of his province. He was an energetic, competent man, knowledgeable about immigrant groups and sympathetic to them. J.W. Dafoe, editor of the *Winnipeg Free Press*, rightly described him as "a sociable, lively, and agreeable person of first-rate ability."[33]

In Davis, Canada's underprivileged immigrants found a true friend. He had developed respect and trust for immigrants in Saskatchewan, where the proportion of European immigrants in the population was high and where these people were accepted as Canadian citizens, equal in status to native-born Canadians. When Davis came East, he discovered, to his consternation, that the situation was not the same in that part of Canada. In February 1942, he explained his discovery to an acquaintance, H.R. MacMillan of the Wartime Merchant Shipping Ltd.:

> [In the West] ... we accept [immigrants] as Canadian citizens, and we do not discriminate against them because of the land of their origin.... When I came

east, I was literally astounded to find the different attitude which prevails down here. No attempt is made to distinguish between Ukrainians, the Poles, the Swedes, the Norwegians, the Danes or anything else. If the name of an individual happens to be something other than an Anglo-Saxon name, he is immediately branded as a German, and there is a very great tendency on the part of industrial organizations, to refuse to employ persons with foreign-sounding names.[34]

Davis' sympathies for the innocent "enemy alien" immigrants who fell victim to anti-alien feelings in the Canada of 1940 were expressed in a letter he wrote soon after his arrival in Ottawa. He explained that people with German or Italian names were "set upon by the people in their communities and they are more or less harassed and persecuted unjustly and unwisely...." He further complained that such people were not accepted for the armed forces and could not get unemployment or other relief since in some provinces able-bodied men were not eligible for social assistance.[35]

Once established in his Ottawa office that autumn, Davis got down to formulating policy to counterbalance the treatment immigrants were receiving from the Canadian public. Sending Philipps to talk to certain ethnic organizations was only one of his measures. More important steps would follow later. One of these came hard on the heels of a speech Watson Kirkconnell delivered before the Canadian Club of Toronto early in November. The long-time friend of Canadian immigrant groups of European ancestry suggested the creation of a committee to deal with the foreign element in the Canadian population. This suggestion was taken up by Davis, who began lobbying for it among high-ranking officials in Ottawa.[36]

Davis' plan was outlined to his superior, Gardiner, on 13 November. He began by saying that "every step" had to be taken to "create good feeling" among the foreign-born in Canada, and that "there never was a time when the possibility of doing this was better...." The government's first task was to engage in extensive information work among these people, through the Bureau of Public Information, making use of the facilities of the sequestered community halls and ethnic newspapers. The other necessary measure, in Davis' view, was the creation of a committee to deal with the whole problem of the foreign-born.[37] At year's end, Davis was working to get the appropriate people together to "begin discussion" of the foreign-born population problem; that is, the question of "getting them behind the war effort." He urged Robertson to bring together Skelton, Coleman, MacNeill, Director of Information G.H. Lash, as well as RCMP Commissioner Wood and his officer in charge of the ethnic problem. Robertson acted without delay. He arranged the desired meeting and invited two other useful people as well: H.G. Reid, of the Office of the Custodian of Enemy Property, and Robert England.[38] After the meeting, its participants were asked to submit their recommendations in writing, while Robertson was urged to have a talk with Kirkconnell to get a more precise idea of his views and, in particular, his opinion of the value of the work being done by Philipps.[39]

Philipps meanwhile continued his activities. His most important task during the second half of December and the beginning of 1941 was the completion of a report on his tour of the ethnic communities of the Canadian West. The report contained a lengthy outline of Philipps' ideas on the politics of Canada's immigrant minorities and their relationship to Canadian society at large.

One of Philipps' central arguments was that the worker and peasant immigrants from Central and Eastern Europe expected to be led. Moreover, leadership for them could not come from local authorities or the police. They would have to be guided by the federal government; without that guidance, they would lapse into a "mental and political void." There were two ways the government could deal with these groups, according to Philipps. One was "surgical intervention," the regulation of immigrant political life through government edict. "This, in effect, [was] the only method which, in the time allowed, could be used to unite ... [the] Ukrainians...." It was also the "least satisfactory method." According to Philipps, the "permanence of the cure" depended on the "quality of subsequent nursing."

The second method of dealing with ethnic groups, and one obviously preferred by Philipps, was that "convenient to Nature," where the subject "was given access to the sun." This course of action, which involved the study of the ethnics' apprehensions and the redressing of their grievances, was "slower but surer." Philipps warned that, in the process of transplanting the immigrants to their new environment, the "old soil" should not be excluded. Rather, the old soil "of their old virtues and arts" should be "blended as the basis of the transition to Canadianism." As an instrument to achieve this "transition," this work of "educating," Philipps called for the creation of a "Canadian Council of Education-in-Citizenship."[40]

In addition to writing his report, Philipps began to bombard officials in Ottawa with memoranda containing specific recommendations.[41] And he sought, as was becoming his habit, interviews with the influential. In January 1941, for example, he was received by Judge Davis, Norman Robertson, and T.A. Crerar, the minister of mines and resources and minister responsible for Canadian immigration policy.[42] Throughout that month, Philipps kept hoping that a decision would be made in Ottawa on his proposals for working with the immigrant ethnic population. He no doubt hoped to be associated with this work in an official capacity, along with his friend Kaye. But decisions were not forthcoming. Part of the delay may be explained by the tragic death of Skelton, the most powerful of Ottawa's mandarins, at the end of January. A more important explanation for it probably lies in the fact that officials concerned could not find a suitable person to direct the project.

Early in the deliberations two candidates had emerged for this position. One was Kirkconnell, who was invited to Ottawa to discuss matters with Robertson and Lash.[43] When the professor's trip did not materialize, Davis wrote him a letter early in the New Year. He praised Kirkconnell's Canadian Club address and asked him to come to see him when he had a chance to visit Ottawa.[44] When Davis got no response to his feeler, he asked a mutual friend, Lieutenant-Colonel James E. Mess, the president of the Association of Canadian Clubs, to put the question to Kirkconnell. But the latter proved reluctant. He felt committed to his university (which had only recently taken him on), and to his family.[45] The other man considered qualified for the position was Robert England. As has been mentioned above, he was also unavailable, much to Davis' regret.[46]

Not finding any Canadians, Davis and his associates temporized. In the meantime, all Philipps could do was to renew his appeals for action. During the middle of February he wrote letters to everyone concerned, pointing out his own precarious financial situation.[47] He also made inquiries on behalf of Kaye, who was in a similar financial bind, but there was no positive response. An appeal had been "launched" for him, Philipps informed his Ukrainian friend, but "all in vain." "No one below the P.M. is capable of giving a decision. Too big an affair! ...."[48]

15

Philipps did finally get a reply to his appeals, but it was not the answer he had hoped for. Davis told him that the Canadian Clubs would have to continue to cover some of his expenses when he was on speaking engagements since the government was not in a position to hire him.⁴⁹ In April 1941, however, it was arranged that Philipps enter the service of the RCMP as "Director of the European Section," on a temporary basis, which entitled him to a daily allowance as well as reimbursement of out-of-pocket expenses.⁵⁰ "Ottawa," Philipps explained to Kaye, "has made another ... impossible proposition ... hopeless for the work, pleasant enough for me...." He felt he could not "honestly" accept the deal, yet accept it he did.⁵¹ His first major assignment was a trip to the United States to find out what was being done in that country to deal with the immigrant ethnic population and to ascertain how these groups felt about the question of relations with the federal authorities. Philipps visited Pittsburgh, Chicago, Atlanta and Washington, among other places. From virtually every stop along his route, he sent detailed memoranda to his new superior, Commissioner Wood.

Much of what Philipps had to say concerned his own ideas for dealing with the problem in Canada. In one of his first reports he pointed out that, in spite of the importance of the foreign-born issue in Canada and the influence that immigrants could exercise on their kin in Europe, "no specialized unit" existed to foster a "partnership" between Canadians and immigrants and to organize the latter for "positive cooperation."⁵² That "unit" should be a "link" between External Affairs and the Immigration Branch of the Department of Mines and Resources. Among other things, the unit would "spread among old-established citizens an appreciation of the contribution to the Nation being made by the newer comers [sic]."⁵³ For practical purposes, the "unit" should be small, consisting of several sections, each composed of two persons. Each section was to specialize in one particular ethnic group, and one of its staff members was to reside in Ottawa, while the other would do field-work. The unit was to be counselled by a "National Advisory Panel" made up of distinguished "Assimilated Foreign-born Citizens," selected from the various ethnic communities.⁵⁴

While Philipps was touring the United States, events were taking place in Ottawa that were to have an effect on the formulation of policy regarding the country's foreign-born population. These events had to do with the problem of wartime propaganda and Prime Minister King's approach to the issue.

For more than a year prior to May 1941, this work was being performed by the Bureau of Public Information, directed by Lash and his associate director, Claude Melançon. After the creation of the Department of National War Services, the Bureau was attached to it. It did what it could to discharge its functions, but was not provided with an adequate budget, staff, or guidance to do its work effectively. Although the fault for the Bureau's shortcomings lay probably first and foremost with Mackenzie King himself,[55] he had become unhappy with its performance. "I made up my mind," he recorded in his diary on the twelfth of that month, "that the whole work [of propaganda] would have to be more effectively co-ordinated...." King was particularly unhappy with the report that had been submitted by the Department of National War Services regarding the issue, and he was even more displeased with Gardiner, who wanted to solve the problem simply by hiring more staff. The government decided to undertake a review of the whole problem of war-time information and King also began thinking in earnest about finding someone to replace Gardiner.[56] King's decisions aroused hope in those awaiting positive developments, such as Philipps. But the prime minister's doubts about Gardiner as a suitable minister for handling information work caused delay rather than prompted action.

The fact was that King had no obvious candidate for Gardiner's job. He and his closest advisers were thinking of two Quebec MPs, Brooke Claxton or D.C. Abbott. Minister of National Defence for Air, Charles G. Power, recommended J.T. Thorson, member of Parliament for Selkirk and chairman of the Select Committee on War Expenditures, who was of Icelandic origin. At first King rejected the idea of appointing Thorson partly because he was already doing "a very real job."[57] However, after weeks of indecision, King suddenly changed his mind and, on 11 June, announced Thorson's appointment as minister of national war services. He wrote in his diary: "I had much in mind Thorson's appointment being something that would please those of foreign extraction in the country...." As the man in charge of the War Services portfolio, King expected Thorson to pay much attention to the problem of wartime information.[58] But the change in ministers inevitably delayed decisions on such matters as the establishment of the machinery of dealing with ethnic groups.

Within a fortnight of Thorson's appointment, Davis was in contact with him regarding the question of establishing a unit within his department to deal with immigrant groups. Not much was decided before Thorson had to leave for Winnipeg, and Davis' outline of the proposed unit was not sent to the new minister until after he had left Ottawa. In his memorandum, Davis identified the general purpose of the proposed "Division" as "keeping in contact with that section of our Canadian population who were either born in Europe or whose origin is European." One of the specific tasks of the planned office, according to Davis, was to ensure that people "with foreign names" were not "discriminated against...." "It would be the duty of this Division," he continued, "to carry out plans and propaganda to weave these people into the fabric of our Canadian Nation."

Many immigrants were "confused about the war," Davis claimed. "We went into the war with France as an ally and Russia as an enemy," he explained. "Now Russia is an ally and France is an enemy. It is no wonder there is confusion." The new office had to try to eliminate this confusion and "utilize the foreign press to direct and give leadership to these people." Whether the office was to be a section of the Bureau of Public Information or a "separate Division" had not been settled yet. However, Davis informed his superior that if it was established, Philipps (who was to meet Thorson in Winnipeg) "would be associated with it."[59]

The last days of June and the early part of July were filled with further exchanges of views. In Winnipeg Thorson saw Philipps and possibly also Commissioner Wood. Next, a delegation of Ukrainian-Canadian leaders called on the new minister and were taken into confidence about the planned bureau. The names of Philipps, Kirkconnell, as well as that of Professor George Simpson — an East European specialist with the University of Saskatchewan's History Department — were mentioned to them as possible persons to head the unit.[60]

Late in July matters ground to a halt again. On 6 August, however, an important development took place. The Cabinet War Committee met and considered the question of the extension of the activities of the Bureau of Public Information. Thorson was admitted to the meeting to present his recommendations regarding the reorganization and expansion of his department's publicity division. Among the new "sections" planned was a "Foreign Language Section." He told his colleagues that, in order to give "intelligent encouragement and direction" to the people who read foreign-language newspapers, he intended to appoint "an appropriate supervisory officer familiar with the problems and conditions of these people." Thorson's proposals were discussed and approved in principle. It was agreed that no formal sections were to be established to carry out the planned work and it was unnecessary to pass an order-in-council to effect the proposed changes.[61]

More delays now followed, but on 15 September Davis saw Robertson (who had succeeded Skelton as the head of External Affairs) and discussed a number of matters with him, including the question of the planned unit for his department dealing with New Canadians. The stumbling block continued to be the issue of a manager. Robertson, who seems to have had a dislike for Philipps, was not in favour of giving him an "administrative" position, as opposed to the "roving commission" he held at the time. Davis promised to take the matter up with Thorson.[62] A little more than a week later, Davis decided to report on developments to Philipps. He assured Philipps that it had been "definitely" decided to create the proposed "division." As soon as someone qualified and willing to lead it was found, Philipps' "future services" with the government could be discussed.[63] Obviously, Philipps would not be hired to head the work he had been proposing. As if this was not enough, he was soon thereafter told by Commissioner Wood that his employment with the police force could not be continued beyond the date agreed upon in the spring.[64]

Philipps did not accept the bad news without argument. He began bombarding Davis with long memoranda pointing out the injustice and impropriety of the government's position. To exclude Philipps from the competition for the directorship of the planned section amounted to "discrimination" against him because of his British birth. He also objected to the unit being placed under the Bureau of Public Information.[65]

While Philipps kept complaining, decisions were being made. After discussions with Davis, Thorson took action. He persuaded George Simpson to head the new section. Philipps was to be retained as Simpson's "advisor," and kept travelling "among the foreign element." The unit was to work in close collaboration with the Department of External Affairs in order to prevent its policies from straying out-of-line with those of that department.[66] The question of reporting and lines of communication had yet to be settled, however. Judge Davis would have preferred the branch to be under his control; he was, by his own admission, "intensely interested in the functions of this section." Director of Public Information Lash, however, felt that the unit should be under his direct supervision.[67]

To iron out the remaining issues, an informal group was called together at the end of October. It was decided that a committee would be created to advise the planned unit. This proposed committee, for the time being called the Committee on Cultural-Group Cooperation, was to be chaired by Simpson and was to have three other members, Kirkconnell, England, and Philipps.[68] When the meeting's recommendations were conveyed to Robertson, he asked that the proposed committee be called either the "Committee on Cooperation in Citizenship" or "Committee on Cooperative Citizenship." Robertson felt that both emphasized that cooperation was "to be exercised equally from all persons in Canada" and stressed the "common rights and duties implied in Canadian citizenship."[69] "All present [at the meeting]," Robertson informed the prime minister, "agreed that the Committee did not have as its object the preservation of group differences, but that it should seek to encourage [immigrant ethnics] to identify themselves as closely as possible with the rest of the Canadian community."[70]

Davis informed his minister of the consensus on the need for an administrative unit within the Bureau of Public Information to deal with "those who have come to Canada from other lands, ... including the descendants thereof." Two days later Thorson signed the document adding: "approved ... everything[:] name[,] committee personnel[,] and plan[.]"[71]

Early in November, then, the plans of 1940 and 1941 finally came to fruition. The Nationalities Branch (NB) became a reality, along with its advisory committee, which in the end become known as the (Advisory) Committee on Cooperation in Canadian Citizenship (CCCC). What remained to be done was the appointment of personnel and the ironing out of a few administrative details. This again took time as new developments were about to make heavy demands on the bureaucracy's time. One of these was preparation for a declaration of war by Canada on a number of Axis satellites; another was the escalation of the war in the Pacific with Japan's attack on Pearl Harbor. Nevertheless, once decisions had been made at the highest level, their implementation was only a matter of time, notwithstanding the distractions presented by international developments. By the New Year, the appointments to the two bodies were all but completed. The NB was to have Simpson as its permanent head; Philipps was to be the "European Advisor." The two were later joined by Kaye as "Liaison Officer" as well as head of an "Editorial Section." The CCCC consisted of a dozen prominent individuals, including England and Kirkconnell.

It is beyond the scope of this paper to trace the history of the NB and the CCCC. It must suffice to say that their existence during 1942 and 1943 was most precarious. No sooner did they begin their work during the spring and summer of 1942 than second thoughts emerged in Ottawa about the nature of their activities and about some of the people directing them, especially Philipps. Before the year was out, Simpson resigned for health reasons. As no one was found to take his place, his responsibilities were inherited by Philipps. He continued to work at his usual hectic pace, making policy changes and pronouncements that were often not in tune with ideas held elsewhere in the Ottawa bureaucracy, External Affairs in particular. The situation was aggravated by attacks on Philipps — and his friend Kirkconnell, the notorious red-baiter — by the leftist press of North America. Soon, there were calls by influential people (just about every senior bureaucrat in External Affairs as well as John Grierson of the Wartime Information Board) for the complete revamping of the administrative machinery just created, and above all, for the resignation of the controversial Englishman.[72] These requests were not acted on for a long time. Instead, the NB and the CCCC were relegated to administrative oblivion: the former was denied adequate funds and staff — Philipps was forbidden to engage in lobbying or speech-making — while the latter was simply not called together. A reorganization was completed only in 1944. It resulted in the creation of the Citizenship Division of the Department of National War Services. The new bureaucratic infrastructure, devised by Robert England, avoided some of the deficiencies of the Nationalities Branch. Notably, it eased Philipps out of Canadian government service.

The Citizenship Division, with its increased staff and budget, was to become a lasting fixture of the Ottawa bureaucracy. Although the CCCC, and even the Department of National War Services, were dismantled at the end of the war, the Division survived. It was transferred first to the Department of the Secretary of State, and in 1950 to the newly created Department of Citizenship and Immigration. In the 1970s, this was the administrative machinery that was charged with the implementation of the Canadian government's policy of multiculturalism.

In assessing the importance of the birth of the Nationalities Branch in the chain of events that led to the institution of official multiculturalism in Canada some three decades later, it would be easy to exaggerate. The creation of the NB and the CCCC did not mark the onset of multiculturalism in Canada. The announcement of a federal policy of multiculturalism would not occur until the Trudeau era. It might be argued, furthermore, that the emergence of a truly multicultural Canadian society remains to this day an unfulfilled dream of those who believe in cultural pluralism. Nevertheless, in the evolution of the status of those Canadians who are of neither British nor French ancestry, the developments of 1940-1941 represent a milestone. They mark a perceptible watershed between the age when "ethnics" or "ethnic populations" were generally ignored, and the post-war era when increasing attention was paid to them, not only at election time but on an ongoing basis.

The role the war played in this transformation can hardly be over-emphasized. Before the war, most members of Canada's two million strong ethnic community lived outside of, or at best, on the fringes of the Canadian national existence. They were unfamiliar with the country's political culture, and they were not integrated into its social and economic life. They formed a mass of marginal people whose connection to the host society seemed to consist of nothing more than the fact that they were trying to eke out a material existence here, and not in Brazil or Argentina. For most of them, Canadian culture and society was inaccessible. Their relation with the Canadian government consisted of routine contacts with postmen, taxmen, immigration officials and the RCMP. This unsatisfactory situation could continue in peacetime, but not in a time of prolonged national emergency. The war placed demands on the Canadian economy and its political structure that made it difficult for the country to allow the continued existence of a large bulk of its population outside the mainstream of national life.

By making the need for a change in this situation obvious, the war made it possible for those members of Canada's political elite who were sympathetic to the plight of the ethnics to exert more influence than would have been possible for them otherwise. Moreover, the war resulted in a new group of people becoming involved in the nation's decision-making processes. Most members of this new group had become convinced, during the early part of the war or even before, of the need to involve the New Canadians in national life. To cite concrete examples, the war thrust politicians such as Gardiner and Thorson into positions in which they could act according to their pro-immigrant sympathies. In the higher echelons of the civil service, the same was true of men such as Robertson, Coleman, and MacNeill. Among those called to Ottawa to handle these matters were people of varying backgrounds and approaches such as Davis from Saskatchewan and Philipps from England. Those regularly consulted included such stalwart friends of ethnics as England and Kirkconnell. All of them would call for, and work for, solutions to the best of their abilities.

Although their recommendations were implemented only after constant delays and in a haphazard manner, and resulted often in half-measures and ineffective arrangements, it must be kept in mind that more was done to involve ethnics in Canadian life in 1940 and 1941 than had been done in the nearly three-quarters of a century since Confederation. There can be no doubt that without the war there would not have been the bureaucratic machinery in Ottawa to deal with the ethnics in the 1940s, or even in the following decade.

That the machinery created was considered important and useful at the time, and in the years immediately following its establishment, is indicated by the fact that the Citizenship Division survived the war, despite the bitter controversies that had surrounded the Nationalities Branch, despite the general bureaucratic reshuffling and retrenchment that took place in Ottawa at the end of the war.

The war resulted in the creation of bureaucratic machinery at the federal level to serve as an instrument of the government's policies towards ethnics. The machinery established was admittedly modest. Its permanent staff consisted of five people (during much of 1943 this was reduced to two, Philipps and his by then ailing friend Kaye). The inadequate nature of this arrangement was implicitly acknowledged in 1944. When the Citizenship Division replaced the Nationalities Branch, it was given a larger staff and more money. Gradually, if erratically, the governmental machinery dealing with Canada's ethnic groups has been expanding ever since.

The beginnings of this bureaucratic apparatus were a small but telling and vital aspect of the general process whereby ethnic minorities in Canada have acquired a higher profile and greater influence in the country's national affairs. Another aspect of the process, without doubt wrought by the war, was increased integration of newcomers into the Canadian economy as well as into social and cultural life. A partial picture of this development might be gained from some of the papers that follow in this volume, while a comprehensive analysis of this subject still awaits the attention of historians and social scientists.

Notes

1. C.P. Stacey, *Six Years of War: The Army in Canada, Britain and the Pacific* (Ottawa, 1955); James Eayrs, *In Defence of Canada: Appeasement and Rearmament* (Toronto, 1965), ch. V; Donald Creighton, *The Forked Road: Canada 1939-1957* (Toronto, 1976), 15; Robert Bothwell, "'Who's Paying for Anything These Days?' War Production in Canada 1939-45," in N.F. Dreisziger, ed., *Mobilization for Total War: The Canadian, American, and British Experience 1914-1918, 1939-1945* (Waterloo, Ont., 1981), 57
   Research for this study has been done with the help of a Social Sciences and Humanities Research Council of Canada Leave Fellowship (1984-85) and the 1986-87 Senior Fellowship in Canadian Ethnic Studies. For comments on various drafts of this paper, I am indebted to my colleagues in the organizing committee of the 1986 conference in Kingston, to Ms. Bennett McCardle of the National Archives of Canada, as well as to the Honourable J.W. Pickersgill.

2. National Archives of Canada (NA), W.L.M. King Papers, vol. 348, f. 3771, unsigned memorandum, "Internal Security," 27 June 1940. See also Ramsay Cook, "Canadian Freedom in Wartime, 1939-1945," W.H. Heick and Roger Graham, eds., *His Own Man: Essays in Honour of Arthur Reginald Marsden Lower* (Montreal, 1974), 38. See also Robert H. Keyserlingk, "Which Fatherland in War? The Canadian Government's View of German Canadian Loyalties in World War Two," in Tova Yedlin, ed., *Central and East European Ethnicity in Canada: Adaptation and Preservation* (Edmonton, 1985), 143ff.

3. Ramsay Cook, "Canadian Liberalism in Wartime: A Study of the Defence of Canada Regulations and Some Canadian Attitudes to Civil Liberties in Wartime, 1939-1945," (M.A. thesis, History, Queen's University, 1955), 80

4. See William and Kathleen M. Repka, eds., *Dangerous Patriots: Canada's Unknown Prisoners of War* (Vancouver, 1982). This is a pro-communist account of the subject.

5. See the unsigned memorandum on "Internal Security," 27 June 1940, cited in note 2.

6. King Papers, Diary, 24 May 1940. In the presence of such "inconsistent" advisers, King decided to depend on "spiritual power" in this hour of crisis, rather than on the advice of "other men." *Ibid.* At the time Skelton was under secretary of state for external affairs, Heeney was King's principal secretary, and Pickersgill was the prime minister's private secretary.

7. J.L. Granatstein, *A Man of Influence: Norman A. Robertson and Canadian Statecraft, 1929-68* (Ottawa, 1981), 83-7. Granatstein draws a sharp contrast between the attitudes on this issue of Robertson and the RCMP. Other works dealing with the treatment of enemy aliens include Ann Gomer Sunahara, *The Politics of Racism: The Uprooting of Japanese Canadians during the Second World War* (Toronto, 1981); Robert H. Keyserlingk, "The Canadian Government's Attitude Toward Germans and German Canadians in World War II," *Canadian*

Ethnic Studies, XIV, (Spring 1984), 16-28, his " 'Agents within the Gates': The Search for Nazi Subversives in Canada during World War II," *Canadian Historical Review*, LXVI, (Summer 1985), 211-39; and his "Which Fatherland," 133-71.

8. Granatstein, 81-3

9. *Ibid.*, pp. 86-8; Keyserlingk, "Which Fatherland," 146

10. Granatstein, 83

11. King Papers, J1, vol. 273, J.F. MacNeill to Walter J. Turnbull, 5 December 1939, enclosed in Turnbull to Arnold D.P. Heeney, 6 December 1939. King's letter to the Reverend C.E. Silcox, quoted by MacNeill, was dated 11 November 1939. It appeared in numerous newspapers.

12. King Papers, J1, vol. 273, memorandum of Heeney to King, 12 December 1939

13. *Ibid.*, King's handwritten notes

14. Watson Kirkconnell, *Canadians All: A Primer of Canadian National Unity* (Ottawa, 1941). On this see William R. Young, "Building Citizenship: English Canada and Propaganda during the Second World War," *Journal of Canadian Studies*, XVI, 3 and 4 (Fall and Winter 1981), 123ff.

15. Discussed by a committee consisting of Turnbull, G.H. Lash, Claude Melançon, and Hugh Keenleyside.

16. King Papers, J4, vol. 413, f. 3989, memorandum of L.W. Brockington, n.d. [ca. May 1940]

17. *Ibid.*, vol. 348, f. 3771, two memoranda of Turnbull, 22 May 1940. Another memorandum in the same file lists the sources of the "representations" King had received: 78 came from veterans' organizations, 41 from municipal councils, 11 from citizens' meetings, 22 from boards of trade, 17 from service clubs, 28 from individuals, and others. In total, 228 messages were received.

18. Unsigned memorandum on "Internal Security," 27 June 1940, cited in note 2 above. See also NA, Norman Robertson Papers, vol. 12, the draft of a radio broadcast on "Fifth Column Activity," prepared by Pickersgill and Robertson, 26 May 1940. This document warned that it was "a disservice to spread the news that Canada is full of enemy agents ..." and assured Canadians that the authorities were fully in control of the situation. "Any persecution of racial minorities in this country," it proclaimed, "is unworthy of our people, and a betrayal of our traditions, our national spirit and the very freedom we are fighting to preserve...." It also asked people not to "take the law into their own hands and play detectives...."

19. King Papers, J4, vol. 239. f. 2395, press release, 18 July 1940

20. NA, Records of the Department of National War Services, RG 44, vol. 36, memorandum of Robertson, 13 August 1940. See also *ibid.*, a memorandum of the Committee on Enemy Aliens and Enemy Alien Property (about the same date, listed under an incorrect name).

21. RG 44, vol. 36, copy of letter, E.H. Coleman to E. Lapointe, 14 August 1940, enclosed in Lapointe to J. Gardiner, 21 August 1940

22. NA, Records of the Department of External Affairs, RG 25, G1, vol. 1964, f. 855-E-39, copy of letter, Gardiner to Coleman, encl. in Coleman to Skelton, 16 September 1940. See also RG 44, vol. 36, copy of letter, Gardiner to Lapointe, 9 September 1940.

23. RG 25, G1, vol. 1964, f. 855-E-39, Coleman to Skelton, 21 October 1940

24. *Ibid.*, copy of letter, [Skelton] to Coleman, 19 November 1940

25. NA, Philipps Papers, vol. 2, pamphlet of the National Council of Education of Canada, 15 May 1940, on the forthcoming lecture tour of Philipps. Philipps' knowledge of the major European languages was confirmed to me by Mrs. Lubka Kolessa-Philipps in a telephone interview in December of 1985.

26. *Ibid.*, vol. 2, copy of letter, Philipps to Chester Payne, 20 January 1944. The full story about the purpose of Philipps' North American tour is not known. In several of his letters, he refers to plans that had existed in the spring of 1940 to send him to the Near East. These were abandoned when the invitation came from North America. Some sources have asserted that Philipps was an agent of Lord Halifax and that his task was to unite the right-wing elements of Ukrainians on this continent. See the attack on Philipps in the American left-wing publication, *The Hour*, 21 December 1940. Indeed, one of Philipps' letters refers to his and Kaye's attendance at an Ukrainian-American Congress in May, at the request of the "War Office." *Ibid.*, copy of letter, Philipps to J.N.K. Macalister, CPR commissioner of colonization, 19 October 1940

27. RG 25, accession 83-84/259, box 198, f. 3426-40, pt. 2, memorandum, 7 June [1943?]. Until 1942 Kaye was generally known as "Dr. Kisilevsky"; after his appointment to the civil service, he became officially known as "Dr. Kaye."

28. Philipps Papers, vol. 2, Kaye to Anne Carol, 6 February 1967

29. *Ibid.*, copy of letter, Philipps to Macalister, 19 October 1940. In December 1942, Philipps recalled that in November 1940 he was asked by Judge T.C. Davis, at the suggestion of Ukrainian-Canadian churchmen, to induce the Ukrainians to suspend their political vendettas, and coordinate their committees for war work. *Ibid.*, vol. 1, f. 30, memorandum of Philipps, 26 December 1942. See also RG 44, vol. 36, copy of letter, Davis to Robertson, 25 September 1942.

30. Oleh W. Gerus, "The Ukrainian Canadian Committee," in Manoly R. Lupul, ed., *A Heritage in Transition: Essays in the History of Ukrainians in Canada* (Toronto, 1982), 197ff. Gerus' account contains inaccuracies.

31. RG 44, vol. 36, copy of letter, W.C. Barrie to J.A. MacKinnon, minister of trade and commerce, 14 December 1940

32. *Ibid.*, Robertson to Davis, 26 December 1940. See also *ibid.*, unsigned memorandum, concerning interview of Wasyl Swystun with O.D. Skelton, 18 December 1940.

33. NA, J.W. Dafoe Papers, (microfilm) M 80, Dafoe to Sir Edward Cunningham, 30 November 1942. Thomas Clayton Davis was born in Prince Albert, Saskatchewan, in 1889. He was educated at St. John's College in Winnipeg, and at Osgoode Hall in Toronto. He was called to the bar in 1915, served as alderman from 1917 to 1920, and as mayor of Prince Albert from 1921 to 1924. From 1925 to 1939 he was in provincial politics, at various times serving as an MLA, as minister of municipal affairs, and as attorney general. In 1939 he was appointed to the bench of the Saskatchewan appeals court. In June 1940, he offered his services to the federal government. After being associate deputy minister of the Department of National War Services, Davis was appointed Canadian high commissioner to Australia. King Papers, J4, vol. 249, f. 2575, memoranda, one undated, another dated 23 October 1946 (both unsigned)

34. RG 44, vol. 36, copy of letter, Davis to H.R. MacMillan (Wartime Merchant Shipping Ltd), 28 February 1942. Similar sentiments were expressed by Davis in a letter to J.T. Thorson, MP, in October 1941. See also *ibid.*, copy of memorandum of Davis to Thorson, 29 October 1941.

35. *Ibid.*, copy of letter, T.C. Davis to Harry Hereford, commissioner, Unemployment Relief Branch, Department of Labour, 12 October 1940

36. *Ibid.*, copy of letter, Davis to Robertson, 9 November 1940

37. *Ibid.*, Davis to Gardiner, 13 November 1940

38. *Ibid.*, copy of letter, Davis to Robertson, 29 November 1940. See also *ibid.*, Robertson to Davis, 3 December 1940

39. *Ibid.*, copy of letter, Davis to Robertson, 6 December 1940

40. Philipps Papers, vol. 1, f. 16, memorandum of Philipps, "Tour in Western Canada, November-December 1941 [sic, 1940]," 8 January 1941. Reprinted in part in Bohdan S. Kordan and Lubomyr Y. Luciuk, eds., *A Delicate and Difficult Question: Documents in the History of Ukrainians in Canada, 1899-1962* (Kingston, Ont., 1986), 74-6.

41. In one of these, dated 13 January 1941, he urged that the community halls that were taken away from Ukrainian workingmen in the Canadian West and closed down by the government should be placed in the hands of trustees and kept open for the use of the ordinary immigrants who had built them. Philipps Papers, vol. 1, f. 16, memorandum of Philipps, 13 January 1941

42. *Ibid.*, vol. 2, Philipps to V.J. Kaye, 13 January and 4 February 1941

43. RG 44, vol. 36, copy of letter, Davis to Robertson, 6 December 1940

44. Archives of Acadia University, Wolfville, Nova Scotia, Watson Kirkconnell Papers, 21/4, Davis to Kirkconnell, 3 January 1941

45. Philipps Papers, vol. 1, f. 17, copy of letter, Kirkconnell to J.E. Mess, 8 February 1941

46. Interview with Robert England, October 1984. Because of injuries suffered in World War I, by the 1940s England was advised against taking a full-time job. As a result, he worked as consultant to the government during the war taking temporary assignments with various departments.

47. Philipps Papers, vol. 1, f. 17, draft of letter, dated 17 February 1941. Copies of this letter seem to have been sent to Davis, Robertson and T.A. Crerar.

48. *Ibid.*, vol. 2, Kaye files, no. 5, Philipps to Kaye, 26 February 1941

49. *Ibid.*, vol. 1, f. 18, Davis to Philipps, 1 March 1941

50. *Ibid.*, vol. 1, Commissioner S.T. Wood to Philipps, 22 April, and 2 and 8 May 1941

51. *Ibid.*, vol. 2, Kaye files, Philipps to Kaye, 15 May 1941

52. *Ibid.*, vol. 1, copy, Philipps to Wood, 1 May 1941

53. *Ibid.*, copy, Philipps to Wood, 9 May 1941

54. *Ibid.*, copy, Philipps to Wood, 28 May 1941

55. One keen observer of the Bureau's work was Watson Kirkconnell. He felt that Mackenzie King was afraid to create a large bureaucracy to deal with propaganda lest it become a "Frankenstein monster." "As a result," according to Kirkconnell, "no hand was lifted to help" Lash and his associates. Watson Kirkconnell, *A Slice of Canada: Memoirs* (Toronto, 1967), 303

56. King Papers, Diary, 12 and 14 May 1941. *Ibid.*, J4, vol. 424, minutes of the meeting of the Cabinet War Committee (CWC), 13 May 1941. See also J.W. Pickersgill, ed., *The Mackenzie King Record*, I (Toronto, 1960), 222.

57. King Papers, Diary, 12 May 1941

58. Pickersgill, 223

59. RG 44, vol. 35, memorandum of Davis to Thorson, 27 June 1941. See also the exchange of telegrams between Davis and Philipps, 24 and 25 June 1941, Philipps Papers, vol. 1, f. 21.

60. Philipps Papers, vol. 1, f. 22, copy of letter, Philipps to Louis Palermo, 13 July 1941. Also an exchange of letters between Wasyl Swystun and Philipps, 16 and 22 July 1941, in the same volume. In writing to Swystun, Philipps disclaimed any interest in the proposed post and confessed his disillusionment with Ukrainians.

Swystun tried to console him: "If the present generation will not understand your efforts, at least history will."

61. King Papers, J4, vol. 424, minutes of the meeting of the CWC, 6 August 1941

62. RG 25, G2, accession 83-84/259, f. 3426-40, memorandum prepared for Robertson by S. Rae, 15 September 1941

63. Philipps Papers, vol. 1, f. 24, Davis to Philipps, 23 September 1941

64. *Ibid.*, f. 7, Wood to Philipps, 2 October 1941

65. *Ibid.*, f. 25, memoranda of Philipps, two dated 24 and 31 October 1941, one undated

66. RG 44, vol. 35, copy of letter, Davis to G.H. Lash, 23 October 1941

67. *Ibid.*, See also, in the same volume, Lash to Davis, 24 October 1941.

68. RG 44, vol. 36, unsigned, undated memorandum [ca. 30 October 1941]. Very soon, other names would be added to the committee's list of members. See also another memorandum, 7 June 1943(?), RG 25, accession 83-84/259, box 198, f. 3426-40, pt. 2. According to this note, the meeting was chaired by Davis and attended by sixteen people. Both Simpson and Philipps were present. The recommendation in favour of establishing the committee was unanimous. For more information on Davis' preparations for this meeting, see his letter to Coleman, 28 October 1941, copy in RG 25, G2, file 3426-40, 83-84/258.

69. RG 44, vol. 36, Robertson to Davis, 3 November 1941

70. RG 25, G2, f. 3426-40, 83-84/259, copy, memorandum of Robertson to King, 3 November 1941

71. RG 44, vol. 36, memorandum of Davis to Thorson, 4 November 1941

72. John Grierson even found a successor to Philipps: H. Gordon Skilling, a young East European specialist. Skilling was interviewed for the job by Grierson, but nothing came of his appointment. General L.R. LaFlèche, the successor to Thorson in the national war services portfolio, refused to fire the Englishman or to transfer the Nationalities Branch to Grierson's organization. Information in part from Professor H.G. Skilling, March 1987. I plan to tell this story in some detail in a paper which I am preparing on the work of the Nationalities Branch and the Committee on Cooperation in Canadian Citizenship during 1942-1944.

Chauvinism and Canadianism: Canadian Ethnic Groups and the Failure of Wartime Information

William R. Young

On 16 October 1942, Mackenzie King went to Montreal. The reason for the prime ministerial visit was to open the Third Victory Loan Campaign at a rally and to make a speech for broadcast across Canada. As on all such grand ceremonial occasions, King in his orotund manner set about putting forward the official view of Canada's reasons for joining the struggle and the aims of his government's war effort. Naturally enough, the prime minister took advantage of his visit to Montreal to attempt to paper over the deep differences over conscripting men for the armed forces, an issue that split French and English Canadians. In addition to praising the contribution of both these communities, he contrasted Canada to Germany and Japan, countries which had created an evil nationalism that strove to destroy the traditions and culture of other nations. He decried the enemy's claim of constituting a master race and the doctrine of superiority of one people over another as a "blasphemy against our common humanity." In contrast to this, King posited that "only by extending throughout the world the ideals of mutual tolerance, of racial co-operation and of equality among men, which form the basis of Canada's nationhood, can nationality come to serve mankind."

Tucked into the prime minister's oratory were a few neat phrases that reinforced the contrast between the Axis and the Allies and as well attempted to broaden the concept of Canadian nationality to include those with an origin neither English nor French. "Into our equal partnership ...," he told his audience:

we have admitted thousands who were born of other racial stocks, and who speak other tongues. They, one and all, have sought a homeland where nationality means not domination and slavery, but equality and freedom. Without the ideal of equality among men, without the vision of human brotherhood, the Canadian nation could never have come into being; without them, it cannot survive.[1]

Mackenzie King's nationwide address encapsulated the official view of Canadian nationhood in sentiments that were echoed over the airwaves, on the movie screens and in print by the government agencies concerned with keeping up morale and uniting the population behind the war effort. Shortly after the war broke out, the government had begun attempting to allay suspicions of more recent immigrants, particularly those with origins in enemy countries. The exception to this, after December 1941, was the Japanese, who were written off entirely. The government, and more particularly its information organizations, made efforts to convince the ethnic communities that their future lay in Canada and that living in a common Canadian environment had molded them into citizens with a future shared by all citizens of the country.

Admirable though these aims remained throughout the war, the government could not penetrate the latent xenophobia of French and English Canadians, nor could it escape entanglement in the rivalries of ethnic groups unwilling to leave behind the feuds which had riven their European homelands. As a consequence, the government retreated behind platitudes or tried to ignore the problem altogether.

Quickly after the outbreak of war in September 1939, there emerged the triangular relationship among the government, the Canadian majority and the ethnic community that was to last for the next six years. One reason that a reluctant prime minister set up a propaganda operation, the Bureau of Public Information, in December 1939 was to "keep the lunatics in leash" and to prevent the privately-owned media from usurping the job of explaining government policies to Canadians.[2] Despite this intention, the bureau lingered in the doldrums until after the 1940 general election and the Allied defeats in Europe in the spring of that year. The fear of the effect of the disastrous military situation on public morale forced Mackenzie King to overcome an innate distrust of government propaganda. He handed responsibility for the bureau and its work to a new Department of National War Services set up in that disastrous Spring.

Encouraged both by inclination and by circumstance to authorize a more activist role for government information, the minister of national war services, James G. Gardiner, moved into action. He allowed the restricted activities of the Bureau of Public Information to expand greatly. The bureau's director, G. Herbert Lash, undertook the publication of hundreds of pamphlets and arranged for news stories, magazine articles, and radio broadcasts that tried to patch up divisive issues and unite public opinion behind the country's war effort. Not least of Lash's concerns were the relations between French and English Canadians and the ethnic community.

Lash's initial approaches were based not on trust but on suspicion. Both the government and the public information bureau held the premise that ethnic Canadians with sentimental ties outside the country continually faced 'exploitation' by foreign governments.³ Naturally enough, this meant that the government tried to keep track of any such contact, particularly in Canada's foreign language press. Although all such periodicals were monitored by the Department of National Revenue, the government's readers paid particular attention to left-of centre publications. The press censors insisted that the periodical readers in the department plough through all Canadian radical and pro-Soviet newspapers. Even after the Soviet Union joined the Allies in 1941, such ideologically-based newspapers, either English or foreign-language, were not trusted. The censors made continuous suggestions that the bureau should attempt to refute the radical (but legal) press which continued to argue that the government supported profiteers and exploited workers.⁴ In an effort to check undesirable influences and to foster the 'proper' viewpoint, the King Cabinet approved the Department of National War Services' suggestion that concealed subsidies for the 'loyal' segments of the foreign-language press be made in the RCMP estimates. The department also tried to secure private as well as government advertising for these periodicals.⁵

The public shared the government's suspicion and in the first six months of the war, excessive xenophobia was leading some Canadians to find enemies behind every tree. In Edmonton, a candidate for the Board of Education election in November 1939 urged, as a means of eradicating "enemy activities in our midst," the censoring of schoolbooks that mentioned Germany. Obviously, most of the venom was directed at enemy aliens, and in April and May 1940, the prime minister received many representations — including those of the mayor of Vancouver and of various branches of the Canadian Legion — to intern all enemy aliens. The Canadian Corps Association called for the establishment of home defence forces recruited from "British sons of British-born people."[6]

Even the government's own Bureau of Public Information warned the public about the growth of a German fifth column movement in Canada. The suspected organization, the *Deutscher Bund*, had disappeared from view in 1939 when the police interned its leaders. But it was an embarrassment to have to deal with home-grown nazi sympathizers possessing a German-Canadian organization spread across the country and strong in western Canada. Nonetheless, the bureau issued largely redundant releases warning about "the fifth columnist who may have escaped the net." Such scare tactics could not but have strengthened popular suspicions of anyone who bore a German name.

To be fair, however, direct attacks on naturalized Canadians with origins in the enemy countries did not get out of hand, and the Bureau of Public Information saved its nastiest assaults for nonconformist groups with purely Anglo-Saxon or French origin. In one press release, the journalist James Oastler presented a vicious attack on the Jehovah's Witnesses who, he claimed, left in their wake "disunity where all had been peaceful and happy before...."[7]

Once the propaganda campaigns got going in mid-1940, the thread which runs through the bureau's products was unity — or at least the avoidance of discord. Official information tried to counter interference from abroad and to prevent racial splits and antagonism by convincing the ethnic community as well as French and English Canadians that the existence of a distinctive ethnic population posed no threat to Canadian nationhood. The bureau commissioned speakers to visit various communities of eastern European origin. In addition, it arranged film showings, news releases, and pamphlets to inspire the ethnic community with a sense of Canadian identity.[8]

The bureau's most important effort — carried out in conjunction with the Canadian Broadcasting Corporation — consisted of a series of radio broadcasts, accompanied by a pamphlet, on the theme "Canadians All." The pamphlet, prepared by Watson Kirkconnell of McMaster University, was not specifically aimed at the immigrant community, although along with the radio series, it tried to dampen anti-immigrant sentiments and quarrels among ethnic groups by directly attacking racism. And yet some of the inferences in language sounded very much like the promotion of racial solidarity among Canadians of 'white' origin. Kirkconnell pointed out that 98 percent of the population of Canada originated from similar stock in Europe. Differences in culture or in language, he argued, did not constitute a difference in race. "To the scientist," Kirkconnell went on, "race is simply and solely a matter of physical characteristics.... Just as we classify our cows as Aberdeens or Guernseys by their bodily types and not because they moo in a certain fashion...." In Canada, he concluded that no European national group could be considered "alien." Forgetting totally about any group that did not share this European origin, he postulated that, at least among Europeans, no superior race existed and Canadians should "never assume that our fellow Canadians of any origin are *by nature* [sic] unworthy of our sympathy, respect and goodwill...."[9]

The official 'line' tried to inspire a sense of unity and identification with the idea of Canadian nationhood. The government had begun in 1939 by trying to bring the country together behind the war effort by using the war itself as a common symbol. To sustain support for battles fought thousands of miles away, the members of the government and their officials had to emphasize the total contribution by Canadians of all descents. In 1940, "Canadians All" exemplified this theme in its message that the war brought about "sharing together in common experience, working and striving together in great causes...."[10] Apart from this, the official view emphasized the place of the war in the advancement of the nation in "strength and stature" and the important role of the federal government in interpreting citizens' wishes.

The script writers for the radio series "Canadians All" expounded the view that the greatness of the country depended on all citizens accepting the principles of a common citizenship so that out of the war "the golden metal of true Canadianism will emerge."[11] For a truly strong nation, the broadcasts preached, Canadians had to "widen the range of our nationbuilding to include ... a fuller knowledge of our fellow Canadians and particularly those who are not of our race or creed."[12] Taking aim at the super-patriotic claims of those of British origin, the bureau emphasized that the enlistment rate in the prairie ethnic communities surpassed that of the native born.[13] Excerpts from the foreign-language press were distributed to English and French newspapers. They all expanded upon variations on the theme that the ethnic community supported the war effort.

35

Although the official view of the war went a considerable distance to excuse the enemy peoples from the guilt of their leaders, the Bureau of Public Information set about counteracting any hostility that might have carried over to the German and Italian Canadians. From Mackenzie King on down, the government had publicly exorciated the nazis' "pagan conception of the social order which ignores the individual and is based upon the doctrine of Might."[14] When Italy entered the war in June 1940, King told Canadians that "with a callousness and treachery second only to that of Hitler ... the dictator who holds the Italian people in thrall has chosen ... to strike ... to satiate his lust for conquest, and ... for such glory as calculated duplicity and treachery can bring."[15] To prevent any carryover, one of the "Canadians All" broadcasts explicitly stressed the loyalty of the German ethnic press and the historic roots of German settlement in Canada. Optimistically, the script pointed out that Germans had been among the first to enlist in all three branches of the Canadian armed forces and to contribute to all patriotic fundraising.[16] The producers of this radio series also put together a programme that praised Italian Canadians and their place in national life. The narrator — again Watson Kirkconnell — emphasized to the radio audience that Italian Canadians had for over eighteen years borne the brunt of "unscrupulous and unremitting propaganda" put out by fascist agents operating in the country. The Canadian government could take no credit for their loyalty because it had done nothing to counter these subversive efforts until after Italy entered the war in 1940. For this steadfastness, he argued, the rest of the country should take pride in the Italian community despite "the shadow that the Fascist conspiracy has, for many persons, cast upon their whole group."[17]

The impact of such work is rather difficult to assess. There is indirect evidence that it at least controlled the ethnocentrism of some English Canadians. For example, English-language newspapers supported the right of the foreign-language press to publish throughout the war. And yet, because the bureau's propaganda was mainly published or broadcast in English, it could not have made much of an impact on those who did not speak or read the language.

Indeed, there are indications that the propaganda directed at the ethnic community had a divisive rather than a unifying effect. The seeds of future difficulties began with the "Canadians All" propaganda campaign. Kirkconnell's pamphlet, distributed before Germany attacked the USSR in June 1941, had made the point that the Soviet communists along with the German and Italian fascists looked for converts in Canada among the immigrant community. Comparing communism and fascism, the pamphlet explained that both systems, despite their opposing philosophies, worked for the destruction of the British Empire and operated "hand-in-hand against the Allied cause." The dictatorships centred in Moscow, Rome and Berlin, avowed Kirkconnell, demonstrated little difference in their extinction of individual rights, in their treatment of conquered territories, or in their creation of problems among the ethnic minorities of allied countries. Obviously, the anti-communism of this approach would force the government to search for 'weasel words' once the Soviets joined the Allies.

The organization of propaganda operations involved with the ethnic community amplified the dangers inherent in Kirkconnell's approach. The information director, Lash, continued to prepare and distribute his products to the ethnic community, but the Department of National War Services — the ministry responsible for the director's work — also set up a Nationalities Branch in 1941 to oversee the wartime activities of ethnic groups. Then in December of that year, the bureau and the department created an advisory body, the Committee on Cooperation in Canadian Citizenship, to advise the director and the branch. Because of the prestige of its members and the pressure that the committee applied, it soon became the driving force in propaganda activities directed at ethnic groups. In its own words, the committee aimed to provide Canadian news for the domestic foreign-language press and to give stories of the activities of the ethnic communities to the French and English newspapers. It wanted to provide the immigrant groups with information about their homelands but without reviving nationalistic ambitions or antagonism. "In their first generation and in wartime," said the committee, "it is better for Canada and for them to get prompt news ... in their mother tongues...."[18]

In some respects, the committee retained the earlier focus on Canadianism as its major principle. At the same time, however, some members indulged in divisive red-baiting. At the outset of the war, the government had recognized the potential embarrassment and divisions that could result from an "anti-red complex" in government operations, particularly in the RCMP, which tended to label any labour organizer or social reformer as a communist. In a memorandum to Mackenzie King shortly after the war began, his aide, J.W. Pickersgill, noted that this tendency led to a failure to discriminate "between legitimate social and political criticism and subversive doctrine." Pickersgill was disturbed by his discovery that the police were "setting themselves up as self-appointed censors of political opinion in the Community, especially when they regard the mildest expressions of liberal views as evidence of Communism." Pickersgill noted that the RCMP's intelligence bulletin referred to the "seditious" nature of the Russian language communist paper in Winnipeg. Then, to illustrate this, the bulletin quoted a paragraph about the Chamberlain government written "in terms which, to say the least, would not be considered outside the limits of legitimate criticism in England." In 1942, King's principal secretary, Walter J. Turnbull, raised the matter again, reporting to the prime minister that some officials were too "concerned with pursuing their old prejudices.... I would think that a change of policy might well be indicated to them, with Russia a valiant ally."[19]

The Committee on Co-operation in Canadian Citizenship nevertheless remained a bastion of "anti-communism." This impetus came from two of the committee's moving spirits, Watson Kirkconnell and Tracy Philipps. Philipps was a former adviser to the British Foreign Office who had visited and lectured to various eastern European ethnic communities under the auspices of the Bureau of Public Information; he also maintained contact with the anti-communist elements in the RCMP.[20] Carried along by this vigorous ideological viewpoint, the committee set about on a disastrous course of trying to 'help' ethnic groups — the Ukrainians for example — settle ideological conflicts between anti- and pro-communist sympathizers.[21] The committee began serving as a reference section that answered government's enquiries about the "ideological background" of ethnic organizations. It also prepared detailed reports of the communist-fascist feuding within the eastern European community after Germany attacked the Soviet Union.[22] All this, of course, was done with an anti-communist bias. After a year in operation, however, the committee complained that "our straw, our raw material is ... so colourless, so scanty and so belated ..." that it could not compete with the established ideological interests.[23] This was perhaps just as well.

It had grown all too apparent that the committee's anti-communist bias was creating rather than solving problems, and the situation did not change when the Wartime Information Board (WIB) superseded the Bureau of Public Information in the fall of 1942. The latter had come under attack for failing to take a firm lead and to guide opinion in a manner that prevented aimless agitation and conflict over controversial symbols. Although this criticism applied to the propaganda directed towards the ethnic community, the most glaring problem was the failure to bridge the gap between French and English Canada, which had shown up clearly in the strong "no" vote against conscription in Quebec during the plebiscite on 27 April 1942. A month later, Mackenzie King had commissioned Charles Vining, the newsprint controller of the Wartime Prices and Trade Board, to review the government's information operations. Vining's report had recommended that a new body, the WIB, assume responsibility for wartime information. The board would be separate from the Department of National War Services and made responsible to the prime minister.

Cabinet approved Vining's proposals and set up the new board, but the Nationalities Branch and the Committee on Cooperation in Canadian Citizenship remained, under the jurisdiction of the Department of War Services. Charles Vining, the WIB's chairman for its first four months, posed little trouble for the committee because he too recruited generally right-wing staff members. René Perrault, one of Vining's recruits, stirred up a storm when he suggested that George Ferguson, the respected Liberal editor of *The Winnipeg Free Press*, was a jail-worthy left-winger.[24] Apart from this, the chairman believed that government information should operate from behind the scenes; he declined to undertake active propaganda campaigns. Therefore, he refused to have anything to do with the committee and transferred the responsibility for administering its budget to the Department of National War Services on 24 December 1942.[25]

Although it was more good luck than good management, Vining's hands-off stance with regard to ethnic information saved the board from becoming a target. In the fall of 1942, the foreign language newspapers began a sustained attack on Philipps. The man was too prominently anti-communist at a time when Russia had joined the Allies. Mackenzie King himself, after all, did not hesitate to appear on the platform at Aid-to-Russia rallies. Communist sympathizers among the ethnic community in Canada made certain that members of the government learned about an article in the American periodical, *The New Republic*, that labelled Philipps as a nazi sympathizer and former intimate of the then-despised Cliveden set in England, which had been associated with appeasement throughout the 1930s.[26] Philipps rebutted the attacks in a letter to *The Globe and Mail* on 1 November.

At this point, the bureaucratic politics of the situation get a little murky. At a meeting on 13 November, the associate deputy minister of national war services, T.C. Davis, agreed with representatives of the Department of External Affairs, G.P. Glazebrook and Saul Rae, as well as Davidson Dunton of the WIB, that he would accept Philipps' offer to resign. They further agreed that the Committee on Co-operation in Canadian Citizenship should disband as a result of the withdrawal due to illness of its respected chairman, Professor George Simpson of the University of Saskatchewan. Glazebrook felt that it would be best to reappoint only a few of the permanent staff attached to the committee, implying the elimination of the more strident anti-communists. But Simpson had written to his friend Davis and strongly supported Philipps' work in promoting citizenship education in the immigrant community. And even before the meeting, Davis "unhesitatingly" backed Philipps in a letter to the minister of national war services, L.R. LaFlèche. Although he was leaving the department to become high commissioner to Australia, Davis must have convinced the minister that the furor had been the result of communist elements out to get Philipps. Even Norman Robertson, the under secretary of state for external affairs, felt that Philipps was the target of some unfair criticism, and accepted his argument that he should have an opportunity to clear up the false charges before leaving.[27]

Although this episode forced Philipps to retire from his public lecturing, he retained an influential position in the Nationalities Branch.[28] The furor provided clear evidence that, despite the optimistic statements of "Canadians All," the traditional divisions in the ethnic community proved stronger than any government statements about the unity that they could find in 'Canadianism' and their attachment to their new homeland.

To make matters even worse, the information programmes had not made a dent in the ethnocentrism of the English and French Canadians. This became obvious in the activities of private patriotic organizations established to counter rumours. A group of Montrealers had set up The Canadian Column, an organization designed to collect and to disprove rumours harmful to the war effort. Originally, the committee on morale associated with the Bureau of Public Information had recommended a programme of public information to counter rumours partly because the members, mainly psychologists, felt that this work could foster unity among Canadians and reconcile antagonistic ethnic groups. The campaign could point out the falsity of issues that led to quarrelling and misunderstandings.[29] Although the cabinet did not approve the bureau's proposal, the Montreal group began to operate on its own initiative in the summer of 1942.

When the Wartime Information Board superseded the bureau later that year, the first chairman, Charles Vining, wanted to provide the Montreal rumour clinic with encouragement but give no traceable financial assistance. By these means, he hoped to control the clinic without giving it an opportunity to claim government support for any potential controversy it might stir up. The WIB, therefore, proposed that if the clinic referred rumours to the board, its officers would investigate them and send back detailed denials that could be used for publication.[30] The WIB's vice-chairman, Philippe Brais, continued to press the case and The Canadian Column eventually received $400 per month to collect and forward lists of rumours to Ottawa and to distribute the WIB's rebuttals to its thirty client newspapers.[31] The board suggested that the rumour collection committees, both in Montreal and across the country, pay particular attention to grudge rumours that caused disunity and resentment among Canadian ethnic groups.[32]

Very quickly, however, the disadvantages of using private patriots outweighed any positive result in terms of creating unity. The Canadian Jewish Congress complained to the board that The Canadian Column had slandered the Jews. In publicizing a denial that Jews ran black markets in rationed goods, the Montreal group had only created an impression which supported the rumour.[33] Appalled at these developments, the WIB staff told its administrators that the Montrealers were not only spreading "undesirable propaganda" but also "retailing inaccurate information."[34] Finally, the experiment came to an end in November 1943 when the board cut off its connection with The Canadian Column. The group disappeared.[35]

The problems of information to the ethnic community, however, did not sink as quickly from view. The organizers of the Victory Loan drives reported to the Wartime Information Board that even the low fundraising quota allotted for ethnic contributions had gone unfilled.[36] Some of the publishers of the foreign language newspapers complained to the government that the lack lustre information campaigns directed at their audience had left the ethnic community open to subversive influences.[37] One German-Canadian publisher estimated that about 75 percent of his readers favoured a German victory, although they held these sentiments quietly and harmlessly. Because he had adopted a strongly pro-Allied stance, he reported, his circulation had dropped.[38] The studies of the Wartime Information Board highlighted the ideological split among the eastern European groups. It had widened to the extent that right-wing Poles, for example, felt closer to right-wing Ukrainians than to left-wing Poles. Each faction was denouncing the other and demanding the supression of their adversaries' activities.

The prescriptions for remedying this situation all contained the same basic recommendations. One editor sensibly argued that:

> There is no place in Canada for chauvinistic points of view or for narrow racial hatreds born of centuries of strife. This does not mean, however, that cultural values brought from Europe should be suppressed or even allowed to die away. On the contrary such should be fostered with care, for through them Canadian life will be enriched and through them the New Canadian will make his own contribution to his new environment.

Wartime information activities should take cognizance of this and of the fact that the role of the new Canadians would loom large in the country's future. An effective interchange of translations between the foreign language and the English and French press should be supplemented by foreign language radio broadcasts. Furthermore, all work should be carried out in conjunction with the respected leaders of the various communities.[39]

Even Tracy Philipps accepted this line of argument, and proposed that a directive be prepared for the editors of the foreign language press. He told the WIB that the directive should urge unity and avoidance of old hatreds as well as reminding them that the Soviet Union, an ally, should not come under unjustified attack. Finally, it would emphasize that Canada's groups were not threatened by each other. The WIB conveniently 'lost' Philipps' memorandum and then, when reminded, declined to accept his suggestion.[40]

The likely reason for this was that in April 1943, the Wartime Information Board decided to make a new start in solving some of these problems.[41] Charles Vining had suddenly resigned in January and the government chose John Grierson, the commissioner of the National Film Board, to take over as general manager of the WIB. Grierson possessed a far more activist attitude to public information work and set about organizing programmes to disseminate information to the armed forces and industrial workers, to popularize wartime restrictions, and to promote consumer awareness. The general manager believed that government information activities could bridge the gap between the citizen and his community. Furthermore, he believed in using his work to promote social change: "under the stress of war, we articulate the terms of our faith in progressive democracy, we learn to integrate the loyalties and forces of the community in the name of positive and highly constructive ideas."[42]

Given the nature of Grierson's philosophy of propaganda and his progressive social attitude, it is hardly surprising that he wanted to establish an information programme for ethnic groups. The WIB's research reinforced his determination and, in April 1943, reported that isolated groups had particularly low morale and that immigrant groups fit this category. The report argued that:

> Letters still appear in the press complaining that "foreigners" are staying home and taking the jobs of "real" Canadians who enlist. If this is so, it is not surprising, for numbers of these people, naturalized or not, have suffered years of humiliating discrimination because of their names, accents or appearance ... it cuts its victims off from the only experience which can make them feel like Canadians. And until they feel like Canadians they can have little urge to fight for Canada.[43]

Yet the WIB felt that if it were to move to correct the situation, the board would have to reduce the influence of Watson Kirkconnell and Tracy Philipps. Grierson recommended that the board not fund a proposed ethnic newspaper under Kirkconnell's patronage. Grierson commented that Donald Cameron, a member of the Committee on Cooperation in Canadian Citizenship and the head of the extension department of the University of Alberta, assessed Kirkconnell's influence as "inflammatory."[44] When Philipps made some anti-Soviet speeches in May 1943, Grierson quietly investigated his status as a public official who spoke out of turn.[45]

The WIB's general manager also tried to undermine the position of the Nationalities Branch and of Philipps by meeting with and supporting the Canadian Unity Council, an alliance of ethnic organizations that opposed Philipps' tactics. The council reported that the Committee on Cooperation in Canadian Citizenship had not done a proper job and had failed to meet the needs of the situation. Philipps, complained his opponents, behaved in a patronizing way as though he should maintain a "guardianship" over the "helpless and divided" ethnic groups and lead them into the Canadian community. This irritating attitude was compounded by his uncompromising anti-communist crusade. Under his influence, the council felt that the Nationalities Branch itself had created "bitter resentment," excluding new Canadians from its advisory committees and, thereby, affirming the second-class citizenship of members of the ethnic community.[46] On 9 October, *The Winnipeg Free Press* claimed that new Canadians remained loyal throughout the war because of the work of the Nationalities Branch and a large section of the ethnic press — this time many of moderate views — took umbrage. This set off another crusade against Philipps and Kirkconnell.[47]

At the end of October, Grierson reported on these findings to L.R. LaFlèche, the minister of national war services, and commented that:

> The interest of the Wartime Information Board is naturally in the provision of information, but you will appreciate that it is also interested in the whole matter of unity, particularly as between the various ethnic groups in the country. I need not say that the strength of the war effort depends upon securing as wise a solution to problems of this kind as can be devised.

Norman Robertson, the under secretary of state for external affairs, gave Mackenzie King a copy of this letter. For his part, Robertson had tried to reduce "the possible mischief which might arise from the activities of the Nationalities Branch" by suggesting to Philipps that he had reached the limit of his useful work in Canada. Robertson endorsed Grierson's proposal and sympathized with his opinion that no solution would appear until Philipps left government service.[48]

Despite this influential support to remove Philipps, Grierson failed to replace his work with a substantial programme run by the WIB. In August 1943, following a meeting with External Affairs, the examiner of publications for the Department of National Revenue and the WIB, the board began putting out a fortnightly survey of editorial opinion voiced in foreign language newspapers. But this set the limits of the WIB's involvement, apart from printing a few speeches by the minister of national war services, who in the conventional vein praised new Canadians' contribution to the war effort. For its armed forces education programme, the board also prepared a pamphlet outlining the history of immigration to Canada and asked the question: "Under just what conditions would we welcome new people and in what numbers?" In response, the pamphlet provided few answers. It noted that immigrants would have to have jobs and then commented that race should not be a barrier, but that the real qualification should be based on the skills desired. Essentially, however, the pamphlet was designed to stimulate discussion and not to editorialize.[49]

LaFlèche refused to remove Philipps on the grounds that the government would then abandon the ethnic community to communist agitators.[50] The prime minister's office also did not support Grierson's position because by January 1944 the general manager had himself come under a cloud for too close an association with left-wing elements.[51] Given these roadblocks, Grierson left the board, and the WIB abandoned any initiatives in the field of ethnic information.[52]

Grierson's withdrawal highlighted the WIB's most noticeable failure in its ethnic information programmes. Prejudice against orientals, long a feature of Canadian public opinion, had permeated the government. During the war, it surfaced as a racist approach towards the Japanese enemies. A National Film Board production, *The Mask of Nippon*, exemplifies the attitude: The film expressed the idea that the racial traits of the Japanese led to a duality in their 'character' which made them unreliable. On the one hand, they trained their children as a master race and, on the other, their custom of hara-kiri showed that they held all life in contempt. As a race, the Japanese could practice deceit and treachery in such a manner that their every action held a double meaning.[53]

The reaction of occidental Canadians to the Canadian Japanese population also strongly reflected this racial prejudice. Fear of subversion strengthened this xenophobia, especially in British Columbia, where public opinion forced the government to move Japanese Canadians from the west coast to internment camps in the interior.[54] The government did little to moderate anti-Japanese sentiment. In fact, arguing that the first obligation was to get the job done, and "if necessary override a democratic principal [sic]," the information board refused to hire a Canadian Japanese to prepare research for its reconstruction information programme.[55] Although the board made no effort to rationalize the displacement of the Japanese in Canada, a subtle amount of racist language surfaced in one of the pamphlets dealing with the post-war future of the Japanese in the country. A.R.M. Lower, a prominent historian who was commissioned to write the pamphlet, noted that while the Chinese Canadians were "unobtrusive and likeable," the Japanese were not. Lower reported that the Japanese had "a knack of getting themselves disliked." They were aggressive. They had large families. Their young people went on to university where the "good showings of many of them created ... enemies as well as friends." Lower concluded that, of all the ethnic groups in the country, the Japanese constituted the "real riddle" and that the government might have to deport them after the war. In August 1944, Mackenzie King announced the government's policy towards the Japanese: those who were judged disloyal were to be deported, the others dispersed throughout the country and no more immigration allowed.[56]

By the end of the war, the efforts to promote an official line that promoted unity among the ethnic communities and the English and French Canadians had failed to alter long-held prejudices. One-half of the population expressed an unwillingness to live beside a Japanese family; poorer and less-educated Canadians showed an even higher level of intolerance. But in a very telling comment, many of those who objected to the Japanese did not justify their attitudes on economic grounds but stated that they disliked "foreigners" in general. They did not believe that immigrants could become "good Canadians." In 1943, the WIB reported that "it is obvious that prejudice against 'foreigners' in general and Jews in particular has grown during the war."[57] A year later, a board survey reported that Canadians who desired a "closed door" immigration policy had increased from 21 percent to almost 30 percent of the population compared to 13 percent who advocated an "open door."

At a loss in June 1945, the information board's analysts recommended promoting acceptance of the Japanese and the ethnic community by capitalizing on a "latent" body of goodwill. For the Japanese, the board recommended a dispersal over the country and particularly a move to the cities as a means of lowering their profile and promoting assimilation.[58] The age of the cultural mosaic and multiculturalism lay far in the future.

Notes

1. W.L.M. King, "Nothing Matters Now But Victory," in his *Canada and the Fight for Freedom* (New York, 1944), 210-20

2. National Archives of Canada (NA), W.L.M. King Papers, J4, vol. 230, C155856, memorandum of A.D.P. Heeney to King, 10 November 1939; *ibid.*, C155853, memorandum of Walter Turnbull to Heeney, 8 November 1939; *ibid.*, vol. 155, C111174, summary of a discussion, 15 November 1939 (the participants were Heeney, John Grierson, J.W. Pickersgill and Turnbull)

3. *Ibid.*, vol. 230, C155877, memorandum of Heeney to King, 12 December 1939; NA, Privy Council Office Records (PCO), ser. 18, vol. 6, f. PCO-D-27, memorandum for the prime minister, n.d. [July 1940]

4. NA, Pierre Casgrain Papers, vol. 10, censorship file, pt. 3, memorandum of censors to Casgrain, 8 June 1940. The Canadian foreign language press which was checked included *Hlas L'Udu* (Slovak, Toronto), *Jiskra* (Czech, Toronto), *Glas Pracy* (Polish, Toronto), *Vapaus* (Finnish, Sudbury) *Pravda* (Serbian, Toronto), *Farmasky Zhitya* (Ukrainian, Winnipeg), *Narodnaja Gazeta* (Ukrainian, Winnipeg), *Slobodna Misao* (Croatian, Toronto), *The Canadian Tribune*, (English, Toronto), *The Advocate* (English, Vancouver), *The MidWest Clarion* (English, Winnipeg). See also W.H. Kesterton, *A History of Journalism in Canada* (Toronto, 1967), 248; NA, Wartime Information Board (WIB) Records, vol. 22, f. 23-22, R.W. Baldwin to Walter Herbert, 16 June 1941

5. NA, Department of National War Services Records, vol. 35, newspaper file, memorandum of T.C. Davis to J.G. Gardiner, 26 March 1941; *ibid.*, Davis to Pierre Casgrain, 27 August 1941; *ibid.*, Davis to members of the Cabinet, 22 September 1941; PCO Records, 7C ser., vol. 4, minutes of Cabinet War Committee, 3 April 1941

6. Provincial Museum and Archives of Alberta, Premiers' Papers, f. 1115, broadside, "Canada at War: Nazi Propaganda in our Schools," November 1939; King Papers, J4, vol. 349, C241240; *ibid.*, C257918, memorandum of Turnbull to King, 27 May 1940

7. For more on the origins and fate of the *Deutscher Bund*, see Jonathan Wagner, "The *Deutscher Bund Canada*, 1934-1939," *Canadian Historical Review*, LVIII, 2 (June 1977), 176ff

8. War Services Records, telegram of G.H. Lash to T.C. Davis, 25 February 1941

9. Watson Kirkconnell, *Canadians All: A Primer of Canadian National Unity* (Ottawa, 1941), 13ff

10. *Ibid.*

11. WIB Records, vol. 19, f. 10-A-7, script, "Canadians All," 23 April 1941

12. *Ibid.*, 16 April 1941

13. Kirkconnell, 16

14. W.L.M. King, "Canada Enters the War," in his *Canada at Britain's Side* (Toronto, 1941), 9 (speech delivered in the House of Commons, 8 September 1939)

15. *Ibid.*, "Italy Enters the War," 123-4

16. WIB Records, vol. 19, f. 10-A-47, script, "Canadians All," 7 May 1941

17. *Ibid.*, script, "Canadians All," 30 April 1941

18. The officers of the committee were G.W. Simpson (chairman), Tracy Philipps (European adviser), Dr. V.J. Kaye (liaison officer with foreign language groups). The members were Professor H.F. Angus, Hon. C.H. Blakeney, Major J.S.A. Bois, Major Donald Cameron, Dr. S.D. Clark, Robert England, J. Murray Gibbon, Professor Watson Kirkconnell, Mrs. R.J. McWilliams, and Mrs. O.D. Skelton. In fact, the order-in-council setting up the committee was never passed, but the body was called together by the Department of National War Services on 10 January 1942. WIB Records, vol. 13, f. 8-9-1, memorandum of Malcolm Ross to D.W. Buchanan, 7 June 1943. See also *ibid.*, memorandum of Philipps to D.B. Rogers, 30 October 1942, for an outline of the committee's plan of work.

19. King Papers, J4, vol. 372, C257903ff, [Pickersgill to King], 27 November 1939. In November 1940, J.A. Gibson commented in an attached memorandum that in his opinion "the points raised have increased, rather than lessened in importance." *Ibid.*, C257902, memorandum of Gibson to King, 16 November 1940. In July 1942, Turnbull reiterated his comments and urged King to intercede with Louis St. Laurent, the minister of justice, to stop the red-baiting. *Ibid.*, vol. 328, C227104, memorandum of Turnbull to King, 6 July 1942

20. Watson Kirkconnell, *A Slice of Canada: Memoirs* (Toronto, 1967), 315; WIB Records, vol. 13, f. 8-9-1, memorandum of Philipps to A.D. Dunton, 7 February 1943

21. NA, Department of Labour Records, vol. 125, f. 601-3, National War Services script sent out by Philipps for approval, n.d.; WIB Records, vol. 12, f. 8-2-2, minutes of committee on morale, 15 October 1942

22. Labour Records, vol. 125, f. 601-3, J.T. Thorson to Humphrey Mitchell, 8 September 1942; WIB Records, vol. 13, f. 8-9-1, memorandum of Philipps to deputy minister, 15 October 1942

23. WIB Records, vol. 13, f. 8-9-1, report of the Canadian Citizenship Committee, 7 October 1942

24. NA, Department of External Affairs Records, G2 ser., vol. 2252, f. 4210-40C, pt. 2, H.L. Keenleyside to L.B. Pearson, 16 September 1942; *ibid.*, memorandum of Saul Rae to Norman Robertson, 16 October 1942; *ibid.*, memorandum of Keenleyside to Robertson, 16 November 1942; *ibid.*, G1 ser., vol. 1978, f. 973, John

Grierson to Robertson, 27 October 1942. Those who objected to Vining's appointments remained anonymous in Keenleyside's memorandum, but are easily identified as Norman Mackenzie, president of the University of New Brunswick, Sidney Smith, president of the University of Manitoba, E.A. Corbett and T.W.L. MacDermott of the Canadian Association for Adult Education, Joe Clark, publicity director of the Department of National Defence, and Brooke Claxton, Liberal MP for St Lawrence-St George.

25. WIB Records, vol. 13, f. 8-9-1, memorandum of Campbell Smart to Vining, 8 September 1942; *ibid.*, memorandum of George Hosken to Malcolm Ross, 7 June 1943

26. The article appeared in *The New Republic*, 26 October 1942, 545, and was sent to the minister of national war services by *The Canadian Tribune*, a Toronto communist newspaper. WIB Records, vol. 13, f. 8-9-1, *The Canadian Tribune* to L.R. LaFlèche, 29 October 1942. R.B. Bryce of the Department of Finance and Pearson of the Department of External Affairs also received copies. *Ibid.*, Bryce to Clare Moyer, 27 October 1942

27. WIB Records, vol. 13, f. 8-9-1, memorandum of Dunton to D.B. Rogers, 13 November 1942; *ibid.*, letter of n.d. T.C. Davis told Simpson that the Nationalities Branch and the committee might disband. *Ibid.*, memorandum of Davis to LaFlèche, 7 November 1942, and Simpson to Davis, 17 November 1942; King Papers, J4, vol. 376, C260746, memorandum of Robertson to King, 1 November 1943

28. *Ibid.*, Davis to Donald Cameron, 25 November 1942; *ibid.*, George Simpson to T.C. Davis, 17 November 1942; War Services Records, vol. 35, Foreign Language Section file, Davis to Robertson, 26 October 1942

29. WIB Records, vol. 12, f. 8-2-2, minutes of committee on morale, 19 June 1942

30. *Ibid.*, f. 8-5-1A, J.W.G. Clark to Vining, 7 September 1942; *ibid.*, Harold Connolly to Vining, 8 September 1942; *ibid.*, Vining to Connolly, 20 November 1942; *ibid.*, Dunton to F.P. Healey, 13 November 1942; *ibid.*, f. 8-5-2, Ken H. Olive to Dunton, 10 November 1942; *ibid.*, 30 October 1942

31. *Ibid.*, Olive to Vining, 30 November 1942; *ibid.*, vol. 5, f. 2-1-2-2, submission of 30 December 1942

32. *Ibid.*, f. 8-5-1C, "Lists of Rumours," 30 January 1943

33. McGill University Archives, F. Cyril James Papers, box 2, Canadian Column file, circular letter, Saul Hayes to J.M. Schmauder, 30 September 1943. As a board member of the rumour clinic, James insisted that the Canadian Column publish a retraction. *Ibid.*, James to Schmauder, 22 September 1943

34. WIB Records, vol. 12, f. 8-5-2, memorandum of J.D. Ketchum to Dunton, 12 November 1943

35. *Ibid.*, Olive to Grierson, 3 April 1943

36. *Ibid.*, f. 8-9-1, David B. Mansur to Dunton, 23 December 1942

37. *Ibid.*, Humphrey Mitchell to Norman Senior, 28 December 1942

38. *Ibid.*, f. 8-9-2, memorandum of Dunton to Grierson, 17 February 1943. Dunton had spoken to Frank Dojacek, publisher of *Canadian Farmer* (a Ukrainian paper), *The Canadian Voice* (Croatian) and *Der Nordwesten* (German).

39. *Ibid.*, f. 8-9-1, speech by Ed. Yardash, 15 October 1942

40. *Ibid.*, Tracy Philipps, "Background Information for Foreign Language Publications," 5 December 1942; *ibid.*, memorandum of Dunton to Philipps, 12 March 1943

41. *Ibid.*, f. 8-9-2, Grierson to H.R.L. Henry, 20 February 1943; *ibid.*, C.F. Crandall to Dojacek, 22 April 1943

42. *Ibid.*, vol. 6, f. 2-1-3, "The Necessity and Nature of Public Information," speech made in Montreal, June 1943

43. WIB, "Low Morale," Information Briefs, 6, 19 April 1943

44. *Ibid.*, vol. 13, f. 8-9-2, Grierson to Henry, 20 February 1943

45. *Ibid.*, memorandum of Gordon Hosken to Grierson, 14 May 1943

46. *Ibid.*, Grierson to LaFlèche, 28 October 1943; *ibid.*, Canadian Unity Council to Grierson, n.d. [November 1943]

47. *Ibid.*, f. 8-9-1, special report for the press censors, 29 November 1943; *ibid.*, memorandum of Grierson to Heeney, 30 November 1943; *ibid.*, special report for the chief press censors of Canada, 20 December 1943. A translation from *La Vittoria*, Toronto, called Kirkconnell "a professional anti-Soviet, red-baiter and pro-fascist who supported Horthy's fascist regime in Hungary."

48. King Papers, J4, vol. 376, C260746, memorandum of Robertson to King, 1 November 1943. This encloses Grierson's letter to LaFlèche of 28 October.

49. WIB, f. 8-9-3, draft release for a speech by LaFlèche, June 1944; Arthur Neal and Morley Callaghan, "Millions of Immigrants?" *Canadian Affairs*, I, 21 (1 March 1944)

50. *Ibid.*, vol. 1, f. 1-2-19, minutes of WIB, 2 November 1943

51. *Ibid.*, vol. 13, f. 8-9-2, Grierson to Robertson, 28 December 1943

52. *Ibid.*, vol. 1, f. 1-2-19, minutes of WIB, 10 January 1944; *ibid.*, G.C. Andrew to C.H. Payne, 12 January 1944

53. National Film Board of Canada, *The Mask of Nippon*, The World in Action, produced by Grierson, October 1942

54. W. Peter Ward, "British Columbia and the Japanese Evacuation," *Canadian Historical Review*, LVII, 3 (September 1976), 289-308

55. WIB Records, vol. 4, f. 2-1-1, memorandum of R. Boyd to G.C. Andrew, 24 May 1945

56. A.R.M. Lower, "Canada as a Pacific Power," *Canadian Affairs* (Canadian Edition), I, 4 (1 March 1944), 7

57. King Papers, J4, vol. 376, C260781, memorandum to Cabinet, 27 December 1943

58. WIB Survey, 30 (12 February 1944); *ibid.*, 66 (30 June 1945). On the 1944 survey the question read: "After the war, do you think Canada should open its doors to permit people from all parts of the world to settle here or do you think we should be careful about the type of people we let into our country?" The results were:

	Jan 1943	Jan 1944
Open its doors	14%	13%
Allow some in	59	50
Keep all out	21	29
Undecided	6	8

Broken down by ethnic background, the results were:

	Open Doors	Be Careful	Undecided
British origin	11%	84%	5%
French origin	7	76	17
Other origin	22	69	9

Breaking the Nazi Plot: Canadian Government Attitudes Towards German Canadians, 1939-1945

Robert H. Keyserlingk

Throughout the Second World War, the *Globe and Mail* was one of Canada's severest critics of the wartime Defence of Canada Regulations (DOCR). In July 1945, not surprisingly, the newspaper greeted their demise with enthusiasm. The end of "years of injustices and irregularities committed in the name of national security" had finally come.[1] Issued in September 1939 under authority of the War Measures Act, the DCOR had given the Canadian government arbitrary domestic powers over all Canadian residents, whether citizens or not. The application of these tough regulations to Italian and Japanese Canadians, and to domestic fascist and communist or left-wing elements, is well known. But what of the many thousands of immigrants and Canadian citizens of German background who were similarly forced during the war to register under the DOCR as enemy aliens? What of those interned by the hundreds without a trial as dangerous security risks?

The generally-accepted version of the government's Second World War policy regarding these German Canadians is that they represented a special case, a real threat. There existed in Canada a large-scale nazi conspiracy, which had to be broken by firm government actions. Even authors normally critical of the Royal Canadian Mounted Police's (RCMP) past or present intelligence capabilities have accepted that there was in Canada before, and during the Second World War, a widespread nazi spy and saboteur network, which was smashed by the

53

government.² Because of the RCMP's stirling undercover work and the government's quick actions, especially in 1939 and 1940, this very real plot was smashed and the highly-dangerous security risks interned.³ Towards the end of the war the RCMP itself admitted that there had been no wartime acts of sabotage by German Canadians in Canada. But, they boasted, this record was attributable to their keen police work.⁴ In other words, great elements of Canada's large German-Canadian community, the third largest population group in Canada after the English and French, had probably been disloyal to this country in wartime.

However, a semi-official history of the RCMP written by an ex-head of RCMP intelligence puts the matter a good deal more tentatively. According to this book, the police checkmated "any plans Germans may have had for espionage in Canada."⁵ The key words "may have had" escaped subsequent students of this matter. Could it be that a domestic nazi network of agents never existed, despite Hitler's wild, propagandistic trumpetings about the mystical unity of race and leader? Printed RCMP records tell of only three nazi spies discovered during the war. Of one nothing is revealed. The second was landed in the Gaspé by submarine and was turned in to the police by a local hotel keeper. The third was also infiltrated into Canada from outside, and turned himself into the Ottawa RCMP once the capital given him in Germany ran out and he became indigent. Until then he had lived quietly in Ottawa, doing no spying.⁶ The government did not, in fact, turn up any real cases of domestic subversion among German Canadians.

Nor did the RCMP possess the capability to do so. It could not investigate the loyalties of such a large and diverse ethnic group like the German Canadians, and had not been required by its political masters to do so before the war. Once war broke out, this paper will show, government moves against German Canadians had much less to do with uncovering real security threats than with domestic political aims. Politicians were suddenly pushed by an alarmed public opinion to take action towards disarming a perceived domestic nazi threat. They in turn drove the police and bureaucrats to present them as quickly as possible with some 'dangerous' nazi agents in order to give the public the impression that the government was in control of the domestic subversion problem and to calm public opinion. However, the policemen and bureaucrats possessed too little hard information about possible domestic nazi infiltration, and were granted too little time to respond properly to this harried request. To cover their unpreparedness, they threw together in great haste haphazard lists of hundreds of Canadian residents and citizens without much chance of turning up truly dangerous agents. Over 800 German Canadians were arrested and interned on the grounds that membership in pro-nazi organizations or neighbours' denunciations made them dangerous agents. Most were fairly simple workers or farmers from the rural west. Those interned were swept up in two waves of panic in September 1939 and during the fifth column scare of mid-1940. Whenever these public panics subsided, the government was prepared to admit to itself that the grounds for these German-Canadian roundups were very weak, and it began to release the internees. Secure in the knowledge that its hurried internment or release actions were hidden behind the impenetrable screen of secrecy guaranteed by the arbitrary DOCR powers, the government operated against German Canadians for domestic political rather than legitimate security reasons. The German-Canadian case was the dress rehearsal for subsequent actions against Italian, Japanese, or fascist and communist Canadians.

It was commonly held in 1939-1940 by proponents of the myth of a dangerous nazi conspiracy in Canada that German Canadians' roots led back to the German state. The truth was that the vast majority of Germans in Canada came from everywhere else in Europe but Germany. Only about eighteen percent of these people, either before the First World War or the Second World War, had come to Canada from Germany itself. The vast majority of the others arrived from eastern European countries, especially from the Tsarist Russian Empire, where they had been settled for centuries before coming to Canada. By 1939 only 16,000 of the over half a million German-Canadians were not Canadian citizens.[7] Among these non-citizens were thousands of refugees of Jewish, Austrian or Czech background.[8] Before the First World War the Imperial German and Austro-Hungarian governments had not regarded naturalization in Canada as relieving their ex-citizens of allegiance to their old homelands in time of war, but the interwar republican German and Austrian governments had been prompt to do so.[9]

In the 1930s, the Canadian government had not worried much about the problem of possible nazi subversion in Canada. The prime minister and his closest associates long remained convinced that Hitler did not intend to fight.[10] When war finally broke out, they were prepared to turn against Hitler and his "gang," while retaining a trust in the German people as basically anti-nazi; as a decent people held in bond by the evil nazi clique.¹¹ Yet, even if they rejected notions of the basic disloyalty or innate depravity of the German groups in Canada, the thorny problem remained of seeking out any possibly dangerous elements which might be harmful to the Canadian war effort. This was the task of the RCMP.

The RCMP at war's beginning was under-staffed, possessed very little intelligence capability, and had been assigned the task of looking for subversion on the left. The government's sudden search for nazi agents in September 1939 caught the force unawares and unready. In 1939 the RCMP had a strength of only 2,541 mainly uniformed officers spread across the country. In most provinces they were responsible for enforcement of both federal and provincial laws and regulations.¹² In Ontario and Quebec, where separate provincial police forces existed, only 100 and 160 RCMP officers and men respectively were stationed.¹³ Protected from military call up, the RCMP expanded its wartime responsibilities enormously to cover protection of vulnerable points, registrations of arms and aliens, break up of black markets, and aid to the military police. At the same time their number actually decreased.¹⁴ Simply from the point of view of numbers, additional intelligence work was hardly possible.

Nor were members of the RCMP trained for intelligence work. RCMP commissioners and their staff saw themselves as policemen. A small intelligence branch was formed after the First World War which had broken a secret communist ring in the 1920s. The force continued to look leftwards for traces of subversion in Canada. Head of this small two-man branch in 1939 was the young Charles Rivett-Carnac, just returned from years of Arctic patrol. He later wrote in his memoirs of his shock at finding himself appointed to this sort of work. "To anyone who had been used to driving dogs and facing the storm and stress of the elements, those two tasks [intelligence and the editorship of the RCMP *Quarterly Magazine*] might have been more than enough to tax anyone's capabilities."¹⁵

Tax and overtax him they did. He was told to draw up intricate plans to protect King George VI when he visited Canada in 1939; later that year he set about the guarding of Canada's industrial plants, harbours, canals, bridges, and other sprawling vulnerable points in case of war.¹⁶ For local intelligence information Rivett-Carnac had to depend on uniformed RCMP policemen with little knowledge of nazism. Three months into the war, indeed, the prime minister's office realized that the

RCMP was a dead letter as far as anti-nazi investigations were concerned. A November 1940 report for the prime minister pointed out that the RCMP had failed to turn up any nazi spies and saboteurs: it still looked to the left and failed "to appreciate the direction from which serious danger might threaten us." Judging from RCMP reports, the memorandum continued, "one would scarcely realize that Canada was at war with Germany."[17] On the other hand, several of the provinces continued to agree with the RCMP that the left presented the real security danger to Canada.[18] In early 1941 the RCMP commissioner himself took the unprecedented step of taking to print to berate the public and members of parliament who refused to see this truth.[19]

In fact, the government had not asked the RCMP before the war to look for danger from the right instead of from the left. As a result, the RCMP collected only an anecdotal record of the printed, public nazi material issued by the three main pro-nazi organizations in Canada.[20] This information was obviously superficial. The RCMP remained unconvinced of any possible danger from ethnic Germans as a whole, or from members of the small 250-man nazi Party (NSDAP) in Canada, the 500-man German Workers Party (DAF), or the 2,000-strong Canadian Society for German Culture or *Bund*.[21] The first two groups were reserved for German citizens, the RCMP appreciated, while the *Bund* was aimed at Canadians of German background.[22] A recent study of the *Bund* has indicated that many Canadians joined it for cultural or nostalgic reasons. Among its members were many Lutherans and Mennonites, who were supplied with very un-nazi German Bibles by the German government.[23]

Nor did the RCMP possess agents to cover or infiltrate these groups. The printed pro-nazi material was collected at headquarters, lay largely untranslated into English, and none was sent to the provincial divisions.[24] Translations reflected great unfamiliarity with nazi terminology. Thus "HJ" and "BDM," acronyms for the Hitler Youth and its sister group for girls, remained mysteries. The term *Wehrmacht*, or German Army, received the following convoluted explanation: "A 'Wehrmann' in the German language, is a militia man, a soldier or swordsman. It is therefore assumed that the above 'Wehrmacht' is some sort of military organization. 'Macht' in German (might, in English) means power, authority or force. It thus means a military or defence force."[25] Some of these interpretations, laughable to us, were to become more serious following the internment of individuals for 'disloyal' tendencies.[26]

Certainly the three pro-nazi organizations, small as they were, were fascist in tone, although more mutedly so in the case of the *Bund*. But many members, especially of the *Bund*, claimed that they were at the same time loyal Canadians who had joined for other than political reasons. The *Bund* refused to employ, for instance, the Hitler salute or to sing the nazi anthem at its meetings and national conventions. Many recent immigrants had come to Canada just before the depression, were victims of it, and claimed they merely huddled together for economic self-help.[27] Whatever the truth, the government at war's beginning was not in possession of enough reliable information to allow a hasty decision about who were the dangerous nazis.

By May 1939 the government had managed to put together a basic war plan for its various departments in case hostilities broke out. In its section on aliens, *The Provisional War Book* of May 1939 stated that enemy aliens should, in case of war, register with the police, and that those against whom there existed real proof of disloyalty or subversion could be arrested and interned.[28] These draft Defence of Canada Regulations therefore spoke only of enemy aliens, and stressed the need for proof of disloyalty before internment could be envisaged. Yet those limitations on arbitrary action fell away when the crisis arrived. On 1 September 1939, the day Hitler invaded Poland and nine days before Canada went to war, the government hurriedly established an advisory internment committee headed by Norman Robertson of the Department of External Affairs. The committee, however, quickly realized that the DOCR did not go far enough.[29] Ordered by their political masters to produce and intern dangerous nazis, the three-man bureaucratic committee found itself with no other source of information than a hastily-assembled RCMP list, to which no real evidence had been attached, of several hundred names turned in by local police detachments.[30] The RCMP list included not only enemy aliens, but Canadians as well. After rejecting the RCMP list at first, the committee realized that it had no choice but to return to the document in the absence of any proof of disloyalty or other relevant information.[31] It therefore recommended to the government that, in order to intern these men, the DOCR should be changed to include others than enemy aliens, and should not require hard evidence for internment. Then the police list would suffice.[32] And so began the notorious internment process under which Italian and Japanese Canadians, and domestic fascists and communists, would later be so lightly jailed as well.

The government toughened the DOCR as recommended, and passed on the directive that both Germans and German Canadians on the RCMP list could be arrested and interned without trial.³³ The Robertson committee's (and the government's) main fear, it turned out, was public panic about a widespread sabotage and spy threat and the danger of local riots if the men turned in locally to the police as nazis were not quickly interned.³⁴ The justice department admitted privately to the prime minister that this process was not in nature different from that employed in totalitarian countries, but claimed that these actions were necessary in wartime.³⁵ Consequently, in the early morning of 4 September, six days before Canada went to war, 303 Germans and German Canadians were arrested, their homes were searched for evidence, and then they were sent off to internment.³⁶ The government was immensely gratified by the positive public response to the arrests, which it gave out were the result of long, painstaking police investigation and infiltration of nazi organizations.³⁷

The government had no idea whom it had really interned. The minister of justice felt they must all be highly educated nazi leaders.³⁸ The truth was that the vast majority were simple workers and farmers.³⁹ Gradually made aware that the swift internment process had not sinned on the side of justice, the government decided to open an internal review of the internees. Fifteen were released over the next few months as not disloyal nor members of any pro-nazi organization. Nine NSDAP members, 45 DAF and *Bund* members were also judged not dangerous and released.⁴⁰ The review judges realised that in many cases they had little to go on, but the review transcripts reveal that evidence consisted mainly of vague unsubstantiated police statements, and that judgements as often as not depended on little more than an internee's demeanor. The RCMP resisted the review judges' calls for hard evidence as shocking.⁴¹ But by early 1940 even the RCMP was willing to admit that "in fact we have doubtless erred in recommending internments when actual evidence was not available."⁴² Review tribunal members and Robertson's advisory internment committee began to admit that people had often joined these ethnic, if pro-nazi, groups for apolitical reasons. It was decided that membership in DAF and the *Bund* was probably not harmful to Canada.⁴³ Robertson admitted his own embarrassment at having to administer retroactive justice to people who had been members of perfectly legal organizations in Canada.⁴⁴ By early May 1940 even the judge advocate general of the Canadian Army recommended to the prime minister that the DOCR be liberalized.⁴⁵ The government agreed, and a special committee was convened to carry out this plan.[46]

However, before the first meeting could take place, Hitler suddenly struck in the west and the Phoney War came to an abrupt end. And with this attack disappeared the plans to liberalize the DOCR and release more internees. Suddenly, a new public panic exploded, directed at the spectre of notorious, hidden fifth columns of agents and saboteurs thought to be everywhere. Norway, the Low Countries and France, it was claimed, had fallen not to German military might, but because their domestic morale and fighting ability were broken by secret fifth column agents doing their hideous work behind allied lines.[47] Canada too, the RCMP told a fearful Canadian public, had been infiltrated by hundreds of thousands of these dangerous agents in the guise of German immigrants, refugees, German-Canadian citizens, even discontented Eskimos or Indians, and who knew what else.[48] An aroused public demanded once again that the government take strong measures against nazis. Conservative members of parliament called for the internment of all Italians, Germans, communists and other fifth columnists. Patriotic organizations flooded the government with petitions demanding immediate and firm action.[49] The prime minister even foresaw the possibility of a *coup* by angry paramilitary groups in the country.[50] Something had to be done, and be seen to be done, against dangerous nazi fifth columnists.

As a result, the DOCR was not liberalized, but instead toughened so that all ethnic nazi and fascist, as well as communist, organizations could be banned and closed. Registration as enemy aliens was made obligatory for wider groups of ethnic Canadians whose date of entry into Canada went back to 1922. In practice this regulation caught up persons who had emigrated to Canada since 1914, as almost no German immigration had taken place between 1914 and 1922.[51] Most important, the government needed to find nazi agents to be interned so that the public would feel once more secure. The 1939 RCMP lists were dusted off, and new ones provided.[52] By the end of 1940 the number of internees had quadrupled to 1200, half of whom were Germans and German Canadians, the rest fascists and communists.[53] These actions achieved the government's public relations goal. As a local RCMP officer guilelessly expressed it, "the effect of periodic internments is very beneficial in stabilizing public feeling."[54] Once again, those interned were put away solely on the basis of bald RCMP lists without any additional information. Most of the names were assembled through local denunciations, while in some cases the RCMP even advertised publicly for confidential denunciations.[55]

Interest in German Canadians peaked in 1941 as the government began to turn its attention to the Japanese Canadians. By mid-year the high point of German-Canadian internments was reached. During 1942 internee releases again began, until by the end of the war only 89 pro-nazi internees were still held in camps.[56] Indeed, government policy began to swing towards a renewed confidence in its German-Canadian population. In December 1942 all naturalized German Canadians were finally exempted from reporting to the registrars of enemy aliens because of their "exceptionally good behavior" since the war's beginning, a decision applied to Italian Canadians as well.[57] By mid-1943 enemy aliens of German or Italian background were permitted to join the Canadian armed forces if their applications for naturalization had been accepted by the government and they obtained security clearance.[58] By this time, most of the administrative restrictions against Germans and German Canadians had been lifted. Forty German Canadians were denaturalized during the course of the war, but further action was halted for fear of losing Liberal votes in German ethnic constituencies.[59] In addition, a dozen jailed German women and their children were exchanged in 1940 for a similar group of Canadian women captured at sea.[60]

Despite these harsh wartime measures invoked against many Germans in Canada and Canadians of German origin, no evidence or trace of a subversive nazi organization or individual domestic spies and saboteurs was turned up. Neither the RCMP nor other bureaucrats possessed the required intelligence capability and knowledge of the domestic ethnic scene — or even the language ability — to be effective. As a result, they were unable to sort out differences within the splintered German-Canadian community or distinguish loyal from disloyal German Canadians. On the face of it, it would appear that no real subversive threat existed to Canada from among this ethnic community. This conclusion supports research elsewhere which indicates that the nazis had no plans in the Second World War to organize subversive networks among North American German ethnic communities.[61] Instead, the main purpose of moves against German Canadians was less to turn up dangerous agents than to calm the public and make it appear that the government was in control of the nazi threat at home. Forced quickly and without even minimum preparation to turn up dangerous nazi agents for arrest and internment, the

Canadian police and bureaucrats responded as best they could in the circumstances to the unrealistic orders of their political masters. The German-Canadian experience was the forerunner of the Italian, communist and Japanese experiences after mid-1940. It does not give the citizen much confidence that over-hasty security or intelligence actions in a crisis are more judiciously restrained when directed by politicians rather than policemen.

Table 1

**Canadian Civilian Internment Statistics
4 September 1939 — 18 August 1945**[62]

	Defence of Canada Regulation 21, 24 & 25(8)	
Pro-Germans:		
Total arrested		847
Released	814	
Deceased	8	
Mental cases — release orders issued	5	
Presently detained		20
Italians:		
Total arrested		632
Released	630	
Mental cases — release orders issued	2	
Presently detained		Nil
Communists:		
Total arrested		133
Released	133	
Presently detained		Nil
N.U.P:		
Total arrested		27
Released	26	
Deceased	1	
Presently detained		Nil
Japanese:		
Total arrested		782
Released	359	
Deceased	3	
Presently detained		420
Miscellaneous:		
Total arrested		2
Released	2	
Presently detained		Nil
Grand Total Presently Detained		440

Table 2

**Recapitulation of Internments
4 September 1939 — 18 August 1945**[63]

	Reg 21	24	25(8)	Totals
Total arrested	1,776	46	601	2,423
Released	1,507	38	419	1,964
Deceased	5	0	7	12
Mental cases	1	0	6	7
Presently detained	263	8	169	440

Notes

1. "Restore Civil Liberties," Toronto *Globe and Mail*, 5 July 1945. See Table 1 for figures.

2. J. Sawatsky, *Men in the Shadows* (Toronto, 1980), 67ff. J. Wagner follows this account in his *Brothers Beyond the Seas: National Socialism in Canada* (Waterloo, 1981), 131-2.

3. C.W. Harvison, *The Horsemen* (Toronto, 1967), 86, 93, 101; V.A.M. Kemp, *Without Fear, Favour or Affection: Thirty-five Years with the Royal Canadian Mounted Police* (Toronto, New York, 1958), 202

4. "Recalls No Act of Sabotage in Dominion," Toronto *Globe and Mail*, 26 August 1944

5. Norma and W.H. Kelly, *The Royal Canadian Mounted Police: A Century of History* (Edmonton, 1973), 190

6. Sawatsky, 68-9, following a version by Harvison

7. H. Lehmann, *Das Deutschtum in Westkanada* (Berlin, Leipzig, 1939), 93. Lehmann estimates that there were probably about 720,000 persons of German origin in Canada by the late 1930s, because many immigrated under other national labels. *Kanada und Newfundland* (Berlin, 1944), 32

8. National Archives of Canada (NA), Department of External Affairs Records (DEA), RG 25, G1, vol. 1871, F.C. Blair (Immigration Branch) to O.D. Skelton, 10 October 1939; NA, Norman A. Robertson Papers, MG 30, E165, vol. 12, MW statistics, 13 March 1939; DEA, G1, vol. 1964, f. 855-D, dominion statistician to Skelton, 12 October 1939

9. Desmond Morton, *The Canadian General: Sir William Otter* (Toronto, 1974), 325. Otter headed Canada's First World War internment programme, and was active in the early stage of the same operation during the Second World War.

10. James Eayrs, *In Defence of Canada: Appeasement and Rearmament* (Toronto, 1965), 73-4, 77-8, 232ff

11. O.D. Skelton and his successor as under secretary of state for external affairs, Norman A. Robertson, both distinguished between the mass of "good" Germans and the small Nazi clique. DEA, G1, vol. 1980, memorandum of Skelton to HLK, 28 August 1940; NA, William Lyon Mackenzie King Papers, MG 26, J4, vol. 358, Robertson to King, 21 June, 14 August, and 1 October 1941

12. NA, Ernest Lapointe Papers, MG III, B10, RCMP Commissioner S.T. Wood to Minister of Justice Lapointe, 25 August 1939; King Papers, J1, vol. 273, J F MacNeill to PM's secretary, J.W. Pickersgill, 4 December 1939

13. Kemp, 201; Harvison, 100

14. Kelly, 190; King Papers, J1, vol. 298, memorandum of RCMP, 10 January 1940

15. C. Rivett-Carnac, *In Pursuit of Wilderness* (Toronto, 1965), 293

16. Harvison, 87

17. King Papers, J4, vol. 372, Prime Minister's Office to prime minister, 16 November 1940

18. *Ibid.*, vol. 424, record of meeting of federal Cabinet with representatives of the Ontario Legislature, 3 October 1940.

19. S.T. Wood, "Tools for Treachery," *The Canadian Spokesman*, I,2 (February 1941), in King Papers, J4, vol. 355. See also Pickersgill to King, 18 February 1941.

20. RCMP Security Services Archives, Ottawa (files kindly sent to the author by C/Supt P.E.J. Banning, whose assistance is gratefully acknowledged), Toronto *Globe and Mail*, 27 November 1939, *Deutsche Zeitung fur Kanada*, 28 October 1937, Inspector F.A. Blake to commissioner, 6 December 1937, memorandum of Spl. Cst. Black, "F" Division, 17 December 1937

21. Robertson Papers, vol. 12, RCMP HQ to Robertson, 4 January 1939, and Robertson to MacNeill, 20 March 1940. Candidates for naturalization were only checked for extreme left-wing links. See DEA, G1, vol. 1964.

22. RCMP Security Services Archives, Supt H.A.R. Gagnon, "C" Division, to RCMP commissioner, 18 March 1939

23. Wagner, 68, 130. Wagner writes about the *Bund* using mainly German sources and reports from Canada by German officials responsible for organizing these groups. He estimates *Bund* membership between 1,800 and 2,000, but admits the membership was very unstable and fluctuated greatly.

24. RCMP Security Services Archives, A/A/Cmd. "K" Division, W.F.W. Hancock, to commissioner, 20 February 1939

25. *Ibid.*, "Directions Respecting Membership in the German Labour Front Abroad," summarized by MHA at RCMP Headquarters. The translation from the German speaks of dispensation from DAF dues in cases where the person serves with the *Arbeitsdienst* (Nazi Labour Service) or *Wehrmacht* (army) as follows: "service to the German Labour Front (whatever that might be), when a member is engaged in WEHRMACHT." All sections dealing with social welfare were not translated or summarized. Later translations (dates unsure, some date from 1942) improve.

26. *Ibid.*, memorandum of Criminal Investigation Branch, Vancouver, 26 June 1939. *Bund* regulations were received at RCMP HQ in early 1939, but only translated in 1942. Exhibit report, Lethbridge to RCMP HQ, 30 January 1939, translated 25 November 1942 by MH at RCMP HQ. Much of the rest of this RCMP material on the *Bund* was only translated in 1983 for transmission to the author by the RCMP Security Services.

27. Toronto *Globe and Mail*, 15 and 17 May 1939

28. Department of National Defence, Directorate of History, Ottawa (DHist), 192 (D1), "Report of the Committee on Emergency Legislation," July 1938, and *Government of Canada War Book (Provisional): Coordination of Departmental Action in the Event of War or Emergency Real or Apprehended*, May 1939

29. DEA, G1, vol. 1964, f. 855-D, Robertson to Skelton, 28 August 1939, and Cabinet decision, 31 August 1939

30. *Ibid.*, Wood to Lapointe, 26 August 1939; King Papers, J1, vol. 273, MacNeill to Pickersgill, internment report for prime minister, 4 December 1939; J.L. Granatstein, *A Man of Influence: Norman A. Robertson and Canadian Statecraft* (Ottawa, 1981), 80-91

31. King Papers, J1, vol. 273, MacNeill to Pickersgill, 4 December 1939, and Robertson to King, 2 September 1939

32. DEA, G1, vol. 1964, f. 855-D, advisory internment committee minutes, 1 September 1939

33. *Ibid.*, meeting of 3 September 1939

34. *Ibid.*, meeting of 1 September 1939

35. King Papers, J1, vol. 273, MacNeill to Pickersgill, 4 December 1939

36. PC 2483, "Defence of Canada Regulations," 3 September 1939; PC 2485, "Registrars of Enemy Aliens," 3 September 1939; DEA, G1, vol. 1964, f. 855-D, Skelton to Robertson, 4 September 1939. Versions of RCMP arrest dates differ. For example, "Canada's formal declaration came on September 10. During the next forty-eight hours two hundred local Nazi leaders and subleaders were arrested." Harvison, 101. "Within a few hours of the declaration of war," nazis were arrested across Canada. Kelly, 190. See also Kemp, 203.

37. "Nazi Activities Here Crushed by Arrest of Over 70 Leaders," Montreal *Star*, 4 September 1939; King Papers, J1, vol. 273, MacNeill to Pickersgill, 4 December 1939

38. King Papers, J1, vol. 270, Lapointe to T.B. McQuesten, 17 October 1939

39. NA, Department of Justice Records, RG 13, C1, vols. 966-971, for the transcripts of the approximately 300 review tribunals held between October 1939 and April 1940. Work profiles: 27 labourers, 61 semi-skilled labourers, 104 skilled workers and artisans, 80 farmers and farmhands. Included were 11 waiters, 9 butchers, 9 bakers, 6 shoemakers, 5 tailors, 2 musicians and 2 hairdressers.

40. *Ibid.*, for decisions and recommendations

41. RCMP Records, box 1, f. C 11-19-4, 1, Wood to Lapointe, 1 November 1939

42. *Ibid.*, Supt. V.A.M. Kemp to Wood, 13 July 1940

43. Justice Records, C1, vol. 970, P. Schaetzle case

44. Robertson Papers, vol. 12, f. 145, Robertson to MacNeill, 19 March 1940; DEA, G1, vol. 1964, Robertson to RCMP Ins. Bavin, MacNeill and Skelton, 17 April 1940

45. King Papers, J4, vol. 355, judge advocate general to King, 2 May 1940

46. *Ibid.*

47. *Ibid.*, J2, vol. 213, J.R. Bowler to King, 24 July 1940, enclosing a copy of A. Warren's *The Nazi Bluff* (Ottawa, 1940). Warren wrote: "Armed conflict plays a subordinate role. The real arm of aggression on the Nazi side is the propaganda division of the 'Fifth Column'."

48. Robertson Papers, vol. 13, f. 149, Skelton to Bavin, 8 July 1940; *ibid.*, vol. 14, f. 158, Civil Service Commission to Robertson, "Organization of the Internal Defence of Canada"; "More than 50,000 Potential Fifth Columnists," Ottawa *Evening Journal*, 8 October 1940; DEA, G1, vol. 1964, f. 844-E, record of conversation between RCMP Sergeant Barnes and Mr. Justice Hyndman, text sent to Robertson, 30 September 1940

49. King Papers, J2, vols. 223-224, contain most of these petitions; *ibid.*, vol. 348, "Summary of Representations Re: Enemy Aliens and So-called 'Fifth Column' Menace," May 1940; *ibid.*, vol. 232, sabotage files for other petitions

50. *Ibid.*, J4, vol. 348, WJT to King, 22 May 1940; *ibid.*, J13, King Diary, 22 October 1940. King feared "tendencies of military organizations like the Canadian Corps to take matters in their own hands."

51. *Ibid.*, vol. 355, memorandum of Justice Department, "Defence of Canada Regulations (1.4.-30.6.1940)"; DOCR (consolidated 1940) under PC 4750, 12 September 1940

52. DEA, G1, vol. 1964, f. 855-E, 2, King to Lapointe, 3 June 1940, and Robertson to Coleman, 5 July 1940; Robertson Papers, vol. 12, for committee's checked lists

53. Figures compiled from RCMP Records, box 5; Robertson Papers, vol. 14; DEA, G1, vol. 1964, 855-D; NA, Department of National Defence Records, RG 24, vol. 4-1-5 (1), f. 6585 for internment lists; *ibid.*, vol. C4, f. 6577, and Department of External Affairs Archives, Ottawa, (f.) 3033b-40 for interned women in Canada

54. RCMP Records, vol. 1, f. C 11-19-4, 2, asst. commander, "F" Division, to commissioner, 15 August 1940

55. Department of National Defence Records, vol. 4-1-5 (1), f. 6585, Robertson to minister of justice, 5 July 1940; RCMP Records, vol. 1, f. C 11-19-4, 2, R.R. Tait to "F" Division, 6 September 1940, and Tait to all RCMP commanding officers, 12 July 1940

56. See footnote 53 above.

57. DEA, G1, vol. 1964, SFR secret memorandum, 11 November 1942, SFR memorandum to King, 8 December 1942, and External Affairs to Canadian high commissioner, London, 24 December 1942

58. DHist, enlistment schemes of 1 August 1942 and July 1943 (revised).

59. King Papers, J4, vol. 246, Pickersgill to King, 7 July 1944; *ibid.*, J2, vol. 224, W.J. Pratt to Heeney, n.d., 1940

60. External Affairs Archives, f. 3033B-40

61. David Kahn, *Hitler's Spies* (Long Island, N.Y., 1981)

62. NA, RG 18, box 5, C116-19-4

63. *Ibid.*

Ethnicity on Trial: The Italians of Montreal and the Second World War

Bruno Ramirez

Not long ago, while working on the screenplay of a docudrama on the history of Montreal's Italians, I had the occasion to realize the extent to which the Second World War period stood as a sort of 'dark age' in the history of that community.[1] The war had in fact brought punishment and humiliation to a community that — because of the particular course of events in world affairs — had been harshly criticized (along with others) for harbouring in its midst potential threats to Canada's national security. The harsh treatment that the community had suffered, dramatized by the internment of several hundreds of its members, was of course a matter of public knowledge. At least three persons who had lived through those critical years had written and published books that dealt with that topic. Two of those three books were published in one of the two official languages and thus, at least in principle, were accessible to a Canadian readership.[2]

But for most of the surviving internees I met in my research, that episode was something in their experience that they preferred to treat as a taboo. When, in the course of my interviews, the discussion touched on the internment issue, it was as if a thick veil of selfimposed censure fell on their memory. Those who did not outrightly refuse to talk about it spoke with great reticence, wanting to bring the subject to a rapid close, or making very vague and general references. Finally, between one conversation and another, between one silence and another, between one confident smile and another, I was allowed to share some painful memories that had been seldom turned into words. As it turned out, those reminiscences became one of the most touching moments of our documentary. The whole experience was enough to convince me that the reasons behind that secretive attitude must be more complex than I had originally thought.

For an historian of immigration and ethnicity, this little known chapter in our national history posed itself as a double challenge. On the one hand, it meant trying to understand how the Italian community had experienced those critical events: what internal dynamics they had unleashed, how they had translated themselves in terms of collective identity and public stance, and how much they had weighed on the subsequent development of the community. On the other hand, it seemed important to pose the question why a modern and pluri-ethnic state had proceeded in imposing security measures in a situation of national emergency, measures that called forth a political and cultural judgement on the ethnicity of a given community.

These are the major issues with which the following text tries to grapple.

The essential facts of that drama are well known and will be briefly summarized here.

On 10 June 1940, the day in which Italy entered the conflict against the Allies, Canadian authorities launched a vast operation of emergency aimed at extending a thorough control and surveillance over the Italian communities in Canada. This would allow authorities to neutralize promptly potential individuals or groups apt to undertake actions that could endanger the security of the Canadian state. Individuals considered to belong to the latter category were rounded up by the RCMP and the police, and held temporarily in local jails. After preliminary interrogations, some were released; those considered to be dangerous to the national security were detained for internment procedures. The majority of them would be sent to Camp Petawawa in eastern Ontario. At the height of the operation, the internee population of Italian origin was estimated at about 450, one-half of which were from the Montreal region.

As far as the rest of the Italian population was concerned, authorities applied the status of "enemy alien" to all those individuals born in a territory that, as of 10 June 1940, was under Italian sovereignty and who were not naturalized British subjects. Those who had been naturalized after 1 September 1929 were also included in the category of "enemy aliens." People falling into this category — clearly a substantial proportion of the adult population — were required to register immediately at the local RCMP headquarters, where they were fingerprinted and photographed. Moreover, aliens were required to report periodically to the police, a procedure that could be suspended if police authorities were satisfied of the "good intentions and loyalty" of the persons in question.[3] In the course of the war years, in fact, no act of sabotage was ever committed by Italo-Canadians; perhaps more importantly, no "fifth column" was ever seen or heard about.

Of all Italian communities in Canada, Montreal was perhaps where these measures had the most devastating effect. Partly because Montreal had the oldest and largest Italian community, including also the largest proportion of "enemy aliens," partly because more than in any other city Italian associational life had taken on strong political overtones, authorities must have felt that they had to act with particular swiftness and severity.

On the day the measures went into effect, a force of almost one thousand agents (combining RCMP officers, local police units and specially sworn-in civilians) was unleashed upon the Italian community. With an enemy-alien population of nearly five thousand and with hundreds of names of individuals reported as being dangerous, clearly authorities did not want to take any chances. Searches and arrests without warrant went on in private homes, in stores, offices, factories, and in the streets and public places.[4] Vicenzo Monaco, a baker who on that day was delivering bread with his horse-driven cart, was arrested on the spot without being allowed to warn his family and then sent to internment.[5] Costanzo D'Amico, a night worker at Canadian National, was sleeping when two agents came to his house. The agents ordered him to dress and follow them, assuring his wife that it would be only a matter of an hour or so. Mrs. D'Amico would not see her husband again for eleven months.[6] So sweeping was the extent of these orders and so frantic their execution that the whole operation must have taken on a semi-military character. One of the things that remained most vivid in Mrs. Amadory's memory was the sound of police sirens going on all day long as if the part of the city in which she worked and lived was under a state of siege.[7]

Though at a smaller rate, searches and abductions continued for days and weeks, often in the middle of the night or early in the morning. Very soon consternation gave way to fear as no information was available on the fate of the arrested people or on the treatment reserved to enemy aliens in general. The community's information network had ceased to exist once the *Casa d'Italia* (the most important centre of associational life) was closed down and taken over by authorities, and the local Italian newspaper dismantled. Italians turning to the local Canadian press for information had to swallow the humiliation of headlines such as "Mopping Up of Italians is Started," or of sensationalist (and untrue) articles trumpetting large quantities of arms and explosives seized during round-up operations, or editorials praising the authorities for their "careful planning" and for the "smooth manner" in which the operations were carried out.[8]

It was inevitable that an operation of such a magnitude, and one which was publicized in such discriminatory terms, would cast a dark cloud over the community, and thus would awake sentiments of prejudice among the Canadian population. And prejudice vented against defenceless and trapped people is more likely to produce a sense of humiliation than one of anger or rage. Probably no one felt this humiliation more profoundly than Mr. D'Amico when he and some fellow Italians were led to the Montreal train station to be taken to the internment camp at Petawawa: "The worst moment in this story was when they took us to the Windsor station. They made us stand in line outside, surrounded by two cordons of soldiers. And all the crowd that was around us cried: 'kill them! Shoot them ... these traitors of Canada.' I really wept."[9]

One of the most insidious sources of fear for many Italians who have recounted those events to me was the fact that no precise charge for acts committed was ever produced to justify searches and arrests. This, coupled with the fact that authorities acted on the basis of reports supplied by anonymous Italian informers, engendered a climate of mutual suspicion which had the immediate effect of paralyzing public activities and reducing social intercourse to a bare minimum. Even religious functions suffered from this climate of fear and suspicion. The parish priest of *Madonna della Difesa* — the institution that had been for two generations of Italian Canadians the centre of their religious and social life — saw attendance at Sunday mass decline sharply. Those parishioners courageous or fervent enough to attend were told by Father Vangelisti "... to stay on the alert, to check one's own actions, to censure one's own words, and in general to behave like real Canadians." Father Vangelisti added that for about seven or eight months after the round-up campaign he could recognize among the Sunday congregation

RCMP agents in civilian clothes sent "to spy on the preacher and to try to catch him on some dubious word."[10]

By the end of 1940 it seems that authorities were satisfied that Italian enemy aliens posed no threat to our national security. House searches came to a gradual halt, compulsory reporting at police headquarters dwindled, and the general operations of surveillance over the Italian community became more discreet — if they did not cease altogether. The anti-enemy alien campaign entered into its legal-bureaucratic phase. Decisions had to be made, for instance, about when and on what grounds to release Italian internees, and when and how to turn back property that had been seized from or the frozen business assets of abducted individuals. Some sectors of Canadian public opinion even began to voice criticism concerning the severity and ruthlessness with which Canadian authorities had acted against Italian Canadians. But by then most of the damage had already been done.

To a large extent, most of that damage defies calculation because it resulted from injuries that were psychological, moral, and cultural in character. Think of those families in which certain members were branded "enemy aliens" while others were considered loyal Canadians just because some functionary or other decided to draw a chronological line — 1929 — on the individual and collective history of an ethnic community. Or think of those cases — few but highly ironical — in which the father was interned as a potential subversive or traitor while one or two of his sons were serving in the Canadian Armed Forces.

Most important was the consequence of having to carry, for the rest of one's life, the burden of a punishment that one firmly believed was not deserved, without ever receiving the satisfaction of an acknowledgement that a mistake had been made. Those repressive measures dealt a major blow to the very essence of Italian-Canadian ethnicity and to some of the most visible ways in which it had manifested itself. For, beyond the individual dramas and their cumulative effect on the community's life, it was ethnicity itself that was *put on trial* (however inadequate the term "trial" is for the circumstance to which I am applying it).

On the eve of the Second World War, as the international situation was growing darker and more threatening, Montreal's Italians were behaving too much like Italians (to borrow Father Vangelisti's euphemism). One could see this in the community's degree of seclusion from mainstream Canadian life, in the resilience of their cultural institutions, in the type of issues community leaders fought around, and in the fact that too many Italian residents had not become naturalized or that those who were had done it too slowly. Yet a keen observer could see here signs of an ethnicity coming into its own; they represented the efforts of two generations of Italo-Canadians trying to define themselves as a community after the disruptive impact that immigration and economic hardship had wrought on their individual and collective life. And there is no question that of all places of Italian settlement in Canada during the interwar period, Montreal was the one that most deserved the title of 'cradle' of Italian-Canadian ethnicity.

Probably in no other sphere of social intercourse was this ethnicity more visible than in the rich and diversified associational life. All the multifarious aspects of an ethnicity in its becoming were present in the community's associational network: *'paesani'* lodges; national organizations; leisure associations; religious clubs (both catholic and protestant); economic associations, such as mutual aid societies and businessmen's organizations. Some of these associations were vehicles through which the Italians of Montreal sought to forge a common identity and convey to the wider public a newly gained ethnic status. Some other associations, the majority of them, operated at a semi-private level, and served primarily to meet the most immediate material, psychic and cultural needs of their members, thus engendering forms of sociality that gave expression to this particular brand of ethnicity. By the 1930s the Italian community of Montreal had achieved — to use Raymond Breton's well-known concept — its institutional completeness.

Institutional completeness, however, was far from meaning homogeneity and consensus. *"Campanilismo"* — the stressing of one's own village origin — was widespread, engendering group sentiments which often competed with the efforts of some community leaders to forge an identity based on a common national origin. Moreover, the community had reached a certain degree of territorial decentralization — with neighbourhoods and enclaves spread throughout the metropolitan territory, some of them inserted within a francophone milieu, others in a prevailingly anglophone milieu, which also meant different itineraries of integration. After more than fifty years of organized community life, a leadership had emerged, made up mostly of businessmen, clergymen, some professionals and a sprinkling of intellectuals. Prestige was viewed as being directly proportional to the ability of these groups to control the community.[11]

Immigration and ethnic historians know quite well that many of these dynamics were by no means peculiar to the Italian-Canadian community. There was, however, one aspect that informed this process of becoming ethnic and that made the Italian experience a particular one. The years during which the process of community and institutional formation was unfolding coincided with the most dramatic political event in the history of the Italian Kingdom. In 1922 Mussolini had seized power in Italy, imposing on that country a repressive regime whose immediate results were law, order, and stability, attributes that were soon interpreted by many western observers both in Europe and in North America as the trade-marks of progress.

For many Italians — whether in Montreal or elsewhere in Canada — their search for an ethnic identity could hardly be divorced from the political developments that had occurred in their old motherland. For an immigrant population in which two out of three adult persons had left Italy before the advent of fascism, in which an overwhelming proportion had little or no formal education, and whose image of the Italy they had left was one of oppression and political exclusion, the transformations that fascism advertised could not but be perceived as signs of progress. For many of those Italians, then, fascism was seen less as a political ideology and form of government, and more as synonymous with a renewed "*italianità.*" Fascism, as it was imported into many immigrant communities of the humble and uneducated, served several purposes at the same time. It brought a sense of respect toward social hierarchy that played very well into the hands of the community's *prominenti*. It brought an elaborate system of public ceremonial that many Italian immigrants could easily appropriate for themselves in their longing for ethnic respectability.

And ethnic respectability did come in the 1930s for the Italians of Montreal. To my knowledge, no comparative study of the Italian communities of Montreal and Toronto in the interwar period has ever been done. But there could be an important difference in the experience of the two cities. In Montreal, it seems to me, the socio-economic and cultural context was more propitious to a fuller expression of Italian-Canadian ethnicity in the public sphere. For one thing, the corporatist leanings of important sectors of the French-Canadian elite translated themselves into a benevolent attitude by civic and church authorities toward manifestations of Italian patriotism. Moreover, it seems to me that by the 1930s the initial phase of competition, friction and conflict between Italian immigrants and the Montreal French-Canadian

77

working class had given way to forms of accommodation and co-existence which made Italians feel much more secure of their public visibility than in the past.

Unquestionably, this situation produced a very fertile terrain for the propaganda activities undertaken by Italian consular authorities. As historian Roberto Perin has shown in an excellent article, these activities were accelerated considerably after the hard blow that Italy suffered in the international community following the invasion of Ethiopia.[12] It was very important that Italy's decline in prestige be at least partially counter-balanced by a show of unity and solidarity among Italian immigrant communities abroad. More concretely, this meant using the Consulate — its personnel, its organizational resources, its public prestige — to mobilize the community and to impose on it a political and ideological hegemony. In Montreal this operation was carried out by consuls extremely skilled in exploiting the *notabili's* thirst for rank and public recognition (in itself an ethnic phenomenon through and through), and with a clear cognizance of the potential support that might come from some sectors of French-Canadian public opinion.

There is one aspect of this scenario that needs to be stressed in order to evaluate the appropriateness of the Canadian state's repressive intervention during the Second World War and its impact on the community. In Quebec, very seldom if at all were Italian immigrants made to feel guilty about their pro-fascist attitudes by the Canadian public at large or even by Canadian authorities. Was this due to a neglect on the part of the host society — as the diplomat Norman Robertson seemed later to maintain?[13] Or was it because, for most Canadians who cared to notice, the outward manifestations of Italian patriotism appeared as nothing more than expressions of ethnicity? Those who did try to make Italian immigrants feel guilty came from their own ranks, from those belonging to the anti-fascist faction. Their counterpropaganda and denunciations undoubtedly represented the most important source of conflictual dynamics marking the community's associational life, particularly during the late 1930s. To most external observers, however, this was a typical sign of community in-fighting, as much an expression of ethnicity as growing tomatoes in one's own backyard or hanging one-dollar bills on a Madonna statue during a religious procession. The overwhelming majority of Italian Canadians who harboured pro-fascist feelings kept away from this type of in-fighting. For most of them the anti-fascist denunciations hardly had the result of making them feel guilty; they were rather perceived as expressions of rivalry and jealousy coming from individuals who sought to legitimize their leadership status within the community (which in part they were!).

On the eve of the Second World War, therefore, the Italian community of Montreal was well advanced in its process of ethnic self-definition. It was a growth and development that had very much its own socio-cultural dynamics, dynamics quite distinct from the timetable of international relations. It also had been a process which had produced among those immigrants a political culture that — if put to the test of a rigid and intransigent rationality — would undoubtedly reveal elements of confusion and apparent contradiction. How did their sentiment of *'italianità'* translate itself in terms of allegiance toward a state? Would this allegiance — whatever its destination — affect the sense of responsibility that Italian Canadians had toward the new society they had chosen for themselves and their children? Could one differentiate between cultural or sentimental loyalty and political and civic responsibility? To one pro-fascist community leader interviewed in the late 1930s, this sort of question must have appeared eminently academic. In my view, however, his answer is quite representative of the attitude that prevailed among the majority of Montreal's Italian Canadians who harboured patriotic sentiments:

> We have tried to educate our people to be better citizens and I know for a fact that this is the first time the colony as a whole has had any prestige. We know that the people here will never go back; neither will the young people. Fascism is for us an idea; we don't try to create any organization among Canadians, but it is something to make the Italians better people and to unite them. We don't see anything wrong in swearing allegiance to the King of England and to Mussolini.[14]

Of course, Italian Canadians who had actually sworn allegiance to Mussolini were very few in number. The majority instead had sworn allegiance to the English Crown, while at the same time preserving a sense of pride in their national origin.

I am purposely trying not to use the term "ethnic identity" because, as American historian Philip Gleason has shown so well, it is a relatively recent concept that only in the late 1950s and 1960s was transposed from Eriksonian psychological theory into the realm of ethnic studies.[15] We may be on a safer ground if we adopt instead the term used by a

McGill Master of Arts student who, in the late 1930s, did his thesis on Italian and Ukrainian ethnicity. (Incidentally, his thesis shows that the scientific knowledge necessary to understand and evaluate immigrant society and culture existed; clearly authorities either did not know about or simply ignored it.) Charles Bayley, the student in question, used the concept "immigrant self-consciousness" in the following terms:

> ... as the result of conflict with ensuing social distance from the greater community (i.e., Italy) and of the fact that they are drawn together intimately in social life, the immigrants develop a self-consciousness. By this they become aware of being foreign, Italian ... or some other nationality, yet simultaneously, individually and as a group, they desire status; they want to be accepted by Canadians....[16]

He then concluded his study with a very perceptive statement on the various organizational and behavioural forms in which the "selfconsciousness" of Italian immigrants concretized itself in Montreal, adding that in his study "... no test was made of their loyalties for such are only revealed during an international crisis."[17]

As we know, the international crisis was not late in coming — in the form of Italy's declaration of war against the Allies. But this crisis was not allowed to serve as a test of the allegiances and loyalties of Italian Canadians. For those individuals who after 10 June 1940 realized what was happening and started making public statements declaring their total support to the Canadian war effort, it was too late. State authorities had already intervened, throwing a thick net of suspicion over the community, and deciding unilaterally for thousands of Montreal's Italians the question of their allegiances and loyalties.

As to the many hundreds of Italians who were rounded up and arrested, their allegiance was measured through lengthy and tortuous interrogations based on a long list of questions that the Italian historian Bruti-Liberati has partially reproduced in his excellent book on Italian-Canadian relations during the fascist era.[18] But even for those who managed to get off the hook, the trauma of the arrest, incarceration, and interrogation about sentiments and opinions without the benefit of legal counsel must have been enough to make them doubt that they were dealing (to use the expression contained in question 35c of the interrogation plan) with a "democratic state."

As to those who remained caught in the police net thrown by the state and interned, one wonders what was the sense of those interrogations.

Most of those who were interned were already classified as dangerous individuals, their names having long before been supplied by Italian-Canadian informers, who apparently had resolved their questions of allegiance and loyalty. And what an intelligent intelligence-gathering operation that had been: using as informers individuals who had been passionate opponents of the pro-fascist faction in the bitter in-fighting that for years had divided the community.[19] It took several months before the authorities responsible for the internment operation became aware of the "spirit of vengeance"[20] with which some of the leading informers had been imbued. They tried to correct the situation and as a result some Italian internees were released. But again, it was too late. Their careless and unwise approach in intelligence-gathering had already transformed bitter dissension and rivalries into hatred and profound divisions that were never reconciled in the subsequent history of the community. It would take the massive arrival of new Italian immigrants — from the 1950s on — to change the community landscape and to revive associational life. In the meantime, those associations that did exist and the ethnic newspapers that were created (with governmental backing) were the preserve of anti-fascist leaders and informers, and as such their presence in the community stood more as a reminder of victors and of vanquished, of pride and of humiliation, than as attempts to heal an ethnicity that had been gravely wounded.

On the eve of Italy's declaration of war, the Canadian state was confronted with a very tough challenge: how to act on its legitimate preoccupations in matters of national security without putting in danger the long and delicate process of integration of one of its largest ethnic communities. In a very important sense, this was also a test of political and civic maturity for a liberal state that had long recognized the advantages and the responsibilities that immigration entailed — a test for a society in which ethnic pluralism, though not formally sanctioned, seemed on its way to becoming a concrete reality.

The result was a major blunder that caused incalculable hardship for thousands of people who fell victims of events which were totally beyond their control. This challenge in statecraft turned into a blunder because the Canadian state chose to act as a 'police state' rather than as a 'state of law,' totally neglecting the possibilities that political judgement and a minimum of cultural sensibility could have afforded.

I am not competent to discuss the political culture of the authorities responsible for that choice. But clearly it was a political culture utterly inadequate to confront responsibly some of the social and cultural phenomena unfolding in their own country. This political culture entailed a notion of Canadianization that left little or no room for the reality of ethnicity, a notion which — when the crisis came — led to reductionist imperatives, such as dividing immigrants and neo-Canadians into loyal and disloyal, assimilated and unassimilated, safe and dangerous, Canadians and non-Canadians.

Table 1

Italian Population of Quebec, 1941[21]
(Overwhelmingly Residing in the Montreal Region)

Population of Italian origin	28,051
Total Italian immigrant population	9,615
% of Italian population having immigrated before 1921	66
Italian immigrant population naturalized after 1930	2,568+
Italian immigrant population not naturalized as of 1941	2,638
Italian immigrants classified as "enemy aliens"	5,206*
% of Italian immigrant population of age 35 and older	81

* This total does not include the number of persons naturalized between 1 September 1929 and the date the 1930 data were collected.

Notes

1. "*Caffé Italia*, Montréal," directed by Paul Tana, screenplay by Paul Tana and Bruno Ramirez (1985 ACPAV Productions)

2. Mario Duliani, *La ville sans femmes* (Montreal, 1945); Guglielmo Vangelisti, *Gli Italiani in Canada* (Montreal, 1956); Antonio Spada, *The Italians in Canada* (Ottawa, 1969)

3. Canada, House of Commons *Debates*, vol. 1, 1940, 653ff; "Interning All Italians Under Suspicion — Mr. King," *The Toronto Daily Star*, 11 June 1940, 4; "Several Hundred Held in Mounties' Round-up of Italians in Canada," *The Toronto Globe and Mail*, 12 June 1940, 5. Two Master of Arts theses were particularly helpful for this paper: Joseph A. Ciccocelli, "The Innocuous Enemy Alien: Italians in Canada During World War II," University of Western Ontario (History), 1977; and Marie Le Comte, "Le concept de la sécurité nationale et les atteintes aux droits de la personne: les Italiens du Québec entre 1939 et 1945," Université de Montréal (Science Politique), 1982. An excellent study that sets this episode in the broader context of the relations between Italy and Canada throughout the fascist period is Luigi Bruti-Liberati, *Il Canada, l'Italia e il fascismo 1919-1945* (Rome, 1984).

4. "Emotion de la colonie italienne," *La Presse*, 11 June 1940, 3; "L'intervention italienne a un écho inattendu," *La Presse*, 12 June 1940, 3; "Autres arrestations d'Italiens fascistes," *La Presse*, 14 June 1940; Vangelisti, 233; Ciccocelli, 55; taped interview with Mr. Gelsio Sistilli, Montreal, 15 July 1986; taped interview with Mr. and Mrs. Geleano Londei, Montreal, 15 July 1986

5. Taped interview with Mr. Vincenzo Monaco, Montreal, 24 April 1984

6. Taped interview with Mr. Costanzo D'Amico, Montreal, 20 April 1984

7. Taped interview with Mrs. Giulia Amadori, Montreal, 15 July 1986

8. Ciccocelli, 55, 56; "Mopping Up of Italians Begins," *The Montreal Daily Star*, 12 June 1940, 5; "Vaste système d'espionnage," *La Presse*, 14 June 1940, 3

9. Costanzo D'Amico, in "*Caffé Italia*"

10. Vangelisti, 238

11. For the history of the emergence and consolidation of the Italian community of Montreal, see Bruno Ramirez, *Les premiers Italiens de Montréal* (Montreal 1984); Bruno Ramirez, "Montreal's Italians and the Socio-economy of Settlement, 1900-1930," *Urban History Review*, IX, 1 (June 1981), 39-49; Sylvie Taschereau, "Pays et patries: mariages et lieux d'origine des Italiens de Montréal, 1906-1930," M.A. thesis, Université du Québec à Montréal (History), 1984.

12. Roberto Perin, "Conflits d'identité et d'allégeance: la propagande du consulat italien dans les années 1930," *Questions de culture*, 2 (1982), 81-102

13. J.L. Granatstein, *A Man of Influence: Norman Robertson and Canadian Statecraft, 1929-68* (Toronto, 1981), 84-5

14. Quoted in Charles Bayley, "The Social Structure of the Italian and Ukrainian Immigrant Communities in Montreal, 1935-37," M.A. thesis, McGill University (Sociology), 1939, 183

15. Philip Gleason, "Identifying Identity: A Semantic History," *The Journal of American History*, LXIX, 4 (March 1983), 910-31

16. Bayley, 179

17. *Ibid.*, 238

18. See citation in note 3 above.

19. For a skilful discussion of the intelligence-gathering operation based on thorough archival research, see Bruti-Liberati, 185ff.

20. *Ibid.*, 198

21. *Census of Canada, 1941*, vol. IV (Ottawa, 1944), table 1, 3; table 8, 167; table 9, 173

A Prescription for Nationbuilding: Ukrainian Canadians and the Canadian State, 1939-1945

Bohdan S. Kordan and Lubomyr Y. Luciuk

Ukrainian Canadians constituted the second largest non-British, non-French ethnic group in Canada during the Second World War, and the presence of such a large "foreign-born" population within Canada during this critical period was viewed by Canadian officials as an internal security concern. There were misapprehensions at the most senior levels of the fledgling Canadian bureaucracy regarding the loyalty of Ukrainian Canadians, precipitating debate about the threat that this ethnic group might pose to the state and how best it might be contained. The government involved itself in Ukrainian-Canadian affairs, notably in the creation of an Ukrainian-Canadian committee, thus bequeathing a constraining and inflexible organizational structure that has persisted, largely unmodified, since. The experience of the Ukrainian Canadians may be taken as illustrative of the general failure on the part of authorities adequately to understand and cope with the problems, or opportunities, that presented themselves in the development of genuine solidarity in and among Canada's ethnic groups. The processes of nationbuilding and assuring the security of the state were even somewhat jeopardized by the actions of those whose duty it was to promote both.[1]

Only one official had a real prescription for nationbuilding. Tracy Philipps, after 1941 the European advisor to the Nationalities Branch of the Department of National War Services, believed that the essential task facing the nation's statesmen was to ensure through a process of "Canadianization" that ethnic minorities were handled in a manner that would provide for the internal security of the state while securing their long-term allegiance.[2] For him it was clear that if Ottawa's decision-makers opted for more facile solutions — be they internment operations or more refined interventions into the affairs of any of Canada's ethnic, racial or religious groups — they would risk exposing a contradiction between their publicly-proclaimed commitment to the principles of liberal-democracy and their own actions. Philipps argued that the very political culture of Canada, the only basis upon which Canada's ethnic groups could be effectively integrated, was threatened by the government's apparent preference for heavy-handedness.

Senior officials within the bureaucracy were not entirely unappreciative of the importance of nationbuilding as outlined by Philipps. For example, Norman Robertson, the under secretary of state for external affairs, had long understood that important work needed to be done in the area of ethnic integration.[3] Yet he and his colleagues, intent on meeting the most pressing demands of the war effort and in particular preserving the state against all perceived threats, recommended a variety of direct security measures over the alternative of integrating these minorities into the Canadian mainstream. The Canadian bureaucracy thus seemed to accept the fundamental importance of maintaining the existing political *status quo* and international order.[4] This would become apparent in the relationship between the Canadian state and the nationalist Ukrainian-Canadian community, whose claims and concerns were perceived to be a liability in the conduct of the war effort.

In the final analysis, the government's inconsistent interventions into the Ukrainian-Canadian community during the Second World War would leave much of this population uncertain about the status and future of their community in the wider society.[5] A chance to strengthen the process of nationbuilding was thus squandered, leaving aside the opportunity to nurture a genuine loyalty to Canada.

In the years immediately preceding the outbreak of the Second World War, the prospect of an independent Ukrainian national state appeared possible as German revanchism offered a number of options for the geopolitical restructuring of Europe. For nationality-conscious Ukrainians these were hopeful years, although the collapse in March

1939 of the Carpatho-Ukrainian Republic — conceived by them as being a stepping stone in the creation of a united and independent Ukrainian national state — disabused most Ukrainians who hoped for German support in Eastern Europe.[6] The Molotov-Ribbentrop accord capped the rapidly-evolving developments of the summer of 1939. The unpredictability of events reinforced the view among some senior officials in Canada's Department of External Affairs that a closer watch had to be maintained over Canada's Ukrainians, it still not being clear what German policy on the so-called "Ukrainian Question" would be. As the then under secretary of state for external affairs, O.D. Skelton, wrote in a confidential note to Prime Minister W.L. Mackenzie King: "Ukrainians are still hoping that out of the flux something can be done [and] it would be in the national interest to try to keep this large group from making trouble at home and abroad."[7] Subsequently, increased surveillance of the Ukrainian community in Canada was undertaken by the RCMP.[8]

The need for caution appeared to be further justified with the Nazi-Soviet invasion of Poland during September 1939. British Foreign Office officials communicated to their Canadian counterparts that German strategy in Eastern Europe did not end with the acquisition of Polish territories, that indeed there was every indication Berlin would use the Ukrainian separatist movement to advance its claims against the Soviet Union. Preliminary intelligence obtained by the British from the occupied territories of the so-called "Polish Ukraine" seemed to confirm this belief, as a supposed shift in German policy, favouring Ukrainians at the expense of Poles, was thought to have taken place. Skelton was firmly convinced that any German favouritism toward Ukrainians in Europe would excite Ukrainian-Canadian nationalists about the prospects of a future independent state and inevitably undermine their loyalty to Canada and the Allied cause.[9]

This view was not shared by all. The RCMP's Commissioner Wood was of the opinion that "A further strengthening of Germany's ties with Russia would undoubtedly have a most favourable effect on the part of the Ukrainian nationalists towards the Allies," and that the current sympathy for the Allied cause would continue to exist so long as "the English and French refused to make overtures with Russia."[10] The nationalist community's Canadian-based newspapers not only publicly affirmed the allegiance of Canada's Ukrainians but similar Ukrainian-Canadian representations were frequently received at the office of the prime minister.[11] The authors of these editorials and petitions wished to impress upon both the Canadian public and officialdom that the vast majority of Ukrainian Canadians believed an Allied victory was the best possible, if not the only, hope for the people of Ukraine. Yet these same communications also expressed the confidence of Ukrainian Canadians that, in the ongoing struggle between the democracies and the totalitarian states, Ukrainian claims to national self-determination would be unequivocally recognized by the democratic bloc. Implying a mutual responsibility, these community spokesmen made it clear that, when the time came, Ukrainian Canadians would be more than prepared "to do their duty" for Canada. In return, they fully expected the Canadian government and the other Commonwealth nations to act on their publicly-enunciated support for democratic principles.

Unaware of the government's assessment of its claims, the Ukrainian-Canadian community, predominantly nationalist in its political sympathies, continued to agitate on the question of Ukrainian independence during late 1939 and 1940. A submission presented to the Canadian government by the leadership of the Ukrainian National Federation, for example, suggested that, should an Allied front be opened up against the Soviets in Finland, Ukrainian-Canadian divisions be created for deployment there and possibly later in Ukraine.[12] Although Allied strategy did at one point call for the deployment of Canadian troops in Finland against the Soviets, the idea of creating and employing distinct Ukrainian-Canadian contingents alarmed Canadian political and military authorities.[13] Ottawa grew even more convinced that there was need for political and educational work in this ethnic group. It was thought that the most useful way to bring Ukrainian Canadians into line with the mainstream was to create a national coalition committee representing all the Ukrainian-Canadian nationalist organizations. Such a body, it was felt, could be closely watched and guided in a manner so as to ensure Ukrainian-Canadian adherence to Canadian policies.

In November 1940, as a result of direct government involvement, the Ukrainian Canadian Committee (UCC) came into being. The structure imposed on the contentious parties that formed the UCC — giving each in essence a veto on policy or action — inevitably meant that it would remain inflexible and unadaptive in the future. Sanctioned by the government, the committee would also be the only body which would enjoy official recognition, severely circumscribing the community's ability to work through the internal mechanics of organizational and community development. For the government, admittedly, the committee was a convenient means by which to influence Ukrainian-Canadian society without being visible. To ensure their leverage over the Ukrainian-Canadian leadership, Canada's security forces would periodically use key UCC officials to gauge the political attitudes of their rivals within the umbrella organization. Easy access to the leadership also offered an opportunity to keep abreast of current developments within the community.[14]

In the wake of the committee's formation, Tracy Philipps, the government representative given the task of creating it, reflected on the merits and means employed by the government in its involvement in Ukrainian-Canadian affairs. He remarked that there were two basic means of unifying discordant elements such as those found within the Ukrainian-Canadian population. There was the method actually used, that of "direct action and threat," which he described as being akin "to surgical intervention." Such an approach would be seen in time to be unsatisfactory, the result being often impermanent and potentially dangerous.[15] The preferred method required unearthing the misapprehensions and grievances of each ethnic group and coming to grips with them. It called for patience, sympathy, genuine accommodation and tolerance, for only in this way "[could] the subjects begin to detach themselves from their ancient backgrounds [and get] caught up into Canadianism of which at last they can be helped to feel themselves the co-creators."[16]

Philipps further stressed that a sound political basis was required for this process of Canadianization. He always publicly put forward the thesis that it was in the interests of Ukrainian Canadians to join with other Canadians to win the war; in the long run, by assisting the cause of all oppressed nations they were advancing their own. He cautioned, however, that "It would manifestly be both morally wrong and politically imprudent to raise false hopes or to pretend to Ukrainians that the British peoples were not in a position to implement the guiding war principles that were so often published.... We will not be able to avoid the consequences of our declarations and in view of this, policy would have to be more cautiously molded to reflect the essence of those declarations."[17]

Philipps' views were not motivated by a crass sentimentalism for romantic nationalism but by a hard-nosed analysis of current political conditions and an abiding respect for the monumental task of nation-building which faced Canada. An over-reliance on antiquated political formulas, he argued, had failed Britain in Eastern Europe. Indeed, only radically innovative solutions could resolve the crises in that region and provide the basis for true collective security. In this regard, Ukrainian nationalism — which had served to weaken Poland in the interwar period and destabilize the overall political situation in Eastern Europe — was in Philipps' estimation a reality "whether we like it or not."[18] The point was not to ignore Ukrainian nationalism but to channel it so that it could best serve the democracies in the global struggle against the totalitarianism of the Right and the Left. On one hand, this would prevent Ukrainian nationalism from falling under the influence of Nazi Germany, while by giving public affirmation to the principle of self-determination Canadian statesmen would also secure the support of the majority of Ukrainian Canadians for the war effort.[19] Thus, the twin objectives of security and integration would be achieved.

After Nazi Germany invaded the Soviet Union on 22 June 1941, Commissioner Wood of the RCMP communicated his fear to Norman Robertson at External Affairs that a section of the Ukrainian-Canadian nationalist community could be expected to re-orient themselves toward Germany if the prospect of a German-sponsored independent Ukraine became a reality.[20] Within days of the invasion the banned Communist Party of Canada (CPC) initiated a campaign against Ukrainian nationalism through its affiliated Ukrainian organizations. By referring to statements made during the pre-Munich period, when some nationalists had been lured by the idea of an independent Ukraine arising out of a "New Order" in Europe, pro-Soviet Ukrainian-Canadian organizations began to equate Ukrainian irredentism with fascism. The nationalists felt compelled to respond by defending their ideology, political attitudes and war record.[21] The polemics launched against them, however, did not deter some from continuing to speak out on the issue of Ukrainian self-determination nor from pointing out, given the principles said to be guiding the war aims of the Allies, the responsibility which the democracies had to all the European nations resisting Hitlerism. In February 1942, for example, Anthony Hlynka, Social Credit MP for the Alberta constituency of Vegreville, addressed Parliament, arguing that Ukrainian lands were indivisible and the Ukrainian people were entitled to exercise the right to political self-determination.

When asked to assess the impact of Hlynka's speech on public opinion, the Nationalities Branch of the Department of National War Services reported that the non-Ukrainian public was much dismayed by the raising of the question of Ukrainian independence at a time when the armies of nazism appeared to be on the verge of overwhelming Soviet forces on the eastern front. The report did note, however, that Hlynka had not committed any political transgression since he phrased his address in terms already used and endorsed by Allied statesmen. Furthermore, he had not gone outside the Soviet Constitution itself in suggesting that an independent state might arise through the voluntary secession of the Ukraine SSR. In attempting to explain the rationale behind Hlynka's speech and the fervour of Ukrainian Canadians on such matters, the report indicated there was the widespread belief in the community that "... if they did not at least state their case, then their claims would be entirely ignored and the mind of the public would have been made up even before the matter was fairly discussed."[22]

Hlynka's discourse in the House of Commons was not appreciated by those in External Affairs who considered mention of the "Ukrainian Question" to be unnecessarily disruptive and unproductive. Displeasure with Hlynka's speech was partly rooted in the fear that the statement could be "misinterpreted" abroad. It was clear that guidelines for dealing with such ethnic minority demands had to be established. Accordingly, External Affairs wrote a position paper aimed at the "foreign-born groups" in Canada, especially those originating in "the borderlands of Russia." The authors of the document felt, in principle, that recognition should not be granted to independence movements (with the exception of the Free French movement) because of an unspoken but long-standing belief that it was politically unwise to make any commitments on such contentious issues. Furthermore, it was desirable to make Canadian policy consistent with that of the United States and Great Britain. Since the primary Allied objective was to encourage opposition to fascism, advocacy of a policy likely to promote discord between the Great Powers had to be avoided. The problem, and one clearly recognized by the officials in External Affairs, was that, although it was possible to agree on an anti-nazi and anti-fascist stand, the distinctions between democracy and totalitarianism ought not to be pursued too far.[23]

For those ethnic groups placing what were considered inordinate demands on Canadian statesmen, additional control was deemed the best possible solution. A suggestion to suppress them altogether was dismissed: "To suppress one or more of these independence movements would be difficult to defend and probably do more harm than good."²⁴ Government officials were not in a position to dictate who should lead such movements; therefore, it was decided that warnings would be issued whenever any of the groups stepped "out of bounds." In order to facilitate government action when required, it was recommended that a sufficiently ambiguous censorship ruling be passed which would place the government in a much "stronger position" to deal with ethnic groups.²⁵

External Affairs' concerns that statements made by Ukrainian-Canadian nationalists would provoke a Soviet response were well-founded. Reacting to a March 1943 UCC memorandum on Ukrainian national self-determination,²⁶ a spate of press articles appeared in the leading Soviet newspapers condemning what was termed to be "Ukraine-German fascism" in Canada.²⁷ Diplomatic pressure was also applied by the newly-appointed Soviet emissary to Canada, A. Gousev. In one of his first official acts, Gousev appeared at Canada's Department of External Affairs to deliver a protest regarding the "pro-fascist" resolutions appearing in the Ukrainian-Canadian press. He expressed disappointment with Canadian censorship, enquiring how it was possible that authorities could allow newspapers to publish articles which advocated, in effect, the territorial dismemberment of an ally.²⁸ The under secretary, Robertson, replied that the government of Canada did not as a matter of policy invoke censorship rulings to suppress editorials, for doing so would probably be counter-productive. Robertson asked that Soviet authorities be more patient, claiming the department itself would on the whole "be happier if Ukrainians would look at the world through Canadian eyes and think of themselves as solely Canadian citizens, but the process of assimilation took time." He consoled the Soviet minister by assuring him that "... although the Ukrainians were a very large bloc in Canada ... they were not a factor in influencing Canadian government policy and too much importance should not be attached to the speeches and resolutions of the Canadian nationalists."²⁹

Soviet officials in the wartime capital of Kuibyshev also lodged a series of protests with Canada's minister, Dana Wilgress. The Canadian in turn told Ottawa that Ukrainian-Canadian nationalists were motivated by sentiments hostile to the Soviet Union and that their activities could be interpreted as nothing less than "pro-fascist."³⁰ As a result of recent Soviet military successes, he felt that Ukrainian Canadians were now adopting a new tactic "seeking to promote discord between the rest of the United Nations." Wilgress cited the UCC memorandum of March 1943 to the prime minister as an example. Wilgress believed that an opportunity now presented itself for Canada to improve relations with its wartime ally. A statement condemning the attacks on the Soviet Union would be appreciated by the Soviets and "go a long way" toward increasing Canada's influence with the USSR. He also recommended that the government distance itself from those whose work needlessly excited the nationalists.[31] As for Ukrainian claims, he categorically dismissed these as illegitimate. Indeed, he went so far as to suggest that since the principles of the Atlantic Charter were being used to promote Ukrainian claims to independence, this document might better be abandoned for a narrower statement of war aims.[32]

In Ottawa HumeCed Wrong, assistant under secretary of state for external affairs, now broached the question of restoring property confiscated from the banned Ukrainian Labour Farmer Temple Association (ULFTA), a pro-Soviet, nationwide organization closely associated with the Communist Party of Canada. Restoring ULFTA property was complicated by the fact that several of its halls had already been sold to Ukrainian-Canadian nationalist organizations and church parishes.[33] A special interdepartmental meeting was called to determine if and how compensation should be given and what steps might be taken regarding the disposition of the remaining, unsold properties. The parties involved — the Departments of Justice, External Affairs, and National War Services, the RCMP, and the Office of the Custodian of Alien Property — agreed on a special commission to look into the matter, and a consensus emerged that redress and compensation would improve Canada's relations with the Soviet Union.[34]

Surveillance of the Ukrainian-Canadian community was also stepped up. RCMP intelligence indicated that the conflict between the nationalists and the Ukrainian left would continue unabated so long as the rampant "nationalism" which gripped both sides remained.[35] Tracy Philipps appeared to agree with this analysis but arrived at slightly different conclusions. He argued the conflict was indeed galvanizing attitudes in the community and in this way the essential tasks of war work and Canadianization were being jeopardized. He stressed, however, that the nationalists were advancing their claims in the political framework that Allied and Canadian statesmen had endorsed, a framework within which the larger Canadian population had been mobilized. To simply dismiss Ukrainian claims, while permitting the radical left to continue their attacks on the majority community as fascist-inspired, not only served to undermine the credibility of the government but spotlighted the contradiction between pronouncements and actual policies.[36] He feared that this increasingly apparent difference between the public and private sides of the official position on the question of self-determination and post-war reconstruction had serious implications for the war effort. After all, the bulk of the Ukrainian-Canadian working class was engaged in a number of key heavy industries and agriculture, all vital to Canada's war effort.[37]

Philipps also suggested that there was another important dimension to the problem which was as crucial to the security of Canada as the question of the war effort itself. He argued that under Stalin's leadership the Soviet Union had ceased to be a revolutionary power and therefore had very little in common politically with the foreign movements it previously controlled through the Comintern.[38] As a result, the political orientation of the Communist Party of Canada made the latter a liability to the Soviet Union in its relations with Canada, especially since the Soviet leadership was not always in a position to control the movement. In order not to further embarrass Canada's ally and to prevent an unfortunate situation from developing through misunderstanding, it was either necessary to curb the activities of the group or dissuade them from continuing their attacks on the majority in the Ukrainian-Canadian community.[39]

Philipps felt that this was neither impossible nor controversial. He believed the Soviet Union would accept any action Canadian authorities might take because it too was guided by practical concerns and a desire to place the alliance on an even keel. Evidence of this was already demonstrated by the fact that Soviet authorities appeared to express little interest in the fate of some one hundred Canadian communists interned at the start of the war.[40] For Philipps the issue in general was not a matter of choice nor political predeliction; it was rather an issue that had to be considered from both the perspective of nationbuilding and the security of the Grand Alliance.

In the Department of National War Services, the deputy minister, Chester Payne, failed to appreciate, or, as he admitted, even to understand Philipps' concerns. Other government officials were convinced that he was motivated by an anti-Soviet or anti-left bias,[41] while still others felt that his support for the Ukrainian nationalist position was disruptive at home and potentially dangerous for

Canadian-Soviet relations.[42] External Affairs was certainly apt to think that he was complicating the affairs of state. Robertson was especially concerned, a concern which undoubtedly became more pressing when it was learned that the UCC proposed to call a national conference, the primary objective of which was to inform the public about both the Ukrainian-Canadian contribution to the war effort and the "Ukrainian Question" in general.

Initially scheduled for late 1942, the Congress was repeatedly postponed. It was not clear, in fact, whether the event would be staged at all given the nationalist leadership's anxiety over whether statements made at the conference would call forth a negative reaction on the part of the authorities. The UCC executive recognized, however, that its credibility and authority in the community would have been seriously affected unless such a meeting was held, and thus in the end fixed a conference date of June 1943. In Ottawa steps were taken to distance the prime minister and cabinet ministers from the event so as to avoid any misinterpretation at home or abroad. External Affairs recommended that the prime minister decline an invitation to attend the conference.[43] and the prime minister's office sent a telegram to the UCC national executive indicating that, because Parliament was in session, "absences of Cabinet ministers from the capital [were] very difficult to arrange."[44]

The UCC conference turned out to be innocuous, creating the impression in External Affairs that its behind-the-scenes efforts were successful and that the Ukrainian-Canadian problem could still be managed. Where controversy did arise at the gathering, Robertson was made aware that it emanated from non-Ukrainian sources and specifically those connected with the Nationalities Branch in the Department of National War Services.[45]

The impression that the Ukrainian problem could be contained was reinforced for the Department of External Affairs by reports from the field. One analysis emanating from Winnipeg stated that the Ukrainian-Canadian nationalist leaders "would not deliberately embarrass the government nor betray the interests of the country as a whole for the purpose of supporting Ukrainian independence."[46] Furthermore, although it was recognized that Ukrainian sovereignty remained a major issue in some Ukrainian-Canadian circles, the rate of assimilation among Ukrainians was proceeding at an exceptionally quick pace, suggesting that all such problems would disappear in the near future.[47]

Reports of this nature confirmed for Canadian officials the utility of their tactic of 'waiting out' the problem posed by the organized Ukrainian-Canadian community. In the meantime, it was now thought politically wise to adopt measures to mollify Soviet authorities who continued to express an interest in Canadian developments. The findings of the commission charged with making recommendations on the disposition of confiscated properties were finally approved, calling for full restoration.

By August 1944, the issue of Ukrainian sovereignty was largely academic. Soviet forces were in control of all Ukrainian ethnographic territories. Allied victory was imminent and the urgency of dealing with Ukrainian-Canadian nationalists receded. These factors, in combination with the notion that the 'political edge' would disappear from what was perceived to be an element that was being rapidly assimilated, suggested to the pundits at External Affairs that any representations on the question of Ukrainian sovereignty should simply be set aside. Indeed, it apparently became a standard departmental practice to ignore such appeals.[48]

The imminence of Allied victory also allowed Canadian officials to adopt a less compromising stance with respect to Ukrainian nationalist claims. In July 1944, British Foreign Office officials approached their Canadian counterparts to ascertain their position on a possible exchange of representatives with the Ukraine. The Department of External Affairs replied that a case could be made for such an exchange because the Ukraine was the second largest Slavic state and held an important place in the global economy. Even more important, granting diplomatic recognition to the Soviet Ukraine could with one stroke "drive from the nationalist's minds the mirage of absolute independence and in this way hasten the process of their assimilation."[49]

Although appeals on the issue of Ukrainian independence from Ukrainian Canadians continued throughout late 1944 and early 1945 — asking Canadian officials, for example, to recognize and raise the issue of political self-determination for the Ukraine at the San Francisco conference — these were ignored. Such appeals did, however, set the tone for a meeting between the head of the Soviet desk in External Affairs, L. Malania, and M. Manuilsky, minister for Soviet Ukrainian foreign affairs. The Soviet minister noted that Soviet-Canadian relations had been satisfactory in the past but that Canada could greatly improve its standing with the USSR if a favourable and unequivocal statement were made outlining the Canadian government's position on the question of Ukrainian independence. Malania reiterated that undue importance should not be attached to the sentimental nationalism of Canada's Ukrainians. He added that Soviet authorities were actually only hindering their cause by taking "such vigorous notice of their [the nationalists'] activities." The situation had to be understood from the Canadian perspective; keeping the controversy alive simply excited Ukrainian nationalism and retarded the process of assimilation. Malania encouraged the Soviets to be patient just as the Canadian authorities were prepared to be. The Ukrainian-Canadian problem, he felt, would disappear in time of its own accord.[50]

Ottawa's mandarins, a tight clique assembled primarily as a result of Dr. O.D. Skelton's efforts in creating the Department of External Affairs and a modern bureaucracy for overseeing the nation's business, were a dominantly Anglo-Celtic group. As a collectivity these men knew very little about the Canada's minorities, and often even less about events taking place in the homelands of these various groups. Circumscribed by the need to act, and quickly so, to meet the demands of the war, the mandarins opted to promote security over nationbuilding. It was an understandable decision, but not a wise one. The counsel of Tracy Philipps, who had an astute prescription for nationbuilding, was all but ignored. The measures taken by the Canadian bureaucracy hampered and handicapped Ukrainians well into the postwar period.

Notes

1. See R.L. Rothstein, "On the Costs of Realism," *Political Science Quarterly*, LXXXVII, 3 (1972), 347-62. See also E. Cassirer, *The Myth of the State* (New Haven and London, 1946), 153-6, for a discussion of the "technique" of modern politics and the practice of contemporary statecraft.

2. National Archives of Canada (NA), Philipps Papers, MG 30, E350, vol. 2, f. "Kaye Correspondence with T. Philipps, 1941," report of Philipps, "Hemisphere Defense; Foreign-born Population; Positive Co-operation (Canada)," 13 May 1941

3. NA, RG 2, ser. 18, vol. 43, f. U-15-2, Robertson to Mackenzie King, 1 June 1943

4. See B. Buzan, *People, States and Fear: The National Security Problem in International Relations* (Chapel Hill, N.C., 1983), especially his chapter entitled "National and International Security: The Policy Problem."

5. Ukrainian Canadians had been subjected to more heavy-handed measures between 1914-1920, when public opinion legitimized the role of the state in adopting severe measures against this community, including internment, disenfranchisement, deportations and the registration of so-called "enemy aliens." See L.Y. Luciuk "Internal Security and an Ethnic Minority: The Ukrainians and Internment Operations in Canada, 1914-1920," *Signum*, IV, 2 (1980).

6. P. Stercho, *Diplomacy of Double Morality: Europe's Crossroads in Carpatho-Ukraine, 1919-1939* (New York, 1971)

7. NA, RG 25, G1, vol. 1896, f. 165, pt. 1, Skelton to King, 27 April 1939

8. *Ibid.*, f. 165-A, pt. 2, Skelton's confidential letter to Commissioner Wood, RCMP, asking for increased surveillance of Ukrainian activities, 27 January 1939

9. *Ibid.*, Skelton to Wood, 6 September 1940

10. *Ibid.*, secret RCMP report, 17 May 1940

11. See, for example, editorials in *Ukrains'kui visti* (Ukrainian News), 5 September 1939 and *Ukrains'kui holos* (Ukrainian Voice), 6 September 1939. See also NA, Robertson Papers, MG 30, E163, vol. 12, f. 138, the Ukrainian National Federation (Toronto Branch) to King, 27 November 1939.

12. RG 25, G1, vol. 1896, f. 165, pt. 1, T. Pavlychenko to W.A. Tucker, MP, 9 September 1939. See also Robertson Papers, vol. 12, f. 138, letter and accompanying draft proposal of the Dominion Executive of the Ukrainian National Federation to King, 17 October 1939.

13. Robertson Papers, vol. 12, f. 133, Robertson to H.L. Keenleyside, 6 December 1939

14. See, for example, document 31 in B.S. Kordan and L.Y. Luciuk, eds., *A Delicate and Difficult Question: Documents in the History of Ukrainians in Canada, 1899-1962* (Kingston, Ont., 1986), 80-9; and NA, Philipps Papers, MG 30, E350, vol. 1., f. 15, secret RCMP document, "Report on the Ukrainian Canadian Committee," 18 September 1941

15. See document 28 in Kordan and Luciuk, 74-6.

16. *Ibid.*

17. RG 25, G1, vol. 1896, f. 165-A, pt. 2, Philipps to Colonel Mess, 6 December 1940

18. Philipps Papers, vol. 1, f. 21, report of Philipps, 4 June 1941

19. *Ibid.*

20. RG 25, G1, vol. 1896, f. 165, pt. 3, secret RCMP report, 26 June 1941

21. See, for example, the Ukrainian National Federation publication, *A Program and a Record* (Winnipeg and Saskatoon, 1943).

22. RG 25, G1, vol. 1986, f. 165, pt. 3, Professor G. Simpson to Robertson, 4 April 1942

23. *Ibid.*, "Policy Toward Foreign Groups," 2 July 1942

24. *Ibid.*

25. *Ibid.*

26. The UCC Memorial was dated 13 March 1943. See RG 25, G1, vol. 1896, f. 165-39c, pt. 4.

27. RG 25, G1, vol. 1896, f. 165, pt. 3, Wilgress to King, 15 May 1943

28. *Ibid.*, Robertson to King, 6 May 1943

29. *Ibid.*

30. *Ibid.*, Wilgress to King, 17 May 1943

31. *Ibid.*

32. *Ibid.*, Wilgress to King, 19 May 1943

33. On the question of seized ULFTA properties, see *An Appeal for Justice* (Toronto, Civil Liberties Association of Toronto, 1944). For the government's record of inventory and sales, see NA, RG 14, 02, vol. 452, no. 285a., unpublished *Sessional Papers*, 4th Session of the 19th Parliament, 28 January 1943 — 26 1944. For a history of the ULFTA, see J. Kolasky, *The Shattered Illusion: The History of Pro-Communist Organizations in Canada* (Toronto, 1979).

34. RG 25, G1, vol. 1896, f. 165, pt. 3, undated memorandum of G. Glazebrook and Wrong to Robertson, 22 May 1943

35. *Ibid.*, Glazebrook to A.J. Halpern, British Security Co-ordination, 30 March 1943

36. Philipps Papers, vol. 2, f. "Correspondence, August 1943," Philipps' letter to unidentified correspondent, n.d.

37. The importance of Ukrainian-Canadian participation in key heavy industries and agriculture was raised initially by Philipps in early 1941. See, for example, pt. 2 of Philipps report submitted to the Department of National War Services, 13 January 1941, *ibid.*, vol. 2, f. 16.

38. The thesis first appears in Philipps' memorandum entitled "Communism: Marx-Leninism," 19 June 1942, NA, RG 36/31, vol. 13, f. 8-9-1A.

39. Philipps Papers, vol. 2, f. "Correspondence, May 1943," unofficial report of Philipps, "An Intervention in Canadian Affairs," 14 May 1943

40. For example, see comments on Philipps in an interdepartmental memorandum entitled "The Pan-Slavic Movement in Canada," 31 July 1942, RG 25, Acc. No. 83/84-259, box 223, f. 4174-40.

41. RG 2, ser. 18, vol. 43, f. U-15-2, memorandum of Robertson for King, 1 June 1943; RG 36/31, vol. 13, f. 8-9-3, J. Grierson to Glazebrook, 15 May 1943

42. RG 25, G1, vol. 1896, f. 165, pt. 3, report, "All-Canadian Ukrainian Congress," 28 May 1943

43. RG 2, ser. 18, vol. 43, f. U-15-2, memorandum for King, 1 June 1943

44. RG 25, G1, vol. 1896, f. 165, pt. 3, prime minister's office to J.W. Arsenych, UCC, 14 June 1943

45. See document 37 in Kordan and Luciuk, 111-3.

46. RG 25, G1, vol. 1896, f. 165-A, pt. 4, report, "Ukrainian Canadians," 6 July 1943

47. *Ibid.*

48. *Ibid.*, memorandum of Malania, 25 January 1945, Wrong to King, 27 January 1945

49. See document 38 in Kordan and Luciuk, 113-5.

50. See document 42 in *ibid.*, 135-8.

The Evacuation of the Japanese Canadians, 1942: A Realist Critique of the Received Version

J.L. Granatstein and Gregory A. Johnson

The popularly accepted version of the evacuation of the Japanese Canadians from the Pacific Coast in 1941-1942 and the background to it runs roughly like this. The white population of British Columbia had long cherished resentments against the Asians who lived among them, and most particularly against the Japanese Canadians. Much of this sprang from envy of the Japanese Canadians' hard-work and industry, much at the substantial share held by Japanese Canadians of the fishing, market gardening and lumbering industry. Moreover, white British Columbians (and Canadians generally) had long had fears that the Japanese Canadians were unassimilable into Canadian society and, beginning early in this century and intensifying as the interwar period wore on, that many might secretly be acting as agents of their original homeland, now an aggressive and expansionist Japan. Liberal and Conservative politicians at the federal, provincial and municipal levels played upon the racist fears of the majority for their own political purposes. Thus when the Second World War began in September 1939, and when its early course ran disastrously against the Allies, there was already substantial fear about "aliens" in British Columbia (and elsewhere) and a desire to ensure that Japanese Canadians would be exempted from military training and service. The federal government concurred in this, despite the desire of many young Japanese Canadians to show their loyalty to Canada by enlisting.

After 7 December 1941 and the beginning of the Pacific War, public and political pressures upon the Japanese Canadians increased exponentially. Suspected subversives were rounded up by the RCMP in the first hours of the war, and over the next ten weeks a variety of actions took place that resulted in the seizure of fishing vessels, arms, cars, cameras, radio transmitters and short-wave receivers owned by Japanese Canadians, and then escalated through the evacuation from the coast of male Japanese nationals between the ages of 18 and 45 to the removal of all Japanese, whether Canadian citizens by birth or naturalization and regardless of age or sex, into the interior. The legalized theft of the property of these Japanese Canadians then followed, and even before the war ended the government moved to deport large numbers to Japan. These events occurred despite the facts that the RCMP and Canada's senior military officers considered the removal of the Japanese from the coast unnecessary, there being no credible military or security threat; that the responsible politicians in Ottawa, and particularly Ian Mackenzie, BC's representative in the Cabinet, knew that the Japanese Canadians posed no threat to national security and acted out of a desire to pander to the bigotry of some whites or for political motives relating to the conduct of the war at home.

This bald summary is based on such books as Ken Adachi's *The Enemy that Never Was* (Toronto, 1976), the second volume of Hugh Keenleyside's *Memoirs* (Toronto, 1982), and Ann Gomer Sunahara's *The Politics of Racism* (Toronto, 1981), as well as on the National Association of Japanese Canadians' brief to the federal government, *Democracy Betrayed: The Case for Redress* (1985). There are variations of emphasis in these accounts, naturally enough, but the received version is a composite that does not pay much attention to these differences.

That Canadians should be interested in the events of 1942 is understandable. That they should attempt to fix blame for the events of those days is no less so, and historians, whose trade obliges them to rummage with more or less science through the past, have not been immune from this tendency. It is the responsibility of historians, however, to try to put themselves back into the circumstances of the past and, while never becoming apologists for the horrors of those times, to seek to understand why people acted as they did. This paper is an attempt to do precisely that, and to look afresh at some points which are encompassed in the received version of the 1942 evacuation and open for examination and some which are not.

The Intelligence Services

The first question that must be raised, and one that has not been asked before, is this: what resources did Ottawa's civil, military and police authorities have on the West Coast before the outbreak of war to secure information about the 22,000 Japanese Canadians living in British Columbia? The answer is readily available.

The responsibility for internal security rested with the RCMP, assisted as necessary by the armed forces.[1] In July 1941, five months before the outbreak of war with Japan, the RCMP's "E" Division responsible for the Pacific Coast had on its staff three persons concerned with gathering intelligence on the Japanese Canadians in British Columbia: a sergeant who did not speak Japanese, a constable who did, and a civilian translator. These three were in charge of the "active personnel intelligence work on enemy and potential enemy aliens and agents." There was, in addition, a lieutenant-commander at Naval Headquarters in Esquimalt charged with intelligence duties who was "greatly interested in the Japanese problem generally," but who had many other tasks. The Royal Canadian Air Force's intelligence section in the province, which like the Royal Canadian Navy's had a wide range of duties over and above collecting information on Japanese Canadians, consisted of two officers, both of whom had lived in Japan and spoke Japanese. The senior officer, a Squadron Leader Wynd, however, could read Japanese only with difficulty; whether his colleague was any more fluent is uncertain. The army's intelligence on the coast was in the hands of two very busy officers, neither of whom spoke Japanese. In addition, the British Columbia Provincial Police had four officers working in the Japanese-Canadian community. Cooperation between the various services was hampered by RCMP regulations that forbade the Mounties to share information with their colleagues without first securing permission from Ottawa headquarters. Even so, the West Coast Joint Intelligence Committee had been created to coordinate the information collected by the military and police.[2] There is one additional point worth mentioning: the British intelligence services had some representation on the West Coast, and there exists in RCMP files one very long (and very inflammatory) report on "Japanese Activities in British Columbia," prepared by someone unnamed for William Stephenson's British Security Coordination.[3]

103

This intelligence presence did not amount to very much. As Hugh Keenleyside of the Department of External Affairs, a British Columbian who had served in the Legation in Japan and who was genuinely sympathetic to the Japanese Canadians, wrote in June 1940, there was a danger of subversive activities on the part of some elements in the Japanese community. "The police," he went on, "are not in a position to ferret out the dangerous Japanese as they have done with the Germans and Italians; they have lines on a few Japanese who might be expected to take part in attempts at sabotage.... But that would not really solve the problem."[4] Even, therefore, in the view of someone in a position to know (and understand), the intelligence information gathered on the Japanese Canadians was strictly limited, the officers involved pathetically few in number and largely baffled by the impenetrability of the Japanese language and the tendency of the Japanese Canadians to stay together, separate, and (with good historical reasons) not to trust whites.

The discussion thus far has said nothing about the quality of the information gathered. The available intelligence evidence on the Japanese Canadians is very slim (and the Privacy Act prevents us from seeing whatever else there might be), but we can state with confidence that when the RCMP looked at Communist questions, towards which it had a definite *idée fixe*, or the activities of suspected Nazis in this period, its work was far from competent.[5] In November 1939, J.W. Pickersgill of the prime minister's office complained that the force could not distinguish between facts and hearsay, or discriminate between legitimate social and political criticism and subversive doctrine. There was, moreover, "no suggestion that there is any co-ordination with Military Intelligence, or with the Immigration authorities, or with the Department of External Affairs, or even with the Censorship." More disturbing still to Pickersgill was "the evidence of a total lack of the capacity, education and training required for real intelligence work...."[6] Whether the RCMP's efforts on the Japanese Canadians were any better remains speculative, at least until all the files are open to research; the existing documents offer no grounds for optimism.

There is little more information available on the quality of military intelligence gathered. But as the regular forces before the war were tiny and as military intelligence, a skill requiring years of preparation, was not among the best-developed areas of the permanent forces, there is no reason to believe that the army, navy or air force by 1941 were any less clumsy or more sophisticated in their ability to gather and assess information on the Japanese Canadians than the RCMP. Evidence for this conclusion is suggested by the efforts of the Examination Unit, a secret operation of External Affairs and National Defence set up under the shelter of the National Research Council, among other things to attempt to decipher Japanese diplomatic and military wireless messages in response to a British request before Pearl Harbor. As the just declassified manuscript history of the Examination Unit notes, two people were engaged for this purpose in August 1941, a Mr. and Mrs. T.L. Colton. "It was hoped that Mrs. Colton, who was very well educated in Japanese but could not handle translation into English, might be able to explain the contents of messages to her husband who could then write them out in English. This system," the history notes dryly, "did not prove very satisfactory" and the Coltons were replaced in April 1942.[7]

In this atmosphere of improvisation and amateurism, many of the available reports by the RCMP and the military on the Japanese Canadians tended to focus on investigations of alleged "unlawful drilling [with weapons]" by male Japanese Canadians, reports of caches of Japanese rifles and ammunition, and accounts of suspicious fishing parties of well-dressed Japanese who did not appear to be fishermen. Rumours, plain and fanciful.[8] On the other hand, there were just as many assertions offered with great confidence that 95 percent of Japanese Canadians were law abiding and satisfied with their lot in Canada and that "No fear of sabotage need be expected from the Japanese in Canada." That last statement by Assistant Commissioner Frederick J. Mead of the RCMP, one of the Mounties' specialists in security matters and Communist subversion, was, he added, "broad [but] at the same time I know it to be true."[9]

Mead was soon a member of the British Columbia Security Commission where, activist *Nisei* (or second generation Canadian Japanese) correctly believed, he depended on intelligence from Etsuji Morii, a man suspected of blackmailing other Japanese Canadians and a notorious underworld figure. Morii was in turn the Commission's appointed chairman of the "Japanese Liaison Committee," whose mandate was to convey news and information in 1942 to the community.[10] As Mead was the senior RCMP official on the coast early in 1942, he was almost certainly the main source for RCMP Commissioner S.T. Wood's defence of Morii and his assertion to William Stephenson (in response to the British Security Coordination report mentioned earlier) in August 1942 that "we have searched without let-up for evidence detrimental to the interests of the state and we feel that our coverage has been good, but to date no such evidence has been uncovered."¹¹ The RCMP's firmly-stated position may have been correct, but again the small size of its resources and the lack of sophistication of all its operations in this period tend to raise doubts. From 45 years distance, the fairest thing that can be said is that the RCMP had uncovered relatively little hard information about possible subversion among the Japanese Canadians before 7 December 1941, if there were indeed subversive intentions within the community, because it lacked the competence and skills to do so. Moreover, much of the information that the RCMP had before and after that date came from sources that even many Japanese Canadians considered self-interested and tainted.

The Role of the Japanese Consulate

Such intelligence information as there was tended to agree that the Japanese Consulate in Vancouver was the focus of Japanese nationalism, propaganda and possible subversive activities in BC. One RCMP report surveying the general activities of the Japanese Canadians noted that the Consul and his staff regularly visited areas where Japanese Canadians lived to deliver speeches and to talk privately with individuals about the Tokyo government's views of world events. One RCAF intelligence officer was sufficiently alarmed by these activities to tell his superior that he considered British Columbia's Japanese Canadians to be "directly under the control of the Japanese Government through their consul at Vancouver."¹² The Consul was also thought to exercise considerable influence on the local Japanese language schools and press. Roles of these sorts, of course, were well within the bounds of diplomatic niceties. And since, under Japanese law, *Nisei* born abroad before 1924 were considered as Imperial subjects, while those born abroad after that date could register at Japanese consulates and secure Japanese citizenship in addition to their status as British subjects, the Consul in Vancouver had substantial work to do in dealing with the approximately 7,200 Japanese nationals, 2,400 naturalized British subjects, and the unknown (but very large) number of Japanese Canadians holding dual citizenship in the BC community.¹³ A military intelligence paper surveying the situation on the coast added that the Consul "through his agents, and through the Japanese schoolmasters, and the Japanese patriotic societies cultivates a strong Japanese spirit and a consciousness among the BC Japanese of being 'sons of Japan abroad' rather than Canadian citizens."¹⁴ That was no different than the role of the Italian and German consuls in this pre-war period.

There were, however, grounds for believing that in this instance the Japanese Consulate's officials had duties of a more dangerous kind. On 28 February 1941, Vincent Massey, the high commissioner in London, reported to Prime Minister Mackenzie King that "reliable information of a most secret character" had revealed that "official Japanese circles" were taking great interest in the British Columbia Coast. "Reference is also made to large number of Japanese settled in British Columbia and on Western Coast of United States, who are all said to have their duties,"¹⁵ an ominous phrase.

The source of that information was possibly Britain's Government Code & Cypher School which had been reading some Japanese military and diplomatic messages since the 1920s,¹⁶ or more probably "Magic," the name given by the Americans to their armed forces' decryption operation that in January 1941 had cracked the "Purple" code used for the most secret Japanese diplomatic traffic. Britain and the United States soon started to cooperate in reading Japanese codes, and by the spring of 1941 the two countries had pooled their intelligence.¹⁷ The Americans also began reading their hitherto unbroken files of Japanese messages back to 1938.

The decryption team had intercepted important telegrams from the Foreign Office in Tokyo to the Japanese Embassy in Washington dated 30 January 1941, which gave the *Gaimusho*'s orders to its officials in North America to de-emphasize propaganda and to strengthen intelligence gathering. Special reference was made to "Utilization of our 'Second Generations' [Nisei] and our resident nationals" and to the necessity for great caution so as not to bring persecution down on their heads. Those messages were copied to Ottawa and Vancouver as "Minister's orders" — instructions, in other words, that were to be carried out in Canada just as in the United States. The Consulate's success in carrying out these orders remains unknown.

A further message from Tokyo to Washington, dated 15 February 1941, was also sent to Ottawa and Vancouver as a "Minister's instruction." In this telegram, the Foreign Ministry specified the "information we particularly desire with regard to intelligence involving US and Canada," especially the strengthening of Pacific Coast defences, ship and aircraft movements. In a telegram the day before, the

107

Consulate in Vancouver was instructed to pay special attention to paragraph 10 of the order to Washington: "General outlooks on Alaska and the Aleutian Islands, with particular stress on items involving plane movements and shipment of military supplies to those localities." The next month, the Consulate was asked to report on RCN ship movements. Whether these particular telegrams were the basis for Massey's despatch to Ottawa is unclear.[18]

A thorough search of the "Magic" intercepts in the United States National Archives makes clear that at least as early as 1939 intelligence and counter-intelligence work was carried on from the Vancouver Consulate, exactly as was taking place in the Japanese Consulates all over the United States and throughout the Western Hemisphere. As we have seen, the 1941 telegrams also stress efforts to involve the resident nationals and the second generation *Nisei*, at whom radio broadcasts from Tokyo had been deliberately aimed for some years. How much, if anything, Ottawa knew of all this, beyond the RCMP's suspicions and the information conveyed in the Massey telegram, is still indeterminate. But surely there was ample justification in the light of the Massey telegram for the government to have increased surveillance on the Consulate and the Japanese-Canadian community. There is no sign that it did so.[19]

One contemporary assessment of the Canadian situation by an RCAF intelligence officer noted that "espionage and subversive activity is largely carried on by a few key Japanese working under the Consul and *seriously* involves only a few — say 60 at most — Japanese individuals." This same officer then tried to assess the response of Japanese Canadians in the event of war, particularly if the Japanese authorities instructed them to engage in sabotage, and if such orders were reinforced by "disorderly demonstrations of white antipathy." His answer was that "No one knows; but no one in his senses would take a chance on Japanese loyalty under those circumstances."[20]

The Pre-War Pro-Japan Actions of Japanese Canadians

If that sounds harsh, there were reasons why it should not. Throughout the 1930s and especially after 1937, Japan had aggressively expanded its influences in northern China, and the Imperial Japanese Army had campaigned with great brutality in that country. The Japanese government, naturally enough, tried to put the best face possible on its actions, and it encouraged the creation and spread of propaganda on its behalf abroad, something in which Japanese Canadians directly assisted by writing and distributing leaflets. The most widely distributed pamphlet, dated 1 October 1937 and published by the Canadian Japanese Association, the largest Japanese-Canadian association with over 3,000 members, was "Sino-Japanese Conflict Elucidated," a far from unbiased examination of the struggle in China, despite its claim to be circulated "in the interests of truth, to meet unfair and untrue propaganda." Moreover, money, comforts for the troops, medical supplies and tin foil were collected for Japan by first generation *Issei* and second generation *Nisei* groups.[21] There was, of course, nothing remotely improper about this, and other ethnic groups in Canada at that time (Italians, say, during the Italo-Ethiopian war) and more recently (Jews during the Arab-Israeli wars, for example) have acted similarly in comparable circumstances.

But the wholly justifiable outrage in Canada over such incidents as the brutal rape of Nanking, with its estimated 200,000 or more dead (and Japanese army assaults on Canadian missionaries stationed there) led many Canadians to boycott Japanese products and to call upon the federal government to take steps to cease strategic metal exports to Japan. Such measures were eventually taken.[22] And the *New Canadian*, the newspaper of British Columbia's *Nisei*, began publication in late 1938, noted its founder, Edward Ouchi, the General Secretary of the main *Nisei* organization, the Japanese Canadian Citizens' League, to counter the "vicious" anti-Japanese propaganda of North American Chinese that was hurting Japanese-Canadian businesses. Although the newspaper did not offer frequent support for Japan's war in China in its pages, it did give close and favourable coverage to the activities of the Consul in Vancouver and even ran an occasional rotogravure section of propagandistic photographs on life in Japan.[23]

Inevitably Japanese-Canadian support for Japan's war on China focussed much attention upon the *Issei* and *Nisei*. As Professor Henry Angus of the University of British Columbia wrote in October 1940:

> The young Japanese understand the position well enough. At first they (in all good faith I think) distributed a good deal of pro-Japanese, anti-Chinese propaganda. Now they say, "we are not responsible for what Japan may do." I tell them that they have unfortunately made people feel that they are identified with Japan by their action in distributing propaganda, and that it is very difficult to find a way of removing this impression.[24]

Angus was always very sympathetic to the Japanese Canadians (and after he had joined External Affairs, he and Hugh Keenleyside would find themselves under attack in Parliament because of the vigor of their resistance to the evacuation in January and February 1942),[25] but he was surely correct in his assessment. Even such supportive British Columbia politicians as CCF Member of Parliament Angus MacInnis agreed.[26] The Japanese Canadians by their support for Japan "impaired [their] standing with those circles most disposed to press [their] cause," Professor Angus lamented.[27]

We can say today that Canadians should have understood the difficulties that a small minority would have faced in not supporting its belligerent mother country in those days in the late 1930s and early 1940s. But after the Pearl Harbor attack and the fall of Hong Kong, British Columbians, already predisposed to expect the worst of the Japanese Canadians and motivated by deep-rooted racism against them, and Canadians generally could not reasonably have been expected to make such judgements. Many Japanese Canadians had supported Japan against China before 7 December and few, if any, had opposed her; after Pearl Harbor, China was an ally and Japan an enemy. Therefore, the supporters of Japan before 7 December were now supporters of Canada's enemy and possibly (or probably) disloyal, particularly as there seemed no way of distinguishing the active few from the passive majority. The syllogism was flawed (and certainly the vast majority of German and Italian Canadians had been treated far differently in the comparable circumstances of September 1939 and June 1940), but few were prepared to challenge its logic.

Norman Robertson, the under secretary of state for external affairs, a British Columbian and no bigot, expressed something of the same reasoning when he told Pierrepont Moffat, the American minister to Canada, on 8 December 1941 that "the Government had hoped not to have to intern all Japanese. However, this might be very difficult in view of the treacherous nature of the Japanese attack, [and] the evidences of premeditation...."[28] Robertson's description of the attack mirrored the public's response: "In the wake of Pearl Harbor, the single word favoured by Americans as best characterizing the Japanese people," John Dower has noted, "was 'treacherous' ...."[29]

The Attitudes of Japanese Canadians After 7 December

In August 1944, Prime Minister King told the House of Commons that "no person of Japanese race born in Canada has been charged with any act of sabotage or disloyalty during the years of war." In his account, Ken Adachi added that "no alien Japanese or naturalized citizen had ever been found guilty of the same crime."[30] Those statements are undoubtedly true, but they do not tell the whole story.

Thirty-seven or 38 Japanese nationals were arrested and interned by the RCMP at the outbreak of the war, presumably because they were thought to be engaged in espionage or subversive activities. None of the standard accounts offers any detailed information on the allegations against or the fate of these people.[31]

More important, it seems certain that support for Japan remained strong among some Japanese Canadians after the war began. The *Issei* Takeo Nakano, in his book *Within the Barbed Wire Fence*, notes that "We Japanese, largely working-class immigrants, were, generally speaking, not given to sophisticated political thinking. Rather we had in common a blind faith in Japan's eventual victory." John J. Stephan's study, *Hawaii Under the Rising Sun*, cites the conclusions of Japanese historians Nobuhiro Adachi and Hidehiko Ushijima that most first-generation Japanese in Hawaii remained loyal to Japan: "even among those who considered the Pearl Harbor attack a betrayal were many who believed in and hoped for an ultimate Japanese victory.... Radio reports of Japanese advances ... confirmed for many their motherland's invincibility." Nakano's book demonstrates that the same response existed in British Columbia, and even Sunahara notes that the Japanese vice-consul encouraged some Japanese Canadians to seek internment as a gesture of support for Japan.[32] Those of Japanese origin, of course, formed a greater proportion of the Hawaiian population (about 35 percent) than did the Japanese Canadians in British Columbia (about three percent). Moreover, at this point it is impossible to determine if the links between the Japanese Canadians and Japan were stronger or weaker than those between Hawaiian Japanese and the mother country. These two factors could certainly have affected the situation.

Nakano also underlines the presence in the Japanese-Canadian community of a substantial number of hard-liners or *gambariya*, "best described as rebels against the treatment they were receiving in time of war. The *Nisei gambariya* were protesting such unjust treatment of

Canadian citizens," he continues, an understandable response. He goes on, however, to note that "the *Issei gambariya* firmly believed in Japan's eventual victory and looked forward to the Canadian government's enforced compensation to them."³³ That attitude is less understandable if the revised version is to be accepted. More than 750 *gambariya*, a fairly substantial number of the approximately 9,000 adult males over the age of sixteen in a BC community of 22,000, were interned at Angler in Northern Ontario, and Nakano, in part as a result of misunderstanding, he says, ended up there as well. Nakano's story is stylistically elliptical, but it rings true. None of the historical accounts make much mention of the *gambariya*, other than to skirt the evidence by saying that there were some who refused to have anything to do with the evacuation or to cooperate with the Canadian authorities.

Perhaps a last word here should belong to Stephan, whose study of Hawaii is an exemplary and sensitive one. "It has been common to write about Hawaii's Japanese before and during the Second World War as if their 'loyalty' were a self-evident, quantifiable phenomenon," he said. "In the justifiable impulse to indict the relocation of West Coast Japanese and Japanese Americans ... writers have in many cases dealt simplistically with what is full of complex nuances and ambiguities."³⁴ Those comments apply with equal force to the Canadian accounts, almost all of which have been remarkably one-dimensional.

The Role of the Military in the Evacuation

There is no doubt that senior officers of the armed forces and the RCMP in Ottawa were remarkably unperturbed by the presence of large numbers of Japanese Canadians in British Columbia.³⁵ General Maurice Pope, the vice chief of the General Staff, attended the Conference on the Japanese Problem in British Columbia in Ottawa on 8-9 January 1942, which brought together representatives from British Columbia, the federal bureaucracy, and political figures, and his memoir provides the standard account. The navy, he wrote, had no fears, now that the Japanese-Canadian fishing fleet was in secure hands; the RCMP expressed no concern, and Pope himself, offering the army position, said that if the RCMP was not perturbed, "neither was the Army." Pope adds that several days after the meeting adjourned, the angry and frightened British Columbians who had attended "must have got busy on the telephone" for "we received an urgent message from the [Army's] Pacific Command recommending positive action against the

Japanese in the interests of national security. With the receipt of this message, completely reversing the Command's previous stand," the minister of national defence, Colonel J.L. Ralston, "was anything but pleased."[36]

The evidence simply does not support Pope's account. While it is clear that the Department of National Defence's representatives on the Special Committee on Measures to be Taken in the Event of War With Japan agreed in mid-1941 with the Committee's recommendation to Cabinet that "the bulk of the Japanese population in Canada can continue its normal activities,"[37] and while it is equally certain in mid-December the Chiefs of Staff Committee told the Cabinet War Committee that fears of a Japanese assault on BC were unwarranted,[38] there is absolutely no doubt that the military commanders *in* British Columbia and the military members of the Permanent Joint Board on Defence were seriously concerned about the possible threat posed by the Japanese-Canadian population both before and after 7 December 1941. The real question that remains unanswered is why in this instance the generals, admirals and air marshals in Ottawa were so ready to ignore the advice of their commanders in the field.

Certainly the military advice from BC was completely unambiguous. The Joint Service Committee, Pacific Coast, the key coordinating military body that brought together the three service commanders in British Columbia, had prepared plans in July 1940 for preventive actions directed at the Japanese Canadians in the event of war with Japan.[39] The Committee also recommended on 17 June 1941 that "the Japanese population [of approximately 230] residing in the vicinity of the Royal Canadian Air Force Advanced Base at Ucluelet [on the West Coast of Vancouver Island] should, in the event of an emergency, be evacuated for reasons of security. It was felt that similar steps should be taken in connection with Japanese resident near other important defence areas, and particularly those established near air bases." There were about two hundred Japanese Canadians living at Port Alice near the Coal Harbour RCAF base and the same number in Prince Rupert near another air station. The Committee's recommendations had been forwarded to the Chiefs of Staff Committee in Ottawa no later than 20 September 1941.[40]

In addition, the RCN on the coast had long been concerned with the fleet of up to 1,200 fishing vessels operated by Japanese Canadians. In 1937, for example, the Navy's staff officer (intelligence) at Esquimalt had said that "The fact that there are a large number of Japanese fishermen operating in British Columbia waters ... and having a thorough and practical knowledge of the coast, is in itself a matter of some concern to the Naval authorities."[41] In August 1941, the naval officer commanding on the coast asked Ottawa for authority to round up the fishing boats in the event of war. The Department of External Affairs refused to agree to this *in toto*, however, and in October orders were issued for seizure only of boats "owned and operated by Japanese *nationals*." "Vessels owned and operated by British subjects of Japanese origin," the RCN was told, "will only be interfered with where there are positive grounds for suspicion, comparable to those which would justify the internment of a British subject of Japanese origin."[42] When war came five weeks later, those orders would be overridden in the urgency of the moment.

Furthermore, before the outbreak of war in the Pacific, both the Canadians and the Americans worried about the concentration of Japanese Americans and Canadians living along the common coastline. The Joint Service Committee, Pacific Coast, had urged Ottawa on 20 September 1941 to coordinate any actions with Washington. In its opinion, "inequality in the treatment of persons of Japanese race in the territories of the Dominion of Canada and the United States would be liable to prove a source of danger to the effective prosecution of such measures of control as may be ordered by either government and to furnish grounds for grievance by the persons immediately concerned."[43] The Permanent Joint Board on Defence at its meeting on 10-11 November at Montreal had also considered the question of the "population of Japanese racial origin." Just as the Joint Service Committee on the West Coast had urged, the Canadian and American members agreed that there should be consultation to produce "policies of a similar character in relation to these racial groups" if war with Japan broke out. The aim was "a practicable coincidence of policy."[44] That did not imply evacuation from the Pacific Coast, but it did suggest that there was a shared realization of a "problem." And as John Hickerson, the senior State Department official regularly concerned with Canadian affairs, noted after that PJBD meeting, it would "cause the Canadians considerable political difficulty in British Columbia if we adopted more rigid treatment of Japanese in California than that prescribed in British Columbia." That, he added, is why the Canadians suggest "that at the proper time there be consultation" between the two governments "with the view to adopting similar policies in Canada and in continental United States."[45]

After Pearl Harbor, but before the Conference in Ottawa, the three senior officers on the coast wrote to Ottawa with their views. Major-General R.O. Alexander, the GOC of Pacific Command, told the chief of the General Staff on 30 December that he believed "internment of Japanese males between the ages of 18 and 45, their removal from the coast and their organization into paid units on public works ... would be advisable." Such action, Alexander added, "might prevent inter-racial riots and bloodshed, and will undoubtedly do a great deal to calm the local population." There is no doubt that General Pope saw this letter, because he sent a copy of it to Hugh Keenleyside of the Department of External Affairs and Keenleyside wrote back to him with suggestions on 3 January — before the "Japanese Problem" conference in Ottawa took place.[46]

The senior RCAF officer in BC shared the view of his army colleague. Air Commodore L.F. Stevenson informed RCAF headquarters in Ottawa on 2 January that security "cannot rest on precarious discernment between those who would actively support Japan and those who might at present be apathetic." If the government had doubts about the wisdom of moving the Japanese out, Stevenson said, "I suggest a strong commission be appointed immediately to ... obtain the opinion of a good cross section of the BC public and the officers charged with the defence of the Pacific Coast." The senior naval officer agreed, Commodore W.J.R. Beech telling his headquarters on 27 December that "Public opinion is very much against the Japanese all over the Queen Charlotte Islands and in view of the strategic position of these Islands I would strongly recommend that all the Japanese be removed."[47]

All three officers stressed public opinion at least as much as military needs, and it is reasonable to assume that their positions often put them in close contact with politicians and journalists likely to be pressing for stern action. But this does not alter the fact that the responsible military commanders in British Columbia, after 7 December and before the Ottawa conference, called for removal of the Japanese Canadians from all or part of the coastal region; so too had their staffs urged removal before 7 December from the vicinity of military bases and after Pearl Harbor from coastal areas of the province.[48] Moreover, on 13 February 1942, the Joint Services Committee, Pacific Coast, decided that in view of "the deterioration of the situation in the Pacific theatre of war ... the continued presence of enemy aliens and persons of Japanese racial origin [in the coastal areas] constitutes a serious danger and prejudices

115

the effective defence of the Pacific Coast of Canada."⁴⁹ And as late as 26 February, the RCN commanding officer on the coast was advised by his security intelligence officer that "The removal of all Japanese from this coastal area would undoubtedly relieve what is becoming more and more a very dangerous situation from the point of view of sabotage and aid to the enemy as well as the great danger of development of interracial strife."⁵⁰ Again, public opinion was given equal weight with the fear of sabotage, but it is significant that this advice was proffered after adult male Japanese citizens living on the coast had been ordered inland.

Even after the great majority of Japanese Canadians had been cleared from the government's designated defence zone, moreover, substantial concern was expressed repeatedly by the American military and by the US members of the Permanent Joint Board on Defence on 26-27 May and 1 September 1942 at the relocation of Japanese Canadians inland to road camp sites near railway lines or other strategic points. Under pressure, the Canadian government then acted to resolve matters to reassure its ally. Similar concerns had been expressed in June 1942 in the British Security Coordination report.⁵¹

An additional factor that played an unquantifiable but important part in events in BC were the reports that Japanese living in Hawaii, Hong Kong and Malaya had helped the attacking Japanese forces.⁵² Undoubtedly the lurid tales of fifth column activities from Europe in 1940 also fed popular fears. The Hawaii stories eventually proved to be mere rumours, but their impact was great in the first months of 1942. In Hong Kong and particularly in Malaya, however, there was substantial truth to the reports in January and February that local Japanese had hidden arms and ammunition, planted explosive charges at military installations, docks and ships, and sniped at troops, as well as providing information to the invaders.⁵³ It is virtually immaterial if the stories were true; what is important is that they circulated widely among a generally anti-Japanese public and a fearful military that were prepared to believe them. As the *Vancouver Sun* put it on 2 January 1942, "we may expect Japanese civilians to do all in their power to assist the attacker."⁵⁴

Finally, the stories, all too true, of the brutality of the Japanese victors towards captured Allied servicemen and civilians had substantial impact on both the public and political leaders. As early as 12 February, telegrams from London to Ottawa spoke of atrocities against captured

Hong Kong prisoners and of deplorable conditions in the POW camps. Within the week, Cabinet ministers in Ottawa were talking about the fate of the Hong Kong force with their intimates, and on 10 March, the widespread rumours were given official sanction by statements in Parliament in London and Ottawa. The "devilish" Japanese, or so M.J. Coldwell of the CCF said in the House of Commons, would be punished after the war for their atrocities. The Canadian Japanese, wholly innocent of the crimes of the Imperial Japanese Army, nonetheless were denied sympathy as a result.[55]

Was There a Military Threat to the Coast?

Whether there was a direct military threat to the coast from the Imperial Japanese forces is also worth some consideration, if only because the received version denies any. In September 1941, RCAF headquarters in Ottawa had been confident that the United States Navy was the ultimate guarantor of the safety of the Pacific Coast: "Unless the United States Navy is seriously defeated or loses its northern bases," Air Vice Marshal G.M. Croil told his Minister, C.G. Power, all Canada had to do was remain in "watchful readiness" on the West Coast.[56] With that attitude in the ascendant, the coast of British Columbia was left "poorly defended," the words employed to describe matters by Robert Rossow, Jr., the American Vice-Consul in Vancouver, in August 1941.[57] After Pearl Harbor, however, the worst possible case seemed to have occurred, and Canada was largely unprepared. Certainly there were few modern aircraft, few ships and relatively few trained soldiers in the area until the outbreak of war,[58] and it took some time before more could be rushed to the coast.[59] That caused concern.

So too did the course of the war. The Japanese hit Pearl Harbor on 7 December and simultaneously attacked Malaya, Hong Kong, the Philippines and Wake and Midway Islands. On 8 December, Japan occupied Thailand, captured Guam on 13 December, Wake on 24 December, and Hong Kong on 25 December. Manila fell on 2 January, Singapore followed on 15 February, a staggering blow to the British position in Asia (and something that frightened British Columbia[60]) and the Imperial Japanese Navy crushed an allied fleet in the Java Sea on 27 February, the date that the Canadian government's decision to move all Japanese Canadians inland was in the newspapers. Closer to home, a Japanese submarine had shelled Santa Barbara, California on 23 February, two days later the "Battle of Los Angeles" took place with

117

much ammunition expended against (apparently) imaginary targets, and there were submarine attacks on points in Oregon. (On 20 June a Japanese submarine shelled Estevan point on Vancouver Island.) The Dutch East Indies and most of Burma were then captured in March, capping an extraordinary four months of conquest.

At the beginning of June, the Japanese launched what H.P. Willmott, the leading historian of Pacific war strategy, called "their main endeavour, a twin offensive against the Aleutians," designed to draw the American fleet to battle to protect their territory, "and against the western Hawaiian Islands," intended to lead to an invasion once the Americans' Pacific Fleet had been destroyed. At least two plans for such an invasion existed before and after the attack on Pearl Harbor, and one plan saw the capture of Hawaii "as preparatory to strikes against the United States mainland."[61] (Whether attacks against the Canadian Coast were intended remains unclear until such Japanese military records that survived the war are searched.) Dutch Harbor, Alaska was attacked by carrier-based aircraft on 3 June as part of this plan. Four days later Kiska and Attu in the Aleutian Islands were taken.

Although in retrospect the American naval victory at Midway in June, aided beyond measure by "Magic" intercepts, put an end to the Hawaiian adventure and truly marked the beginning of the end for Japanese imperial ambitions as a whole, its significance was not quite so apparent in mid-1942 as it has since become. Certainly the Canadian government did not slacken its defence efforts on the coast after the American victory. In mid-February 1942, a military appreciation prepared by the chiefs of staff for the minister of national defence's use at a secret session of Parliament noted that "probable" Japanese strategy included containing "North American forces in America" by raids on the North American Pacific seaboard. "Possible" enemy aims included an "invasion of the West Coast of North America," although the chiefs noted that "Under present conditions" such invasion was "not considered to be a practicable operation of war."[62]

The next month, with the Japanese forces seemingly roaming at will throughout the Pacific and with the politicians anxious to satisfy the public clamour for stronger local defences in British Columbia, the chief of the General Staff in Ottawa was estimating the possible scale of a Japanese attack on the Pacific Coast to be two brigades strong (i.e., two Japanese regiments of three battalions each or approximately 5,200 to

6,000 men), and he was recommending the raising of new forces.[63] At the beginning of April, President Roosevelt used the occasion of the first meeting of the Pacific Council, made up of representatives of all the belligerent allies, to say that he had invited Canada because "he thought that Canada might do more than she was now doing."[64] That disturbed Ottawa, perhaps because it mirrored British Columbia public opinion so clearly, and Mackenzie King hastened to discuss the matter with the president.[65]

Later that month, after Lieutenant Colonel James Doolittle's B-25 bombers, launched from the carrier *Hornet*, had hit Tokyo, Canadian intelligence reports predicted that enemy aircraft carriers would launch retaliatory attacks against the West Coast in May.[66] By June, there were nineteen battalions on the coast, a response to Japan's invasion of the Aleutians and continued and growing public concern. Even so, the military commanders were far from satisfied. The Joint Canadian United States Services Committee at Prince Rupert believed that military strength in the area was "entirely inadequate against many types of attack that are possible and probable from the West."[67] The air officer commanding on the coast asked for sixteen squadrons to deal with the maximum scale of attack by battleships, cruisers and carrierborne aircraft. There were also blackouts and dimouts, and active plans underway in July and August 1942 for the evacuation of Vancouver Island and the lower mainland in the event of a Japanese attack.[68]

The Cabinet War Committee was assured by the chief of the General Staff in late September that he saw "no reason to fear any invasion from the Pacific Coast at present time,"[69] but two months later the Combined Chiefs of Staff, the highest Allied military authority, determined that while "carrier-borne air attacks and sporadic naval bombardment" were the most probable form of attack, the possibility of "a small scale destructive raid cannot be ignored." By that, the British and American planners meant "a force comprising 10/15 fast merchant ships carrying up to two brigades."[70] And as late as March 1943, there was a flurry of reports of Japanese activity in North American waters that stirred fears about a possible attack of the precise sort the planners had anticipated.[71] In other words, and contrary to the arguments of those who have argued that there was never any threat from Japan to the coast and hence no justification on grounds of national security for the evacuation of the Japanese Canadians, there *was* a credible — if limited — military threat into 1943.

The intent of this paper was to present some new and re-state some old evidence on several aspects of the Japanese-Canadian question. What has our account done to the received version? It has pointed to the gross weaknesses of and wishful thinking in RCMP and military intelligence about the Japanese Canadians. It has demonstrated irrefutably that the Japanese Consulate in Vancouver had orders from the Foreign Ministry to employ British Columbia *Nisei* in information collection or spying. It has called into question the advice of the military planners in Ottawa, brought forward once more the widespread concerns of the senior officers and staff planners of all three armed forces in British Columbia, and argued that there was a limited but credible military threat to North America from early 1942 into 1943 from the Imperial Japanese forces. It has noted that the attitudes of some Japanese Canadians by their support for Japan's war with China before 7 December 1941 raised understandable concerns on the part of British Columbians and Canadians generally. And although the attitudes of Japanese Canadians before and during the war have yet to be thoroughly studied despite all the work on the subject, Nakano's memoir is important for its account of the wartime attitudes and divisions in the community and especially so because of its resonance with Stephan's account of Hawaii. Finally, although little has been made of this here, it is certainly germane to recall that there was a war on and that Canada and its Allies were losing it at the beginning of 1942. As the civil libertarian and historian Arthur Lower wrote in October 1941, "The temper of the Canadian people seems to be becoming more and more arbitrary and we are fast losing whatever tolerance and magnanimity we once possessed."[72] That explains much that happened.

None of this alters the conclusion that the Japanese Canadians were victims of the racism of the society in which they lived and an uncaring government that failed to defend the ideals for which its leaders claimed to have taken Canada and Canadians to war. Even so, this paper does maintain that there were military and intelligence concerns that, in the face of the sudden attack at Pearl Harbor, could have provided Ottawa with a justification for the evacuation of the Japanese Canadians from the coast. The government in December 1941 was unaware of much of the data that has since emerged, and even if it had had it all, it simply lacked the assessment capability to put it together. If it had had the information and the intelligence capacity to appraise it properly, the arguments for evacuation would certainly have appeared far stronger than they already did.

However arguable this case, there is, of course, no necessary connection between the later confiscation of property and the still later effort to deport the Japanese Canadians and the reasons for the evacuation that seemed compelling to some in January and February 1942. The anger that persists at the evacuation might be misplaced; that at the confiscation of property and the attempt at deportation still seems wholly justifiable. In any case, this paper should demonstrate that there remains ample room for further work, broader interpretations and, perhaps, a changed emphasis in this area of research.

Notes

1. National Archives of Canada (NA), Department of National Defence Records, mf reel 5257, f. 8704, "Instructions for the Guidance of General Officers Commanding-in-Chief Atlantic and Pacific Commands," 26 February 1941

2. NA, Department of External Affairs Records, vol. 2007, f. 1939-212, pt. 2, "Report on the State of Intelligence on the Pacific Coast with Particular Reference to the Problem of the Japanese Minority," 27 July 1941; Department of National Defence Records, vol. 11913, "Japanese" file, Cmdr Hart to R.B.C. Mundy, 21 August 1940

3. PAC, RCMP Records, declassified report, "Japanese Activities in British Columbia" and attached correspondence. See also External Affairs Records, vol. 2007, f. 1939-212, pt. 2, "Report on the State...."

4. External Affairs Records, vol. 2007, f. 1939-212, pt. 1, Keenleyside to H.F. Angus, 28 June 1940. After the order to remove the Japanese from the coast, Keenleyside noted that American "control of enemy aliens seems to be rather more severe than ours while their action with regard to their own citizens is somewhat less severe than ours." *Ibid.*, Acc. 83-84/259, box 171, f. 2915-40, pt. 1, Keenleyside to Wrong, 14 March 1942

5. See, e.g., Robert H. Keyserlingk, " 'Agents Within the Gates': The Search for Nazi Subversives in Canada During World War II," *Canadian Historical Review*, LXVI (June 1985), 216-17; J.L. Granatstein, *A Man of Influence* (Ottawa, 1981), pp. 81ff; Reg Whitaker, "Official Repression of Communism During World War II," *Labour/Le Travail*, XVII (Spring 1986), 137 and *passim*.

6. NA, W.L.M. King Papers, "Note on a War-Time Intelligence Service," 27 November 1939, f. C257903ff. We are indebted to Professor W.R. Young for this reference.

7. Department of National Defence Records, Declassified Examination Unit Files, memorandum for chairman, Supervisory Committee, 15 August 1941, Lt C.H. Little memorandum, 18 April 1942, Draft History, chapter VI, "Japanese Diplomatic Section," 1

8. The spy scares in British Columbia sound much the same as those in Britain before the Great War. See Christopher Andrew, *Secret Service* (London, 1985), 34ff.

9. Department of National Defence Records, vol. 11917, f. 5-1-128, 1938-9, RCMP report, 3 June 1938; *ibid.*, vol. 11913, "Japanese" file, "Vancouver" [an agent] to Cmdr Hart, 30 June and 13 July 1940; External Affairs Records, vol. 2007, f. 1939-212, pt. 2, RCMP report, 29 July 1941; Ann Sunahara, *The Politics of Racism* (Toronto, 1981), 23

10. See Roy Miki, ed., *This is My Own: Letters to Wes & Other Writings on Japanese Canadians, 1941-48 by Muriel Kitagawa* (Vancouver, 1985), 98-9.

11. RCMP Records, declassified material, Commissioner S.T. Wood to Stephenson, 5 August 1942

12. Department of National Defence Records, vol. 3864, f. N.S.S. 1023-18-2, vol. 1, memorandum, F/L Wynd to senior air staff officer, 24 June 1940

13. External Affairs Records, vol. 2007, RCMP report, 29 July 1941. Under a Japanese law of 1899, Japanese men liable for military service did not lose Japanese nationality upon naturalization abroad unless they had performed their military service. After 1934, Canada would not accept Japanese for naturalization without certification that they had completed military service. See *ibid.*, Acc. 83-84/259, box 171, f. 2915-40, pt. 3, memorandum, "Postwar Treatment of Japanese in Canada," n.d.; John J. Stephan, *Hawaii Under the Rising Sun* (Honolulu, 1984), 24; and Ken Adachi, *The Enemy That Never Was* (Toronto, 1976). Adachi, 175, says that in 1934 86 percent of *Nisei* were dual citizens. The population numbers used here are those in the *Report and Recommendations of the Special Committee on Orientals in British Columbia, December 1940* (copy in NA, Privy Council Office Records, vol. 1, f. C-10-3), not those of the 1941 Census which were, of course, not available at the time.

14. External Affairs Records, vol. 2007, f. 1939-212, pt. 2, "Report on the State...." See also the pamphlet by the Vancouver unit of the Fellowship for a Christian Social Order, "Canada's Japanese" (Vancouver [1942?]), 7-8, with its explanation of the role of the Consulate.

15. External Affairs Records, f. 28-C(s), Massey to prime minister, 28 February 1941. This telegram was discussed by the Cabinet War Committee, the key comment being that by Angus L. Macdonald, the minister of national defence (naval services), that there was "little danger of serious attack by Japan" on the Pacific Coast. Privy Council Office Records, Cabinet War Committee Minutes, 5 March 1941. This type of attitude presumably was responsible for the fact that, as late as July 1941, as we have seen above, the RCMP still had only three people responsible for Japanese- Canadian questions. For a plausible hypothesis on how the information might have reached Massey — from US under secretary of state, S. Welles, to the British ambassador, Halifax, to London and thence to Massey — see Ruth Harris, "The 'Magic' Leak of 1941 and Japanese-American Relations," *Pacific Historical Review*, L (1981), 83.

16. Andrew, 261, 353; Ronald Lewin, *The American Magic* (New York, 1982), 44ff

17. *Ibid.*, 45-6

18. United States National Archives (USNA), General Records of the Department of the Navy, RG 80, "Magic" Documents, box 56, Tokyo to Washington, 30 January 1941 (2 parts); *ibid.*, Tokyo to Washington, 15 February 1941; *ibid.*, Los Angeles to Tokyo, 9 May 1941; *ibid.*, Tokyo to Vancouver, March 1941. USNA, Records of the National Security Agency, RG 457, "Magic" Documents, SRH 018, SRDJ nos. 1233-4, 1246-9, 1370, 1525, Vancouver to Tokyo, 7, 14 July, 11, 19 August 1939. Some of this information is contained in *The "Magic" Background to Pearl Harbor* (Washington, 1977), I, no. 131, and especially no. 135, which is the Tokyo to Vancouver, 14 February 1941, telegram referred to. See also *New York Times*, 22 May 1983, and Gregory A. Johnson's doctoral research paper, "Mackenzie King and the Cancer in the Pacific" (York University, 1984).

19. Indeed, as late as 21 October 1941, and despite the Massey telegram referred to above, Hugh Keenleyside, the assistant under secretary of state for external affairs, told the under secretary that "While it might be possible to find Japanese nationals in British Columbia against whom some meagre suspicion exists, there is certainly no Japanese national at large in that Province or elsewhere in Canada against whom any really convincing case can be made out." That comment likely reflected both RCMP advice, which is suspect, and Keenleyside's own extensive knowledge. Whether his certainty was justified — in the light of the Consulate's activities — is another question. D.R. Murray, ed., *Documents on Canadian External Relations*, vol. VIII: *1939-41*, pt. 2 (Ottawa, 1976), 1169

20. External Affairs Records, vol. 2007, f. 1939-212, pt. 2, "Report on the State...." Cf. H.F. Angus' critique of this report in Department of National Defence Records, f. 212-39c, 15 August 1941, and his memorandum of an interview with the officer, F/O Neild, 15 August 1941. We are indebted to Professor Patricia Roy for the Angus critique. It is worth noting that even missionaries shared alarmist views. A United Church China missionary, in Vancouver in January 1941, wrote that "I have had too much experience with the Japanese to trust them ... there is a war in progress and we in Vancouver are in the front line. And the front line is no place for thousands of enemy citizens." United Church Archives, Board of Foreign Missions, Honan, box 11, f. 174, Stewart to Reverend Armstrong, 20 January 1942

21. Adachi, 184-5. Membership figures for the Canadian Japanese Association are in University of British Columbia Archives, Japanese Canadian Collection, Miyazaki Collection, f. 6-4. A copy of the pamphlet is in *ibid.*, P.H. Meadows, Japanese Farmers Association Papers.

22. Granatstein, 98ff; King Papers, f. C144716ff, contains petitions and other material on Canadian policy to Japan after 1937. See also Murray, 1203ff, for extensive documentation on metals export policy.

23. Ed Ouchi, ed., *'Til We See the Light of Hope* (Vernon, BC, 1982[?]), 70. *The New Canadian* is available in the UBC Archives. For support for the war, see the 20 October 1939 issue; on the consul, see, e.g., 8 September 1939. The rotogravure

section began in late 1939 and ran well into 1940. On the economic boycott launched by Chinese groups, see UBC Archives, *Chinese Times* translations for 1937.

24. NA, J.W. Dafoe Papers, Angus to Dafoe, 15 October 1940. Mackenzie King told the Japanese minister to Canada in January 1941 that Japanese Canadians would not be called up for NRMA service: "he must remember that Japan and China were at war and we might be encouraging a little civil war if we supply both Chinese and Japanese with rifles etc., in BC at this time. He laughed very heartily at that." King Papers, Diary, 8 January 1941

25. University of British Columbia, Special Collections, H.F. Angus Papers, vol. 1, folder 2, draft memoir, 320-1; H.L. Keenleyside, *Memoirs of Hugh L. Keenleyside*, vol. II: *On The Bridge of Time* (Toronto, 1982), 171

26. University of British Columbia Archives, Special Collections, MacInnis Papers, Box 54A, f. 8, MacInnis to the Canadian Japanese Association, 11 December 1937; *ibid.*, f. 12, MacInnis to T. Umezuki, 18 April 1939. The CCF did not live up to its ideals once the Pacific War started and the BC party supported removal of Japanese Canadians. See Werner Cohn, "The Persecution of Japanese Canadians and the Political Left in British Columbia, December 1941 — March 1942," *BC Studies*, LXVIII (Winter 1985-6), 3ff.

27. H.F. Angus, "The Effect of the War on Oriental Minorities in Canada," *Canadian Journal of Economics and Political Science*, VII (November 1941), 508

28. Harvard University, J. Pierrepont Moffat Papers, "Memorandum of Conversations with Mr. Norman Robertson ...," 8 December 1941

29. John W. Dower, *War Without Mercy: Race and Power in the Pacific War* (New York, 1986), 36. See also Christopher Thorne, *Racial Aspects of the Far Eastern War of 1941-1945* (London, 1982) and chapter II of his *The Issue of War* (London, 1985).

30. Canada, House of Commons *Debates*, 4 August 1944, 5948; Adachi, 276

31. RCMP Records, "Japanese Activities in British Columbia," Appendix 6, lists the names. Adachi, 199, says 38 were arrested. Sunahara, 28, agrees.

32. Takeo Nakano, *Within the Barbed Wire Fence* (Toronto, 1980), 8; Sunahara, 70; Stephan, 171

33. Nakano, 44-45. Sunahara, 69, says that many *Nisei gambariya* had been educated in Japan.

34. Stephan, 177

35. To what extent the post-7 December military response was a reflection of pre-war contempt for Japanese military capabilities remains unknown. Dower, 98ff, discusses the responses of the American and British military and civilians both before and after the outbreak of war.

36. Maurice Pope, *Soldiers and Politicians* (Toronto, 1962), 176-8. Escott Reid, who attended the Conference for the Department of External Affairs, later wrote that delegates from BC "spoke of the Japanese Canadians in a way that Nazis would have spoken about Jewish Germans. I felt in that room the physical presence of evil." "The Conscience of a Diplomat: A Personal Testament," *Queen's Quarterly*, LXXIV (Winter 1967), 6-8

37. External Affairs Records, Acc. 83-84/259, box 115, f. 1698-A-40, "Report of Special Committee ...," 28 July 1941. Ottawa had not always been so calm. The Joint Staff Committee at Defence Headquarters on 5 September 1936 had foreseen circumstances in which "the Western Coast of Canada will be within the area of hostilities and is likely to be attacked not only by Japanese naval and air forces, but, in the case of important shore objectives, by Japanese landing parties operating in some strength." An abridged version of the document is in James Eayrs, *In Defence of Canada*, vol. II: *Appeasement and Rearmament* (Toronto, 1965), 213ff. Two years later Defence Headquarters had concluded that "there was a problem of possible sabotage in wartime and recommended that Japanese Canadians not be allowed to purchase property adjacent to areas of military importance." Cited in John Saywell, "Canadian Political Dynamics and Canada-Japan Relations: Retrospect and Prospect," 26, a paper published in Japanese only ("Nikkakankei No Kaiko To Tembo," *Kokusai Seiji* (May 1985), 121-36)

38. W.A.B. Douglas, *The Creation of a National Air Force*, vol. II: *The Official History of the Royal Canadian Air Force* (Toronto, 1986), 405. The British and American planners meeting at the Arcadia conference later in December agreed. *Ibid.*, 410. On 29 December 1941, the chief of the General Staff told the Cabinet War Committee that he had just returned from the Pacific Coast where he found the military and police more concerned with the possibility of attacks on Japanese Canadians than with subversion. Cabinet War Committee Minutes, 29 December 1941. The enormous difficulties that the military would have faced in dealing with racist attacks on Japanese Canadians should not be underestimated: the limited number of trained troops in the area and the very real problem of using white troops against white British Columbians in defence of Japanese Canadians would have frightened any realistic commander.

39. Department of National Defence Records, vol. 2730, f. HQS-5199X, "Memorandum of the Joint Service Committee, Pacific Coast, on the matter of the Defences of the Pacific Coast of Canada," 12 July 1940

40. *Ibid.*, vol. 3864, f. N.S.S. 1023-18-2, vol. 1, N.A. Robertson to LCol K.S. Maclachlan, 14 August 1941; *ibid.*, vol. 2730, f. HQS-5199X, "Memorandum of the Joint Service Committee, Pacific Coast, on the Subject of Dealing With Persons of Japanese Origin in the Event of an Emergency," 20 September 1941. See Peter Ward, *White Canada Forever* (Montreal, 1978), 145, which notes that as early as June 1938, the military were thinking of widespread wartime internment of Japanese Canadians. The numbers near RCAF stations are from NA, Ian Mackenzie Papers, vol. 32, f. X-81, Commander Parsons to Attorney General Maitland, 17 February 1942.

41. Department of National Defence Records, vol. 3864, f. N.S.S. 1023-18-2, vol. 1, "Extract from Report on Japanese Activities on the West Coast of Canada," 10 March 1937. See also Privy Council Office Records, vol. 3, f. D-19-1 Pacific Area, for AVM Croil's "Appreciation of the Situation Likely to Arise on the West Coast ...," 11 September 1941.

42. External Affairs Records, Acc. 83-84/259, box 115, f. 1698-A-40, memorandum for Robertson, 21 October 1941. London soon urged that as many Japanese fishing vessels as possible be seized in the event of war. External Affairs Records, f. 28-C(s), secretary of state for dominion affairs to prime minister, 23 October 1941

43. National Defence Records, vol. 2688, f. HQS-5199-1, vol. 1, "Memorandum of the Joint Service Committee, Pacific Coast, on the Subject of Dealing with Persons of Japanese Origin in the Event of an Emergency," 20 September 1941

44. USNA, Department of State Records, RG 59, PJBD Records, box 14, meeting 12

45. *Ibid.*, 842.20 Defense/140 1/2, Hickerson to Hackworth, 2 December 1941. We are indebted to Professor Robert Bothwell for this reference.

46. RCMP Records, vol. 3564, f. C11-19-2-24, General Alexander to CGS, 30 December 1941; *ibid.*, Keenleyside to Pope, 3 January 1942

47. Mackenzie Papers, vol. 32, f. X-81, "Extracts from Secret Letters," 30, 27 December 1941. See also C.P. Stacey, *Six Years of War* (Ottawa, 1955), 169, and W.A.B. Douglas, "The RCAF and the Defence of the Pacific Coast, 1939-1945," an unpublished paper presented to the Western Studies Conference, Banff, Alberta, January 1981, 8.

48. Department of National Defence, Directorate of History, f. 193.009 (D3), Pacific Command, Joint Service Committee, minutes, 9 January 1942

49. Department of National Defence Records, Acc. 83-84/216, f. S-801-100-P5-1, minutes of Joint Service Committee, Pacific Coast, 13 February 1942

50. *Ibid.*, vol. 11767, f. PC019-2-7, P.A. Hoare to commanding officer, 26 February 1942. The Joint Service Committee recommended on 20 February that all aliens and all Japanese regardless of age and sex should be removed from certain areas on the coast, particularly those near defence installations and in isolated areas. Cited in Patricia Roy, "Why Did Canada Evacuate the Japanese?" unpublished paper, 6-7

51. USNA, Records of US Army Commands, RG 338, box 4, f. 291.2, contains ample evidence of US concern from April 1942; RCMP Records, declassified material, "Japanese Activities in British Columbia." See also Department of National Defence Records, mf. reel 5258, f. 8704-11, for indications of National Defence's concern about sabotage in August 1942 and especially the vice chief of the General Staff's fear that the RCMP lacked "a realistic appreciation of the present danger of sabotage." *Ibid.*, General Murchie to Ralston, 19 August 1942

52. Mackenzie papers, vol. 32, f. X-81, BC Police Commissioner T.W.S. Parsons to Attorney General Maitland, 17 February 1941: "With these people neither Canadian birth nor naturalization guarantees good faith. Something to remember in the case of invasion or planned sabotage."

53. On Pearl Harbor, see Roger Daniels, *Concentration Camps USA: Japanese Americans in World War II* (New York, 1972), 36-8 and Gordon W. Prange, *Pearl Harbor: The Verdict of History* (New York, 1986), 348ff; on Hong Kong, see Stacey, 467, Oliver Lindsay, *The Lasting Honour* (London, 1978), 28, Carl Vincent, *No Reason Why* (Stittsville, 1981), 137, 139 and 146, and Ted Ferguson, *Desperate Siege: The Battle of Hong Kong* (Toronto, 1980), 57, 127-8, 137-9; on Malaya, see Ian Morrison, *Malayan Postscript* (London, 1942), 32-3, and the book by the British official historian of the war in Asia, General S. Woodburn Kirby, *Singapore: The Chain of Disaster* (New York, 1971), 30, 37, 152, 251, as well as the British Security Coordination report cited above from declassified RCMP records.

54. *Vancouver Sun*, 2 January 1942

55. External Affairs Records, Acc. 83-84/259, box 160, f. 2670-D-40, high commissioner in Great Britain to secretary of state for external affairs, 12 February 1942; Queen's University Archives, T.A. Crerar Papers, Crerar to J.W. Dafoe, 20 February 1942; Montreal *Gazette*, 11 March 1942. See also *Times* (London), 13 March 1942.

56. Privy Council Office Records, vol. 3, f. D-19-1, Pacific Area, memorandum, AVM Croil to minister for air, 11 September 1941

57. Department of State Records, 842.20 Defense/100, "Observations on the General Defense Status of the Province of British Columbia," 1 August 1941

58. See Stacey, 165ff, and Department of National Defence Records, vol. 2730, f. HQS-5199X, "Memorandum of the Joint Service Committee, Pacific Coast, on the Matter of the Defences of the Pacific Coast of Canada," 12 July 1940; Privy Council Office Records, vol. 3, f. D-19-1, Pacific Area, appreciations of 18 November 1941 and 10 December 1941.

59. See, e.g., Dafoe Papers, Bruce Hutchison to Dafoe, January 1942; Mackenzie Papers, vol. 30, chief of air staff to minister for air, 16 March 1942 and various memoranda.

60. Dower, 112, notes that, as the Japanese victories continued through early 1942, "Suddenly, instead of being treacherous and cunning, the Japanese had become monstrous and inhuman ... invested in the eyes of both civilians and soldiers with superhuman qualities."

61. The best accounts of Pacific war strategy are H.P. Willmott, *Empires in the Balance* (Annapolis, 1982) and *The Barrier and the Javelin* (Annapolis, 1983). On the Aleutian and Midway plans, see Willmott, *Barrier*, chapter 3; Stephan, chapters 6-7. Note, however, Willmott's cool assessment of the difficulties Japan would face in trying to take Hawaii. *Empires*, 437. The importance of the Aleutian

thrust was seen by the Americans' Special Branch, Military Intelligence Service, based on an analysis of "Magic" traffic. See USNA, RG 457, box 2, SRS-668, supplement to Magic summary, 30 July 1942, and on the Special Branch, Lewin, 141ff. One interesting assessment of the Japanese attack in the Aleutians was offered to Japanese Ambassador Oshima in Berlin by General von Boetticher, a former military attaché in Washington: "the Aleutian attack has closed the only practicable route for an attack on Japan and is a serious threat to Canada and the West Coast." *Ibid.*, box 1, SRS-640, Magic summary, 26 June 1942

62. NA, J.L. Ralston Papers, vol. 72, Secret Session file, chiefs of staff appreciation, 19 February 1942

63. Stacey, 171. See also Cabinet War Committee Minutes, 18 February 1942, and National Defence Records, vol. 2688, f. HQS-5159-1, vol. 2, "Report of Meeting Held at Headquarters, 13th Naval District Seattle, ... 6 March 1942," where Canadian and American commanders agreed with the Canadian estimates of scales of attack and suggested that "nuisance raids" were most likely. Additional information on defence preparations is in John F. Hilliker, ed., *Documents on Canadian External Relations*, vol. IX: *1942-1943* (Ottawa, 1980), 1162ff. For a good example of hindsight 20/20 vision on the impossibilities of a Japanese attack on the coast, see Adachi, 207-8.

64. Privy Council Office Records, vol. 14, f. W-29-1, "First Meeting of the Pacific Council in Washington," n.d. [1 April 1942] and attached documents

65. *Ibid.*, "Memorandum re Prime Minister's Visit to Washington, April 14th to 17th, 1942"

66. Department of National Defence Records, vol. 11764, f. PC05-11-5, naval message to NOI/C, Vancouver and Prince Rupert, 29 April 1942

67. *Ibid.*, vol. 11764, f. PC010-9-18, memorandum, "Defence of the West Coast," 7 July 1942

68. See *Vancouver Sun*, 10 August 1942; *Vancouver Province*, 13 August 1942; documents on External Affairs Records, Acc. 83-84/259, box 216, f. 3942-40; Douglas, *Creation*, 354. We are indebted to Professor John Saywell for his recollections of this period on Vancouver Island and to his father's book, John F.T. Saywell, *Kaatza: The Chronicles of Cowichan Lake* (Sidney, BC, 1967), 197-8, which briefly details the role of the Pacific Coast Militia Rangers, a force largely of skilled woodsmen and hunters.

69. King Papers, f. C249469, memorandum for file, 25 September 1942. See also Cabinet War Committee Minutes, 25 September 1942, where the chief of the General Staff said he would be "surprised" if the Japanese attacked the coast.

70. USNA, RG 218, Records of the US Joint Chiefs of Staff, mf. reel 10, f. 39322ff, Combined Chiefs of Staff, "Probable Maximum Scale of Attack on West Coast of North America," CCS 127, 29 November 1942. See also *ibid.*, f. A4024ff, CCS 127/1, "Probable Scale of Attack on the West Coast of North America," 16 January 1943. Not until August 1943 (in CCS 127/3) did the Combined Chiefs

declare the possibility of any serious attack on the coast "very unlikely." Douglas, *Creation*, 368-9. C.P. Stacey's comment in *Arms, Men and Governments* (Ottawa, 1970), 46, that "No informed and competent officer ever suggested that the Japanese were in a position to undertake anything more than nuisance raids" seems exaggerated in the light of the CCS papers. It is worth recalling that the Canadian raid on Dieppe involved about 5,000 men and was intended, among other purposes, to lead the Nazis to strengthen the French Coast at the expense of the Eastern front. The Japanese planners could (and should?) have been thinking similarly. Certainly a raid in force would have resulted in a massive public demand for the stationing of more troops on the coast; indeed, the simple prospect of such a raid did lead to the strengthening of defences.

71. Department of National Defence Records, vol. 11764, f. PC05-11-7, naval messages, 30-31 March 1943. This may have been based on false information. A secret US Federal Communications Commission project had reported on landing barges in the area; Washington discounted these reports but turned the information over to Canada, which sent them to the West Coast and then back into the American intelligence net where "they were believed to be authentic. Hence military action was ordered." See USNA, RG 457, SRMN-007, memorandum, 19 April 1943.

72. Lower to Frank Underhill, 15 October 1941, quoted in Doug Owram, *The Government Generation* (Toronto, 1986), 263

"As Far as Conscience will Allow": Mennonites in Canada during the Second World War

David Fransen

Canada's social landscape in 1939 consisted of not just two but a multitude of solitudes. Immigration policy in an earlier, simpler, more optimistic time had filled the land with a potpourri of people who shared little more in common than their location north of the 49th parallel. Strange people with unpronounceable names struggled to survive, usually by gathering into tightly knit communities with well defined and seldom traversed boundaries.

Historical judgement on the wartime government of Prime Minister W.L. Mackenzie King has inclined to the view that it was not so understanding of ethnic particularities as it might or should have been. Too often, we are told, King caved in, not so much to the imperatives of war but to the bigotry of Cabinet, caucus, or constituency. Discrimination against this or that minority, it would seem, was always politically motivated, and unjustified. One group which could, and did, expect harsh treatment was the Mennonites. There were approximately 110,000 of them in Canada in 1939, concentrated in a few rural areas of southern Ontario, southern Manitoba and Saskatchewan. Always wary of "the English" (and to the Mennonites anyone who was not one of them was an *Englander* (Englishman)), Mennonites had sought to create separate lives for themselves by settling in rural, often previously uninhabited areas. In many of these areas, they had been, in the truest sense of the word, pioneers. This physical separation, however, reflected another, much deeper distinction. According to the Mennonites' theology, they alone belonged to the Kingdom of God. All others who had not been baptized as adults on the public confession of their faith — in other words all non-Mennonites — belonged to the Kingdom of the World, and as such were eternally damned.

Such spiritual arrogance might have annoyed their "English" neighbours, had they been aware of it. Usually they were not, because another traditional emphasis of the Mennonites had been that, as a people, they should be *"die Stillen im Lande"* (the quiet in the land). What neighbours were aware of, and what angered them, was that Mennonites spoke German and refused to fight. Worse yet, in some communities it was known that some Mennonites had expressed admiration for the achievements of Adolf Hitler. The Mennonites felt this animosity and to a certain extent expected, even welcomed it as the burden which they as children of God had to bear in a sinful world. They hoped, however, that the government, divinely ordained by God, would be a little more understanding than their sinful neighbours.

Not willing to leave everything in God's, and the government's, hands, some leaders felt compelled to act. With war in Europe becoming an increasingly distinct possibility, leaders of the many different Mennonite denominations across Canada gathered in the small southern Manitoba town of Winkler on 15 May 1939. Bishop David Toews of Rosthern, Saskatchewan, one of three Canadian Mennonite leaders who had attended a similar gathering in Chicago two months earlier, had been inspired by the advanced state of preparations and the high degree of cooperation among American Mennonites. Unity, however, as Toews knew well, would not be achieved easily. Of the ten different Canadian Mennonite denominations invited to Winkler, one (the *Sommerfelder*) refused even to attend. Of the rest, many were more suspicious of others in the same room than they were of the government.

The primary reason for the anxiety were the *Russlaender*, Mennonites who had only recently come to Canada from the USSR in the 1920s, fleeing famines and Communist oppression. For many of their brethren, they were a distinctly menacing presence. On average, they tended to be better educated than the Mennonites who were already living in Canada. More worrying, as far as these other Mennonites were concerned, the *Russlaender* had strayed a long way from the path of true Mennonitism by compromising on a central tenet of the Mennonite faith, the refusal to bear arms. They had first started down the slippery slope when they accepted the demands of the tsarist government in Russia late in the nineteenth century that they perform some alternative forms of service, such as in the forestry service or the army's medical corps, in return for exemption from military service. Then they had committed the worst sin of all by taking up arms to defend themselves against the bands of anarchists who swept through their villages in the wake of the Russian Revolution.

Those Mennonites who had been in Canada during the First World War remembered a relatively better experience. Both the Swiss Mennonites (a generic term referring to all those of Swiss background who had migrated to Upper Canada from the United States after the American Revolution) and the *Kanadier* Mennonites (those who emigrated from Russia in the 1870s and settled in the west) felt that they had been granted a complete exemption from any form of service. In the event, some were ordered to perform non-combatant service and, refusing, found themselves in prison. Others were forced to endure the taunts and isolated acts of violence of frustrated neighbours. In general, however, the government had stood by earlier promises granting them exemption from military service. Leaders of both the Swiss and the *Kanadier* Mennonites, therefore, believed that the government would once again honour its commitments. Their greatest fear was that the *Russlaender* might undercut their privileged status by unilaterally offering their young men to Ottawa in return for some form of alternative service. Bishop Samuel F. Coffman, an elder statesman among Swiss Mennonites in Ontario who had led several delegations to Ottawa during the First World War, reflected his concerns to a troubled colleague shortly before the Winkler conference: "I hope that the conference will be enlightening. Some of those people are trying to introduce the Russian method into America. We do not ask for such experiences. Our attitude differs from that and we may continue to take the position we have taken in the past. They may profit by our experience."[1]

Coffman himself was unable to attend the Winkler conference. He ensured, however, that his point of view would be forcefully expressed by asking Harold S. Bender, the well-known Mennonite scholar from the United States, to represent him. That Bender shared Coffman's concerns about the new immigrants was clear. "Glad also to learn of your contact with the Russian Mennonite brethren," he had written to Coffman in December 1938. "I think that it is important for us to keep in touch with them and to bring Christian pressure to bear on them to seek to avoid any possibility of compromising on our stand on nonresistance."[2] Having been given the opportunity himself, Bender did what he could to bring Christian pressure to bear on the *Russlaender* at the Winkler conference. As far as the (Old) Mennonite Church was concerned, he said, it was "entirely opposed to any work in any organization which has anything to do with the conduct of the war, such as the medical corps or a war industry."³ Any future war would require the total effort of all people, including women. It was essential that the Mennonites refuse to compromise. Steadfastness would be unpopular and perhaps bring persecution, but was a price they would have to pay.

If Coffman and Bender hoped that the *Russlaender* would profit from the experience of the Swiss Mennonites during the First World War, *Russlaender* leaders were equally eager to convince their Swiss and *Kanadier* counterparts of the virtues of their experience. Passive nonresistance was of little value, said B.B. Janz, the prominent Mennonite Brethren leader from Coaldale, Alberta. Mennonites should be prepared to heal the enemy as well as the friend. The Mennonite Brethren Church, announced Janz, was prepared to render an alternative service, preferably in the medical corps, where they could witness to their faith by displaying their willingness to save life rather than destroy it.⁴ The *Russlaender* bishop in Ontario, Jacob H. Janzen of Waterloo, agreed with Janz. The distinction between military and civilian was artificial. In a nation completely mobilized for war, argued Janzen, they were all under military leadership one way or another. As far as he was concerned, he would permit service in the medical corps, even under military direction, as long as they would not be required to carry guns.⁵

In the end, the gap was too wide. No one was willing to learn from the experiences of the others. "Perhaps half of our people would be willing to do some kind of non-combatant service," wrote David Toews to a friend after the conference, "but a number of them refuse any kind of service.... To me it seems the only way in which we might unite would be that in case of war we offer the government non-combatant service under church supervision, but I am not sure that we will get that far."⁶

Toews' pessimistic prophecy proved accurate. The outbreak of war did bring a flurry of organizational activity as Mennonites sought to establish a single voice. In September 1940, the Conference of Historic Peace Churches (CHPC) was formed in Ontario, representing not only the Swiss and the *Russlaender* Mennonites of that province but the other 'historic' peace churches as well — the Quakers and the Brethren in Christ. The CHPC, however, covered only Ontario. In the west, developments had taken their own course. The Mennonite Central Relief Committee (MCRC) was formed in March 1940, ostensibly representing all prairie Mennonites. But within months even this degree of unity was shattered. The *Kanadier* remained deeply suspicious of the *Russlaender*. Convinced that they were entitled to special consideration because of the arrangements made when they immigrated in the 1870s, and afraid that association with the *Russlaender* would taint them in the eyes of the Mobilization Board in Winnipeg, the *Kanadier* formed their own *Aeltestenkomitee* (Committee of Elders) in September in order to make their own special appeals to government officials.

Although several attempts were made to heal the rift in the west, all failed. A special meeting in Winnipeg in October 1940 between leaders of the MCRC and the *Aeltestenkomitee* shows why. Representing the MCRC, Janz emphasized a point he had already made many times at similar gatherings. The Mennonites in Alberta which he represented were strongly in favour of some form of medical service. In fact, he stated, he had already communicated their willingness to serve to the Mobilization Board in Edmonton, where the news had been received gratefully. This pre-emptive proposal from the *Russlaender*, of course, was precisely what the more conservative *Kanadier* had feared. Speaking for the *Aeltestenkomitee*, Bishop David Schultz chided the *Russlaender* for their willingness to sacrifice the principle of complete exemption from military service. It was a principle, said Schultz, for which their fathers had "endured and suffered and which they had won through prayer and supplication."[7]

There, it was in the open. The *Kanadier* had endured and suffered; the *Russlaender* had compromised. Such explicit condemnation of their experience could not go unchallenged. The *Russlaender* protested that they too had been willing to sacrifice and suffer.

> The medical service [D.P. Reimer has written] was just such a service which gave our brethren the chance to be of service to the State, to practice brotherly and Christian love and to face danger side by side with other fellow citizens, and what was of main importance in this respect: it need not violate the conscience of a non-resistant Mennonite. We also had to take into account that our young men who were especially concerned, felt the same way. They felt it their duty where other young people stake their lifeblood to do something also.[8]

Conviction prevailed over compromise; neither side would give in. Dejected, David Toews wrote to a friend: "I cannot quite grasp why, in the question which we as Mennonites face today, there has to be dissension. I can well understand why a segment of our people would like to perform alternative service — one wants to cooperate with the government as far as conscience will allow, and one wants to pacify the agitation of the Canadian people. On the other hand, one would like to take advantage of the rights which we have to the utmost."9

These conflicting tendencies, confirmed by the split between the *Aeltestenkomitee* and the MCRC, were never completely reconciled in western Canada. A more positive experience was the cooperation between the Mennonite Central Relief Committee and the Conference of Historic Peace Churches. On 12 November 1940, a delegation comprising four representatives from each organization began a series of meetings in Ottawa with officials of the Department of National War Services, meetings which were to have a profound impact on the programme which the government eventually established to handle the problem of conscientious objectors. The impetus for these meetings had come several months earlier with the government's proclamation of the National Resources Mobilization Act. The act, passed in the traumatic aftermath of the fall of France on 14 June 1940, placed a person, his services and his property at the disposal of the government for the war effort. Regulations now called for the establishment of a compulsory military training scheme with the first trainees to be called up in October 1940. Despite earlier official assurances that their exemption from military service was ensured, the Mennonites were worried.

The Conference of Historic Peace Churches had already mailed a lengthy statement, entitled the Canadian Fellowship Service, to the war services department outlining its position on the types of training which Mennonite young men might accept when called up under the NRMA. The MCRC representatives brought their own statement with them. The two documents, similar in nature, requested that the mobilization boards created under the NRMA grant postponement from military training on the basis of lists of names submitted by Mennonite leaders. This would eliminate the need for the young men to appear individually before the boards. Once military training was put off in this way, the Mennonites would willingly perform alternative service provided that it was non-military in nature and under civilian control. The training, or service, was to be somewhere other than in military camps and in groups large enough to make spiritual supervision by a Mennonite minister possible. Those Mennonites currently in military camps —

"mistakenly" so — were to be released and directed to these new centres.[10]

The first response to the delegations' proposals was not encouraging. The associate deputy ministers of National War Services, Justice T.C. Davis and Major General L.R. LaFlèche, saw several problems with the Mennonites' ideas. The number of men which these leaders represented was a very tiny proportion of the overall number which mobilization officials would have to manage. To establish a separate administration would be an unnecessarily cumbersome and unwelcome complication of manpower administration problems. Furthermore, the transportation costs to move the men to the various camps would be great. Davis and LaFlèche wondered too whether there should be any special provision at all for conscientious objectors. Public opinion certainly opposed special treatment. The Mennonites, insisted the judge and the general, should reconsider their opposition to non-combatant service under military control. If it would make it any easier, they would arrange that this could be done in civilian clothes.[11]

Sober second thought did not change the Mennonite leaders' minds. After their meeting with Davis and LaFlèche, another text was produced. This third statement is significant for two reasons. First, it was the first ever to result from a joint east-west inter-Mennonite consultation. Secondly, the form alternative service eventually took closely mirrors the Mennonites' ideas. Work in military camps, they wrote, whether it was performed in uniform or not, would not be acceptable to the young men whom they represented. Instead, they proposed work of an agricultural or forestry nature on government-owned land (so that "the benefit from labour expended should accrue to the Country as a whole") with supervisors selected from the departments of agriculture and lands and forests. While in camp the men would be given first aid courses "to equip them to render service in the event of epidemics or other emergency resulting from war." Such a solution, argued the leaders, should satisfy "any reasonable objection" from those opposed to the accommodation of religious conscience.[12]

The new statement, duly presented to Davis and LaFlèche the next day, 13 November, initially met with no more favourable a response than before. A civilian service under civilian supervision would cause "considerable difficulty," and Mennonite leaders were urged to consider once again the possibility of non-combatant service under military

137

supervision. In any case, the officials assured the churchmen, their position would receive the department's full consideration.

Their brief presented, the Mennonite leaders departed Ottawa — everyone, that is, except the *Russlaender* B.B. Janz. Disappointed with the officials' consistent refusal to allow postponements to Mennonites on the basis of lists prepared by church leaders, Janz insisted that he remain behind to continue pleading their cause. The others, fearing that Janz might compromise their position which they felt had already been clearly stated, attempted to dissuade him, but unsuccessfully.[13] The following day, Janz met again with LaFlèche, presenting him with yet another statement, his revised version of the one submitted by the four delegates from the Mennonite Central Relief Committee on 12 November. While Janz later claimed to his Mennonite brethren that his was simply a strengthening of the original MCRC document, he had in fact dramatically and unilaterally changed the terms of the proposal. The earlier insistence that the training or service be under civilian supervision and not in military camps was dropped, as was the suggestion that the work be on forestry or farm projects. Instead, Janz advocated an alternative service along the lines of a first aid, ambulance, or hospital service under the Red Cross authorities.[14]

LaFlèche, rather taken aback by this unexpected departure from the line consistently taken on the two previous days, wired the other Mennonite leaders to determine whether this new position reflected their own views. It most certainly did not. From Waterloo, Ontario, Bishop Jacob H. Janzen wired Janz to come to a meeting in that city scheduled for 19 November, or, if unable to attend, at least to desist from any further action until informed of that gathering's decisions. David Toews chastised the Alberta Mennonite leader. While he shared Janz's frustrations with the delegation's joint statement, which made no allowance for a non-combatant medical service, the compromise had been necessary to accommodate the Swiss Mennonite leaders of the CHPC. Unity, at this point, was more important than the full adoption of the *Russlaender*'s proposals.[15]

Janz was soon reinforced in Ottawa by his wary colleagues. On 20 November he, J.B. Martin of Waterloo, and C.F. Klassen of Winnipeg met with LaFlèche. LaFlèche pressed Janz's case vigorously: the Mennonites should accept that non-combatant medical service was a legitimate alternative to bearing arms. Martin and Klassen simply heard Laflèche out, and then requested more time so that the rest of the original delegation (with the exception of Toews who had already returned to the west) could return to Ottawa to restate the Mennonite position.

The request granted, the reconstituted delegation put its case once again on 22 November. With Janz present, the other Mennonite leaders unequivocally repudiated his statement of 14 November. Under no circumstances, they emphasized, would their people accept noncombatant service in the medical corps. Undoubtedly irked by the pacifists' obvious determination, LaFlèche clumsily attempted to bully them. "What'll you do if we shoot you?" he demanded. Ernie Swalm, a Brethren in Christ bishop who had been jailed during the First World War for refusing to report for military training, replied calmly that half his people would be willing to die. Jacob Janzen, a *Russlaender* who had survived harrowing times in Russia, was more forceful. "Listen, Major General," he retorted, "I want to tell you something. You can't scare us like that. I've looked down too many rifle-barrels in my time to be scared that way. This thing's in our blood for 400 years and you can't take it away from us like you'd crack a piece of kindling over your knee. I was before a firing squad twice. We believe in this. It's deep in our blood."[16]

No longer confident that LaFlèche would represent them fairly, the delegates made an inspired change in their tactics. They sought a meeting with the war services minister, James Gardiner. When Swalm introduced himself as "bishop of the Brethren in Christ Church, otherwise known as the Tunkers," Gardiner's eyes lit up. He himself had attended a school with a number of Tunkers, he explained. Listening patiently and closely as the men repeated their arguments, Gardiner assured the Mennonites that there were "one hundred and one things that you fellows can do without fighting; we'll see that you get them." With a sigh of relief, the Mennonite leaders (again with the exception of Janz) returned home, satisfied that they had at last received a sympathetic hearing.[17]

And indeed they had. The National War Service regulations laid down the rules governing the mobilization of Canada's manpower. Amended by order-in-council PC 7215 on 24 December 1940, Section 18 of the regulations now stated that conscientious objectors could be sent either to a military camp for non-combatant training, for first-aid training at a civilian camp, or to perform civilian labour at a civilian camp. For the time being at least, there would be no actual service in the medical corps. In other words, the government had accepted the position put forward by the Mennonites on 12 November.

It was not until five months later, on 29 May 1941, that James Gardiner announced to the House of Commons that the first call-up for the Alternative Service Work (ASW) camps would begin immediately.[18] The ASW program as originally conceived involved four months' service in camps established in the following national parks: Riding Mountain, in Manitoba; Prince Albert, in Saskatchewan; Banff and Jasper, in Alberta; and Kootenay, in British Columbia. In Ontario conscientious objectors were assigned to service of the same duration in a road camp at Montreal River, eighty miles north of Sault Ste Marie, clearing the right of way for what would eventually become part of the Trans-Canada Highway. Later, in 1942, three other camps were established. One small and temporary camp, lasting only from July to October, was located at Glacier National Park. Two others were set up at forest experiment stations at Seebe, Alberta and at Petawawa, Ontario.

This system, consisting of camps in national parks, forest experiment stations, and road construction camps under the administration of the federal Department of Mines and Resources, constituted the first stage of the ASW program during the Second World War. While there would be frequent changes in the number of camps, especially after the spring of 1943, the outlines of the camp system remained until the end of the war. This programme of civilian service under civilian supervision, a compromise between the extremes of non-combatant military service on the one hand and complete exemption from any service whatsoever on the other, was a new departure in Canadian policy towards conscientious objectors. It represented a major victory for the *Russlaender* Mennonite leaders, who had succeeded in transplanting the Russian model of alternative service to Canada.

Bureaucrats and businessmen were soon to recognize that, while Mennonites might make poor fighters, they were without doubt good workers. As BC's minister of lands and forests explained to General Laflèche in Ottawa, this cheap and docile form of labour had very quickly become a greatly coveted commodity:

> It is a notable fact that, no sooner were a few of these Alternative Service Workers in camp in this province, than a wide variety of interests were inquiring as to the possibility of securing their services. We have been approached by various mills, logging operators, the E&N Railway, by ... the

CPR in Vancouver, the Lumber and Shingle Manufacturers' Association, the BC Loggers' Association, and even by taxi firms. The services of these men were urgently requested for harvesting crops in the Fraser Valley and for harvesting the fruit in the Okanagan. It was proposed that they should be returned to the Prairies for harvest there and, most of them being farmers we had urgent requests for harvest leaves. These representations have been progressively urgent and pressing as the employment situation has become more aggravated during recent months.[19]

West coast employers were not alone in clamouring for CO labourers. Robert Gardiner, president of the United Farmers of Alberta, complained that Alberta's Mennonites, shuffled off to British Columbia's forestry camps, were desperately needed at home on the farm. From Regina, Justice J.F.L. Embury complained that "labour in the parks is the only service now provided for and it produces no noticeable public benefit, annoys the old Soldier, is of no value as a War Effort, and it is unsuited to the many educated Mennonites, who have expressed to our Board their desire to serve the country in any dangerous war service except that involving the actual taking of life."[20]

Pressure to diversify the available alternatives also came from within the Mennonite community. A delegation from the Conference of Historic Peace Churches travelled to Ottawa in January 1943 to argue that "the best possible use be made of all persons who have special training or skill ... (to) enable each person to make the largest possible contribution to the good of Canada and of all mankind." Specifically, they referred to the availability of doctors, dentists, teachers, and engineers. Once again, consistent with the demands they had made in November 1940, they emphasized that the service be of an entirely civilian nature.[21]

From the west, the Mennonite Central Relief Committee likewise pressed for diversification. Writing in early February 1943, C.F. Klassen urged the government to reconsider its refusal to accept COs into the medical corps:

> We could not understand then — and cannot now — why a medical group of 600 to 1,000 conscientious objectors would not prove of the greatest possible service....
>
> We are convinced that the time will come when those in authority will realize that a serious mistake was made when the willingness of so many of the Mennonites to serve their country in the manner that their conscience permits them to serve, was rejected. Perhaps it is not too late even now to rectify the error.

> If any plans are about to be formulated for the purpose of making available to the country this additional resource, then we would strongly urge you to permit us to share in the working out of the details because we are convinced that our experience gained in the First World War should prove to be of considerable value.[22]

The government, of course, did not need mobilization board chairmen, farm representatives, or ministers (whether provincial or Mennonite) to persuade it of the need for a more efficient utilization of manpower. A great deal of the government's mental and emotional energy had been taken up with precisely this problem during all of 1942.[23] Competition between politicians and officials responsible for the armed forces on the one hand and those responsible for war production on the other grew increasingly intense as the manpower pool dwindled. Conscientious objectors were, granted, only a very small part of this equation. They did, however, have skills to offer.

In April 1943, therefore, an entirely new administrative structure was created. Within the Department of Labour, the alternative service programme, formerly lodged in the mobilization section of the National Selective Service, became the responsibility of the new Alternative Service Branch, under the guidance of a chief alternative service officer, L.E. Westman. In those mobilization districts where there were significantly large numbers of conscientious objectors — Toronto, London, Winnipeg, Regina, Edmonton, and Vancouver — alternative service officers were also appointed.

From this point on, the ASW camps became little more than detention centres for the uncooperative. The vast majority of COs were redirected to farms or essential industries. The diversification of service opportunities had satisfied all Mennonite demands but one. A relatively small, but stubborn, element represented so persistently by B.B. Janz continued to press for non-combatant service in the medical corps. The armed forces, however, continued to oppose the idea, as did Arthur MacNamara, the director of national selective service. It would, the latter argued, remove a valuable source of labour from the Alternative Service Branch's control. But the ASB itself had become persuaded that a limited number of Mennonites should be given the opportunity to serve in the capacity which they so strongly desired.[24] This view, and Janz's persistence, finally prevailed when the enlistment of conscientious objectors in the Royal Canadian Army Medical Corps and the

Canadian Dental Corps was authorized by order-in-council PC 7251, 16 September 1943.

This provision for non-combatant service in the medical and dental corps was the last major development in the alternative service programme during the war. At the outset, there had been nothing more than a strong conviction among government officials and some Mennonites that COs should do something. This was gradually translated, through negotiation, into a government operated camp system. Finally, a diverse structure providing for the relatively flexible utilization of individual skills in both the public and private sectors was created. Throughout, the Mennonites enjoyed a significant degree of influence over its definition. But why? Why had a government, anxious to mobilize millions for a war effort vastly exceeding anything ever before done in Canada, accommodated a few thousand Mennonites firmly opposed to their own direct involvement in that effort?

Certainly there were those not inclined to be tolerant. Justice Adamson, for example, chairman of the Winnipeg mobilization board, actively sought to undermine the pacifist position. Speaking to a large gathering of Mennonite ministers, fathers, and sons before board hearings in Steinbach in 1941, the Manitoba judge urged the older generation to

> let (the boys) go as regular Canadians and come back as heroes, rather than do some secondary work which can never be as useful to the Government or as good for them as permitting them to take the course which I have already suggested....
>
> I am not overlooking the fact that a considerable number of young Mennonites have enlisted, and I am told that many more would go if your leaders would permit them. That is no doubt true, because your Mennonite boys are not slackers and not cowards. They like adventure and honour as well as other boys, and their love for Canada, their native land, is as great as that of other boys. If they are left free they will do their duty to their country just as well as other boys.
>
> To you Bishops, Preachers, Elders, and fathers, I say, do not attempt to influence these young men. Leave them free. Remember it is their conscience, and not yours. If you do influence them, you will do them a great injury and will put a black mark upon your own church. And to you young men, I say you need not be nervous here today. Only speak the truth.[25]

Not content with this appeal, Adamson submitted to the director of national selective service a treatise written by a member of the

Winnipeg mobilization board entitled "Can Christian Principles of Life and Conduct be Harmonized with Active Military Service?" Adamson's idea was that the pamphlet, which of course answered the rhetorical question with a resounding yes, should be printed and circulated to the ASW camps, the jails in which some of the COs were located, and to all those who had yet to appear before the board to gain their 'postponement.' Exposure to this biblically based argument against the CO stance, he believed, would convince many to change their minds. In Ottawa, some may have sympathized with Adamson's plight, plagued as he was in Manitoba with the highest concentration of Mennonites. Still, as one national selective service official noted, while the pamphlet might be an effective weapon against conscientious objection, its distribution would at the same time make the government guilty of the very thing which Adamson himself had repeatedly condemned, namely authorities abusing their power to influence impressionable young men.[26]

Notwithstanding Adamson, LaFlèche, and others, it must be said the Mennonites enjoyed a generally favourable response from government officials. One historian who has made a careful study of the alternative service programme has suggested that this phenomenon was the result of the conscientious objectors' "readiness to do hard work," their "sincerity and faithfulness," their "courage and unselfishness," and their "willingness to cooperate."[27] Certainly it appears true that officials appreciated the calm, reasoned, and cooperative approach which the Mennonites adopted and recognized the good work that they did. Even as difficult and unsympathetic an official as LaFlèche grudgingly admitted respect. In a curiously phrased but obvious attempt to compliment, the associate deputy minister of national war services said of one of his Mennonite opponents: "It is hard not to take such a fine man as Bishop Toews at par. I have now met him a number of times and while he is certainly not lacking in intelligence, he is a very likable and gentle man."[28] Chief Alternative Service Officer Westman noted in an internal memorandum that "when Mines and Resources made arrangements for Camps they had in mind the very excellent Mennonite labour that willingly went to Camps and was the best labour they had ever received."[29]

Their reputation for being likable and hardworking undoubtedly stood the Mennonites in good stead. They appear, moreover, to have benefitted greatly from the contrast, in officials' eyes at least, between them and other conscientious objectors. Doukhobors and Jehovah's Witnesses in particular antagonized mobilization officials. One

Department of Mines and Resources memorandum assessed the work being done by the COs in the various national parks. Distinguishing among the different groups, the report spoke favourably of the Mennonites, "who were so successful as farmers in our new West that it was expected the Doukhobors would be equally successful." That this had turned out not to be the case, it was concluded, reflected a "basic and racial difference": Mennonites belonged to the Nordic race, while the Doukhobors came from the "Semitic Nomadic race."[30]

As for the Jehovah's Witnesses, they weren't in the race at all. Like the Mennonites, the JWs refused to kill their fellow man. Unlike the Mennonites, they refused to cooperate with the government in any way whatsoever. In January 1944, when the Alternative Service Branch was considering providing greater allowances for the dependants of COs, the director supported the idea in general but strongly opposed granting this benefit to the Jehovah's Witnesses. "A distinction must be made," he argued, "between the dependants of Jehovah's Witnesses who are in camp as a result of their refusal to accept any provided employment under AS contracts and other COs. We have had to prosecute 50 such men in Ontario who are willing to claim postponement on grounds of conscience but are unwilling to accept any kind of agreement or do any Alternative Service. As soon as they are placed in camps, they organize a public appeal through their dependants. They will not go to camps without prosecution or escort."[31] The director was simply echoing the exasperation of one of his officials who had written a few months earlier: "Surely there is some more realistic way to deal with Jehovah Witnesses [sic] than what we are doing at present. Jehovah Witnesses [sic] are not Conscientious Objectors, and should not be treated as such."[32]

The private sector was equally unenthusiastic about non-Mennonites. At a meeting in Galt, Ontario late in 1943, businessmen, politicians, officials, and church leaders met to consider the supply and demands for CO labour. Farm and industry representatives were adamant: "no Mennonite CO farm labour could be spared for the entire winter." They were, however, perfectly willing to donate any given number of Jehovah Witnesses [sic]![33]

One final factor must be noted in explaining the generally favourable response Mennonites enjoyed at the federal level. More beneficial perhaps than the hard work in the alternative service programme, and even greater than the impact of the negative image of uncooperative conscientious objectors, was the ample evidence federal officials accumulated of Mennonite accommodation to the state. The delegation of Mennonite leaders which travelled to Ottawa in November 1940 was an early signal that these people who would not fight were not out to shirk their duty to serve. Indeed, despite what their leaders preached, many Mennonite young men were actually enlisting in the armed forces. L.E. Westman, director of the Alternative Service Programme, was prompted to observe that while no amount of argument, biblically based or otherwise, could persuade Hutterites, Doukhobors, or Jehovah's Witnesses to renounce pacifism, Mennonites had proven more cooperative, enlisting in large numbers.[34]

Westman's observation was not one Mennonite leaders would have been proud to hear. But the Second World War experience had fundamentally altered the world for the Canadian Mennonites. Previously isolated, not only from "the world" but from each other as well, the various Mennonite streams now found themselves flowing together. At the higher levels, with various degrees of success, church leaders formed organizations to represent the Mennonite cause before the many levels of wartime administration. Among the laymen, *Russlaender*, *Kanadier*, and Swiss Mennonites found themselves pushing boulders, cutting trees, clearing rights of way, and fighting fires, side by side. The groundwork for post-war inter-Mennonite cooperation had been firmly laid.

At the same time, latent tensions within the Mennonite fabric had been exposed. The teaching on non-resistance had obviously not been assimilated as well as many had assumed. Forced to fend for themselves before intimidating, if not antagonistic, mobilization board officials rather than receive blanket exemption simply by virtue of biological accident, many young Mennonite men could not articulate a non-resistant faith. Many more were not even interested in trying. They simply enlisted. Mennonite congregations across the country had no choice but to come to terms with young men who had had their eyes opened to the world, whether this was in the context of alternative, or military, service.

The Mennonites' experience is also instructive for understanding the government's response to ethnic minorities during the Second World War. Clearly, politicians and officials recognized a legal obligation to allow postponement from military service on the grounds of conscientious objection. Equally clearly, this recognition was easier to grant when the conscientious objection was not consistently applied. Dogmatic, unequivocal resistance met with irritable and increasingly intolerant officials. Accommodation to the state, especially when evidenced by those who had compromised the faith, went a long way to enhancing the ethnic group's image. Dissent, in other words, was most easily accepted when tempered by evidence of compromise. The Mennonites were tolerated because, while non-conformist, they sought to accommodate the government as much as possible. It was an attitude which government officials could respect, if not accept.

Notes

1. Conrad Grebel College Archives (CGCA), Waterloo, Ontario, S.F. Coffman Papers (SFC), Coffman to Moses H. Schmitt, 11 May 1939; Schmitt to Coffman, May 1939

2. CGCA, SFC, file I-3-2.4, Bender to Coffman, 16 December 1938

3. Quoted in David P. Reimer, *Experience of the Mennonites in Canada During World War II* (Steinbach, Manitoba, n.d.), 43

4. *Ibid.*, 41

5. CGCA, J.H. Janzen Papers, Janzen to Toews, 20 April 1939

6. CGCA, Mennonites in Canada files, David Toews to Walter H. Dyck, 26 May 1939

7. These organizational developments, and the differences which prompted the divisions, are explained in greater detail in David Fransen, "Canadian Mennonites and Conscientious Objection in World War II," Master of Arts thesis, University of Waterloo, 1977, 40-58.

8. Reimer, 71

9. CGCA, Mennonites in Canada files, Toews to J.J. Siemens, 5 November 1940

10. Mennonite Brethren Bible College Archives (MBBCA), Winnipeg, Manitoba, B.B. Janz Papers, "ASW-Ottawa Officers" file, Toews, Janz, C.F. Klassen and J.J. Gerbrandt to T.C. Davis, 12 November 1940

11. *Ibid.*, "AS-Mennonite Peace Relief Committee," Report of the Delegation of the CHPC to the Department of National War Services, 12-13 November 1940

12. *Ibid.*

13. *Ibid.*, Jacob H. Janzen, *Bericht der Delegation der Konferenz der historischer Friedensgemeinden ueber ihre Audienzer im Department des Nationalen Kriegsdienstes am 12 u.*, 13 November 1940

14. MBBCA, Janz Papers, "AS-Mennonite Peace Relief Committee," Janz to L.R. LaFlèche, 14 November 1940

15. Canadian Mennonite Bible College Archives (CMBCA), Winnipeg, Manitoba, Benjam Ewert Papers, "*In Militaer Angelegenheiten*" file, Janz, "*An einige leitenden Brueder, zum Teil im Osten, doch vornehmlich im Westen,*" 18 November 1940; MBBCA, Janz Papers, "Correspondence: Janz to David Toews" file, Toews to Janz, 18 November 1940

16. Interview with Bishop Ernie J. Swalm, 26 May 1977

17. *Ibid.*

18. Canada, House of Commons, *Debates*, IV, 29 May 1941, 3261

19. National Archives of Canada (NA), RG 27, vol. 131, file 601.3-6, I, A. Wells Gray to LaFlèche, 29 January 1943

20. CGCA, "Mennonites in Canada" files, J.F.L. Embury to the Departments of National War Services, National Defence, and Mines and Resources, 13 January 1942; cf RG 27, vol. 131, f. 601.3-6, I, H. Harvey to A. MacNamara, 22 January 1943, and *ibid.*, f. 601.3-12, I, A.M. Manson to MacNamara, 1 March 1943

21. CGCA, Conference of Historic Peace Church Papers (CHPC), Janzen, J. Harold Sherk, Fred Haslam, and J.B. Martin to MacNamara, 7-8 January 1943

22. MBBCA, C.F. Klassen Papers (CFK), Klassen to H. Mitchell, 2 February 1943

23. C.P. Stacey, *Arms, Men and Governments: The War Policies of Canada, 1939-1945* (Ottawa, 1970), 397-410

24. RG 27, vol. 131, f. 610.3-6, II, Westman to MacNamara, n.d.

25. CGCA, Mennonites in Canada files, "1940 War" file, speech by J.E. Adamson delivered to the Mennonites at Steinbach, Manitoba, 7 May 1941

26. RG 27, vol. 132, f. 601.3-6, IV, Adamson to MacNamara, 18 March 1944

27. J.A. Toews, *Alternative Service in Canada During World War II* (Winnipeg, 1959), 110-11

28. RG 27, vol. 986, f. 1, LaFlèche to Adamson, 25 August 1941

29. *Ibid.*, vol. 132, f. 601.3-6, V, Westman to MacNamara, 29 July 1944

30. *Ibid.*, vol. 993, f. 2-101-9, pt. 2, "Report on Work Done by COs under Direction of Department of Mines & Resources from June to November 1941," 11

31. *Ibid.*, vol. 138, f. 601.3-12, II, Westman to MacNamara, 7 January 1944

32. *Ibid.*, vol. 131, f. 601.3-6, III, MacKinnon to Westman, 8 October 1943

33. *Ibid.*, "Galt Meeting re CO Labour," memorandum of J.F. MacKinnon, Alternative Service Office, Mobilization Division B, 1

34. *Ibid.*, vol. 132, f. 601.3-6, IV, Westman to MacNamara, 16 May 1944

Fragmented Loyalties: Canadian Jewry, the King Government and the Refugee Dilemma

Paula Jean Draper

> The democracy we were being invited to defend was flawed and hostile to us. Without question it was better for us in Canada than in Europe, but this was still their country, not ours.
>
> Mordecai Richler, *The Street*.[1]

The Second World War forced the Jewish community of Canada to come face to face with its true position in the Canadian body politic. As 17,000 men, ten percent of the entire Jewish population, crossed the Atlantic to fight an enemy which threatened to wipe out European Jewry, their families were confronted with unexpected questions of loyalty at home. Jews in Canada, still close to their immigrant roots, feared for their brethren across Europe. They appealed to the conscience of their own government to protest Nazi policies and then to provide protection and refuge to relatives fleeing the impending catastrophe.[2] Ever grateful to Canada for providing them with a safe home, Canadian Jews were nevertheless mindful of the limitations anti-Semitic sentiments placed on their economic, social and political mobility. What they could not grasp was that the government's conduct in relation to its Jewish citizens was coloured, indeed moulded, by strong undercurrents of prejudice. As the war against the Jews progressed to its final solution, Canadian Jewry coalesced into a united voice in its efforts to open Canada's doors of refuge. But by choosing

Jewish issues as their priority, the community opened itself to accusations of disloyalty. Confronted with the cold fact that the government of W.L. Mackenzie King lacked the conscience to which they appealed so eloquently, Canadian Jewry found that indeed its loyalty was fragmented — between Canadian nationalism, advocacy of a Jewish state, and the survival of world Jewry.

Although the war years forced Jews to focus on the issue of rescue, their problems in Canada were significant. Canadian Jews stood powerless in the face of a rising tide of anti-Semitism which was encouraged by pre-war fascists and exacerbated by the Depression and widespread fear of communism. Indeed, power was the key and Jews had none. They comprised about 1½ percent of the population. There was a general sense of alienation from society — of being in Canada yet at the same time not belonging. Reminders of their separateness were everywhere. On Toronto Island, in restaurants and on beaches signs read "no dogs or Jews allowed."[3] Teaching, nursing and dentistry were virtually closed to Jews. There were quotas in medical schools and hospital posts were restricted. Promotions of Jews were blocked in banks, brokerage houses and real estate companies. Entire suburbs barred Jews from owning homes, and summer resorts were restricted to "Gentiles Only." While Canada won loyalty from an ethnic group seldom before granted the full rights of citizenship, Jews sensed, correctly, that in their case these rights were limited by prejudice. "Whether in Quebec or English Canada," write Troper and Abella in *None is Too Many*:

> few saw Jews as desirable settlers. Folk wisdom understood Jews as clannish, aggressive and cosmopolitan. Jews, many concluded, 'did not fit in,' their political sensitivities were suspect, their loyalty forever in doubt, their religion based on the continued rejection of Christ, their sole preoccupation, making and hording money. In the dark recesses of the public mind there may even have lurked the suspicion that the Nazis were not wrong in pinpointing the Jews as a particular problem — they were just carrying their anti-Semitism much too far.[4]

But the struggle against home-grown racism was overshadowed by the urgent need to provide rescue for others less fortunate than Canadian Jewry. When their representatives approached government, it was as citizens anxious to see Canadian foreign and domestic policy reflect their concerns. This was a democracy. They knew they had the right to ask. Seeking what they thought was reasonable and just, they went quietly and unobtrusively. They returned with empty promises.

The two issues of greatest concern to the Jewish community were interrelated. The United Zionist Council (UZC) represented the interests of those who felt Canada should use its influence as part of the British Empire-Commonwealth to pressure Britain towards a pro-Jewish Palestine policy.[5] During the early part of the war the UZC pursued their previous policy of quiet lobbying through Jewish and non-Jewish allies in government. The enemy was the British White Paper of 1939, which drastically curtailed Jewish immigration to Palestine.[6] Until 1942 Jews could still escape the Nazis. All they needed was a place to go. In Zionist eyes, Palestine offered the clearest solution.

Wary of appearing anti-British, drawing too much attention to itself and wearing out its welcome, the Zionist lobby focused on winning widespread support among non-Jews, especially clergy, in order to further their case with government. They recognized that previous attempts to win favour, through the representations of Jewish MPs and personal approaches to the Prime Minister, had been ignored. This mid-war step towards a more public campaign marked a new phase in Jewish political action. It also coincided with a breakdown of the uneasy war-time truce between the British and the Jewish community in Palestine.

Early in 1944 the UZC saw the forthcoming Commonwealth Prime Ministers' Conference as an opportunity for Canada to press for a suspension of the White Paper. Surely with the indisputable evidence of the extermination of European Jewry, the prime minister would be sympathetic to a plan to distract refugee advocates from Canada's door to that of the Palestinian Mandate. An all-out effort was made at the end of March. The Jewish Agency's representative in Washington, Dr. Nahum Goldmann, was brought in to meet with Mackenzie King. The prime minister then met a Zionist delegation led by Herbert Mowat (a former Anglican minister who led the UZC-financed, non-sectarian Canadian Palestine Committee) and comprised of supporters like CCF leader M.J. Coldwell, Social Credit MP J.H. Blackmore, Liberal MP Arthur Roebuck, Canada's first female Senator Cairine Wilson, as well as the presidents of the Trades and Labour Congress, the Canadian Congress of Labour and the Toronto Board of Trade. They brought evidence of their support from the press and other national organizations. It seemed to work. King committed himself to the cause and told the Commons he would raise the Palestine Question at the Conference. But the Department of External Affairs stepped in, advising King to avoid the volatile Palestine issue. When the prime minister returned, he

153

told CCF member Stanley Knowles that Palestine had been discussed. The Conference minutes told another story.

Undaunted, the UZC continued its campaign with cross-country speeches, radio addresses, luncheons, distribution of literature and personal approaches to influential Canadians. Meanwhile Department of External Affairs officials were experiencing a change of heart. Norman Robertson told King he felt that on compassionate grounds the doors of Palestine should be opened, yet he feared that any pressure on Britain could poison Anglo-Canadian relations. Perhaps sensing this shift in attitude, the UZC stepped up its recruitment activities. During the month of April 1945, seventy-six MPs, MLAs and Senators from across the political and geographic spectrum added their voices to the Zionist cause. Yet three years of concerted lobbying came to naught when that same month, at the San Francisco Conference to draw up the United Nations Charter, Canada remained silent on trusteeship matters regarding Palestine. Ironically, the sole involvement of the Canadian government in the struggle for a Jewish State came after the war when it helped Britain stem the illegal immigration of Displaced Persons by blocking the sale of war surplus ships to those attempting to skirt the regulations. It was only in 1947, when Canada was drafted by the US to participate in the UN Special Committee on Palestine, that Canada was dragged into the conflict.

Despite its sophisticated and conformist approach, the Zionist lobby had failed. Canadian Jewry found its loyalty to Britain and the Commonwealth questioned. As a *Calgary Herald* editorial pointed out in July 1946, Zionists and Jews had shown a shocking lack of gratitude towards Britain for saving European Jewry from the Nazis' gas chambers![7] It was, sadly, only the barest remnant of European Jewry who survived to see the Allied victory. But during the first years of the war there were many chances to save lives. If Canada could not push Britain to alter its position on Palestine, then perhaps shelter could be offered within its own gates.

The leaders of the Jewish community of Canada used various methods to convince the government to open Canada's doors to Jewish refugees in the 1930s. Recent research has shown that neither secret diplomacy nor the vociferous support of prominent Gentiles were successful tools in breaking through the almost impenetrable walls of Canada's restrictive immigration regulations.[8] The declaration of war against Germany added more fuel to the fire of Canadian antiimmigration feeling grounded in economic recession, indifference to the problems of the outside world[9] and an anti-Semitism which was overt in Quebec and socially acceptable among Anglo-Canadians elsewhere. In a period when the term "refugee" meant "Jew," and Jews were seen as undesirable and unassimilable immigrants, few non-Jewish Canadians would support an influx of this group into their country. Overshadowing all this was the fact that the western world was now engaged in a massive war. Under these conditions Canadians were little inclined to display humanitarian sentiment towards any group other than their own fighting boys. It was with the burden of past failure and the community's priority of directing aid to the suffering Jews of Europe that the Canadian Jewish Congress (CJC) approached government in the summer of 1940. They had just discovered that over 2,000 of those very refugees they had struggled to bring into Canada were already here — interned across New Brunswick, Quebec and Ontario in camps for prisoners of war.

The only significant group of Jewish refugees to enter Canada during the war had come by accident,[10] by way of Britain. In the panic days which followed the fall of France, Britain interned thousands of German, Austrian and Italian nationals residing in the country. Internments were meant to be temporary, but during the confusion large numbers of refugees, classified by British Tribunals as "friendly aliens," found themselves bunched with prisoners of war and pro-Nazi Germans on ships bound for Canada and Australia. Having agreed to accept only dangerous internees, Canada gave these men (who ranged in age from sixteen to sixty) an enemy's welcome.

With the arrival of the last ships came word from Britain that these men were mostly innocents whom Canada should release. The British government had itself begun to release the majority of the refugees still interned in the UK. This news was not well received. Canada had absolutely no intention of letting Jewish refugees in through the back door. While over half the men eventually gave up hope of release in Canada and returned to Britain, the remainder lived in internment — some as long as three and a half years.

The saga of Canada and the interned refugees provides a stark example of the dynamics of the Canadian government's relationship with its Jews during the Second World War. It began in July 1940, when Canada's high commissioner, Vincent Massey, demanded that the

British Dominions Office explain why Canada had received "innocent refugees" instead of the dangerous internees it had consented to accept.[11] Meanwhile a member of his office, Charles Ritchie, recorded the commotion in his London diary:

> I now hear that the ferocious internees whom the British Government begged us on bended knee to take to Canada to save this country from their nefarious activities are mostly entirely inoffensive anti-Nazi refugees who have been shovelled out to Canada at a moment's notice where they may have a disagreeable time....[12]

Massey cabled back to Ottawa the unwelcome news that the 2,284 refugees were "persons not regarded as individually or even potentially dangerous." Even the Italians, it was admitted, had only been selected because they were single and between the ages of twenty and thirty. The British government agreed to review the cases of the refugees and return them to England. This procedure could be eliminated, however, if "the Canadian Government are prepared to allow them to remain at liberty in Canada and they themselves wish to be there."[13] Soon representatives from the Canadian Departments of Defence, Justice, External Affairs and the Secretary of State were conferring over this unforeseen dilemma. Despite ample indications of the innocence of these men, government decided to await a proper review by British authorities. Certainly, "there could be no general policy of releasing these people in Canada."[14]

The sticky problem of the refugees was placed in the hands of the Cabinet Sub-Committee on Internment. By September they had agreed that, although it was the "duty" of the UK to take back the internees, who "had been sent by mistake and without any previous information or consultation, it was not practical to expect that this could be done." They hoped many would be admitted to the United States. Yet it was "apparent that we are going to have the great majority on our hands for some time" and the "question is whether some of these people could not be allowed to settle down in Canada". The trouble was, all agreed, that the internees were Jews. They sensed "there will be opposition to the admission of any large proportion of Jews."[15] Yet by October 1940 it was conceded that the problem had to be solved by Canada. "I am afraid," wrote the under secretary of state for external affairs, O.D. Skelton, "we will have to accept the fact that this problem is now on our doorstep as simply one of the fortunes of war, and go about cleaning it up ourselves as quickly and as effectively as possible."[16]

While internal government policies were argued, the refugees remained under the jurisdiction of the Department of National Defence. And the treatment received by these hapless boys and men was strictly by the rules — rules for dangerous internees. While protesting that Britain was totally responsible for the custody of the interned refugees, Canada refused to follow British guidelines in its day-to-day role as jailer. Authorities in London were soon complaining about the Canadian attitude. They certainly did "not like some of the [Canadian] regulations or the spirit in which they have been administered"![17] Under the Dominion's regulations, interned civilians held no special status and were considered 'prisoners of war class two.' The military was geared up to deal with fascist internees under these conditions. But they were nowhere prepared for what arrived from Britain.

General E. de B. Panet, as director of internment operations, was himself horrified at the peculiar group of men that stepped off of British ships into his jurisdiction. He described them to the secretary of state as refugees — members of Kitchener Camp, a camp from which "many were recruited for the British Army," refugees from Czechoslovakia, Catholics and over two hundred orthodox Jews. "These are the most troublesome of all," Panet noted. "They beg to be fed on kosher food — they are unusually dirty and untidy and generally speaking cause more bother than all the others."[18] If General Panet was appalled with his new prisoners, the under secretary of state, E.H. Coleman, seemed more sympathetic, and realistic. He noted that not only were most of "these people ... of Jewish origin," many had suffered in German concentration camps before reaching Britain. He feared that unless some action was taken soon, "the monotony of the existence will begin to fall on the educated people — and most of the civilian internees are highly educated men — and there may be danger of serious discontent arising."[19] Meanwhile, Massey was frantically cabling for the return to Britain of individual refugees, in particular those who had been plucked from secret war research.

Barely a month after the deportations had begun, a number of points were clear. Britain had made a grievous error in deporting the refugees. British public opinion, outraged by the sinking of one of their ships with a great loss in refugee lives, demanded speedy resolution of the problem. But there was no logic in returning the lot. In any event, most had been awaiting their chance to get to the United States, and now they were on America's doorstep. For the Churchill government the best solution, not to mention the easiest, was to leave them in Canada and press for their release. It was clear to Massey that no programme of Canadian release, however temporary, would be accepted. This was government's view, and no one voiced it more clearly than the ever-vigilant director of immigration, F.C. Blair. He noted:

> In last night's press I noticed a statement that there is a row overseas about the ease with which some German people could manage to remain in England and have someone else take their places in the transfer of enemy aliens.... We may find that in the end the presence of so many Jewish people is merely another illustration of their ability to beat others to it.[20]

To Blair, it was just another indication that international Jewry had somehow engineered the internee deportations in order to slip Jews into Canada.

The scene was now set. The refugees were to be separated from nazis but kept incarcerated, their camp commandants complaining constantly about their constantly complaining, unmilitary prisoners; British representatives trying diplomatically to press Canada towards freeing the refugees; Blair conducting a personal battle to block their release in Canada while External Affairs officials like A. Rive argued that it was "impossible to justify their continued detention, or their return to the danger zone";[21] and the refugees and their advocates, the Canadian Jewish community, mounting an increasingly vociferous battle to ameliorate camp conditions and win release. No matter how much the Canadian government wished it were otherwise, the interned refugees had become a Canadian problem.

They had also become a problem for the Canadian Jewish Congress and its director of relief and refugee agencies, Saul Hayes. No sooner had the CJC discovered that anti-Nazi refugees had arrived, it was confronted with the contradiction of a handful of Jews classified as pro-Nazis. For in Camp R, near Fort William, 174 refugees were incarcerated with Nazis. Within a week of their arrival, one elderly refugee had already been removed to a hospital for the insane where he later died. Four others were hurriedly returned to Britain and important war work. The rest remained in this abusive situation for at least six months. Hayes approached these Jews with extreme caution. Their only advocate, the Director of the Western Region of Congress, Louis Rosenberg, begged Hayes for guidance.[22] Yet the CJC steered clear of Camp R. Rosenberg continued to press for:

further information which will enable us to understand how it is possible for orthodox Jews who need prayer books and kosher food, to be classed as pro-Nazi ... there is considerable possibility that these Jews were incorrectly classified, and surely steps should be taken to remedy this situation.[23]

But Hayes remained uneasy. If these men were under suspicion,[24] then the Jewish community could not afford to bring criticism on itself by consorting with declared Nazis. The sensitivity of the interned refugee dilemma was undeniable. Already, Hayes felt, the community was treading on thin ice and openly helping the Camp R refugees would jeopardize the Congress' hold on sympathetic public opinion. For in this case, as in the wider issue of the interned refugees, the first concern of Jewish leaders was not the refugees themselves, but the very security of the Canadian Jewish community. The wider community had to perceive that Jews were unswervingly loyal to Canada and to the government's war policies if any Jewish causes were to succeed.

What Canadian Jewish representatives felt they could or could not do for the interned was largely determined by the relationship they felt they had with the government. The fact that all Jewish community strategies adopted previously on behalf of European refugee immigration had failed utterly and completely left little room for new or innovative approaches to government. Tactics which had repeatedly failed were employed again.

Hayes was slow to take up the case of the interned refugees. By September 1941 he came under intense criticism by CJC members for his inability to solve the internee problem. At the Congress' national meeting, speaker after speaker complained that the continued internment of anti-Nazis and Jews was "deplorable and wretched." "Criticisms were also made of the work of our office," Hayes noted, "and the implication was quite clearly drawn that [we] had neglected the internee problem during these last 14 months. It was clearly implied and even stated that had [we] been more active and persistent the present unhappy position of these internees would not exist." Hayes defended himself by pointing to the difficulties involved, particularly in dealing with government. Convincing government to promise improvements had been hard enough. Getting those promises implemented would prove even harder.

Hayes felt they had good reason to move cautiously. He explained:

> I don't think we did enough at the beginning for these people, because we knew they were safe in Canada and we were trying to rescue people who weren't safe.... The fact that we couldn't get them out only underlies what I'm saying.... We paid more attention to those who were still [in Europe] than we did to those who had three square meals a day and who were in a safe position.[25]

While the internees were safely in Canada, the refugee committee quite openly chose to put all its efforts into getting Jews out of Europe. They felt that the internee problem could wait, fearing that soon there would be no more avenues of escape from Hitler.

By mid-October 1940 the shifting of internees into their own, more permanent camps, was underway. These moves were necessary because the military found itself faced with thousands more internees than it could accommodate. Hayes, however, took credit for this shift. After a meeting with Coleman and Panet in early October, Hayes proclaimed that "the changes are those which we have been working for some time to achieve, and, if proceeded with, will ameliorate conditions considerably and will do much to bring about the state of affairs considered necessary under the conditions." Just what conditions were "considered necessary"? Above all, the question of immigration to the United States occupied the minds of CJC officials and internees alike. Hayes focused his energies on this question, to the virtual exclusion of all else, including services to those in the camps and certainly getting them released into Canada. Of course, wholesale removal of the internees to the United States would preclude any campaign for Canadian release. And Hayes, long experienced with Canadian immigration authorities, knew any release at all in Canada would be difficult indeed.

Numerous schemes were pursued in order to gain US entry for the refugees. Most had been originally admitted to Britain on transit visas or to await the validation of their US quota numbers. Now that emigration from Europe was cut off by war, everyone thought that this handful of men would gain speedy admittance. There was only one obstacle. The American government did not want them. Not only did internment place a stigma on the refugees which proved impossible to erase, but most were Jews and this did not endear them to US immigration authorities any more than it did to Canadian. Anti-refugee lobbies sprung into action in Washington and a series of Bills were passed expressly to block entrance of the internees. By refusing to release refugees from the camps until the US agreed to accept them, the

Canadian government played right into their hands. The CJC now had to look more closely at pushing government towards wholesale release in Canada.

Hayes believed there was merit in the quiet diplomatic approach to government. It was quite clear to him, however, that government was not anxious to deal with Jews. What seemed the best solution was to find a way by which the issue of the interned refugees should be seen as a humanitarian rather than a Jewish cause. In this he had two strong allies. One was the Canadian National Committee for Refugees (CNCR) headed by Senator Cairine Wilson. Although CJC staff continued to do the bulk of the work for the refugees and pay the bills, the CNCR conducted most of the political lobbying. Ironically, the other pro-refugee force was the British government, as represented by Alexander Paterson. His Majesty's commissioner of prisons, Paterson was personally chosen by the home secretary for the job of convincing the Canadian government to release the refugees in Canada.[26] The British, recalled a fellow worker, "assumed that once Paterson came, he was a very famous man, there would be no problem.... No one dreamed that the Canadians would refuse" his advice.[27] But matters did not go smoothly, and Paterson remained in Canada for more than eight months.

Paterson's mission was to return to Britain those refugees who wished to risk the dangerous voyage, and to satisfy the Canadians as to the loyalty of the remainder. He emphasized to all that the transfer of aliens had been a "gigantic and appalling mistake,"[28] remarking to CNCR officials that "over a period of years his work as His Majesty's Commissioner of Prisons had made him familiar with tragedy, but never, he said, had he seen such a degree of misery or heard such tragic stories, as he had encountered in the Internment Camps in Canada.'[29]

Paterson was infuriated with the treatment accorded the internees who remained. For four months he kept silent on Canadian policy. He then unleashed a volley of criticism at the Canadian treatment of the interned refugees. Paterson later reported that his "easy, comfortable policy of silence and appeasement could not be maintained after a visit to a very lonely camp towards the end of winter."

> It brought me [he continued] into a cell of a shy German of seventeen years, whom I asked to read one of the categories of the White Paper [on the release of internees]. He replied he could not read it as he had broken his spectacles five months ago and, although he had the money, was unable to get them

mended. On inquiry it appeared that his story was true. For five months he had been unable to read book or newspaper, and even his mother's letters had to be read aloud to him by another refugee. It was the business of no one to deal with such a simple and urgent situation. That night the policy of appeasement came to an abrupt end. I should have forfeited much of my little self-respect if I had left Canada without making comment on such callous negligence. The time had come to see if the Canadian government had acquired any confidence in a visitor who had maintained silence for four months, to enable him to present a report and make suggestions. Accordingly I called upon Dr. Coleman, the Under Secretary of State, and told him that I should find myself compelled upon my return to England to make some comment on the conditions in the camps, and I should prefer to make known to the Canadian government the substance of my criticism before I left the Dominion.

With the encouragement of Coleman, Paterson submitted a detailed proposal to the Canadian government for the official reorganization of the Internment Camps into Refugee Camps and an alteration of administration and treatment.[30]

On May 2, 1941 Paterson's proposal was approved by Cabinet. The interned refugees had suffered as prisoners of war for ten long months. Now the government moved quickly. Paterson, Hayes and Wilson were relieved; the internees, still in camps but now reclassified as refugees, were ecstatic. At long last real improvement would be made, or so it seemed. Then came another Order in Council detailing new regulations concering the treatment of refugees in the camps.[31] They bore a remarkable resemblance to the old military regulations.

Paterson's work was well received at home, if not in Canada. The remarkably frank and extensive report (41 pages and seven appendices) he presented to the Home Office in July 1941 after his return from Canada made painfully clear the continuing differences in attitude between the British and Canadian governments. A Home Office minute noted:

> This is a most valuable and interesting report.... Mr. Paterson's visit and the reforms which he was instrumental in introducing have done a great deal to restore British credit and I have heard nothing but praise from all quarters.... In one sense it is a pity that the report is written in such an enjoyable and racy style. It can never be published.[32]

The home secretary credited Paterson with infusing "into what might well have become too rigid and soulless administration, a humanitarian spirit." He too reluctantly admitted that the document could not be published, unless some editing was done "particularly from the point of view of not offending the Dominion Government."[33] The Paterson Report was in fact never published. Yet Paterson's activities in Canada accomplished a great deal: the derogatory labelling of internees as prisoners of war had been erased; even more critically, as emigration to the United States receded as a possibility, he lent his weight (as we shall see) to a programme of release in Canada.

With Paterson and Senator Wilson's CNCR behind him, Hayes was able to present a strong case to the government. Not only was their release a humanitarian issue, he argued, but it would prove Canadian Jewry's loyalty to British wishes. Government officials, particularly in External Affairs, quietly promoted this view as well — emphasizing the pragmatic advantages in not provoking the UK and in avoiding adverse publicity. To all concerned, the obstacle lay in the Immigration Branch, in the person of Frederick Charles Blair.

Certainly it had been bad enough that, at first, the refugees had been treated as prisoners of war. Their change in status, however, seemed to place them in an even more tenuous position. Refugees who returned to Britain reported:

> ... the recognition by the authorities of their identity as Jews or political refugees made them appear as "undesirables" in the eyes of the authorities. The official view seemed to be that the interned refugees presented a troublesome problem, if not a danger, in view of the immigration policy of the Canadian government. Both in official communications from the ... Director of Internment Operations ... and in the treatment accorded to the refugees by many Canadian anti-Jewish officers ... political prejudice became apparent.[34]

Blair had been working for many years to bar Jews from Canada. The minister reponsible for immigration, Thomas Crerar, was not particularly interested in Blair's department and the official was left to run the Immigration Branch much as he saw fit. Blair was difficult to deal with. James Gibson, an external affairs department official working for the prime minister, called the Immigration Branch a "holding operation.... There was no give to it, no flexibility. And I think," recalled Gibson, "Blair resented any criticism of his conduct. I found myself keeping out of his way."[35] CJC and CNCR officials had good reason to fear Blair. All their attempts to rescue Jewish refugees had failed miserably before the arrival of the internees. The CNCR even registered a complaint against the director with Prime Minister King.

> The tenor of the resolution is to the effect that the Immigration Branch has scandalously dealt with immigration matters, and that Canada was being deprived of the possibility of a rich increment of immigrants, culturally, artistically, scientifically, and materially because of the attitude of the Department. There will be more than a hint in the resolution that discriminatory attitudes are present, particularly on the part of ... Mr. Blair.[36]

With the arrival of the interned refugees, the problem of Blair and the entrenched anti-Semitism he personified became even more relevant. Here were men with skills and potential value to the war effort. Indeed, requests for Canadian release of the internees began to flood the Immigration Department as early as August 1940. Individual members of the Jewish community wrote to Blair, offering maintenance, homes and jobs to internees. But all such offers were turned down, even those from first degree relations.[37] Dr. Mendel, a refugee from nazism who had entered Canada in the early 1930s, approached Blair regarding the release of some internees. This Jewish immigrant was a favourite of Blair. Dr. Mendel worked in the Connaught laboratories for Dr. Frederick Banting, without salary and, as far as Blair was concerned, represented the lone exception to prove the rule that refugees would only take jobs from Canadians. Mendel felt that "he and other more fortunately placed refugees should try to help those boys when they are released." He went to the director's office where, Blair noted, he "made himself rather objectionable ... through his persistence." Blair's standard reply to everyone who approached him on the matter was that he had absolutely no jurisdiction since the interned refugees were wards of the British government.[38] That he had more power in this matter than he let on fooled few.

In a memorandum for his own files Blair made special note of "the widespread information that the Jewish people have got and got apparently long before we knew anything about the inclusion of so many Jewish people." The fact that 47 Youth Aliyah boys were among the internees also made Blair suspicious. For months Canadian Zionists had been attempting to acquire entry permits for 370 boys stranded in England. The 47 youths were originally part of this larger group.

> Apparently [Blair wrote] with the closing of the Mediterranean these Jewish people saw an opportunity of appealing for admission to this country and used it.... These Jewish people had apparently been able to get from the Home Office a statement that there was no objection to the release of these people in Canada.

Blair was mortified. Could the British be conspiring with the Jews to squeeze open Canada's door? Blair wondered whether "the Home Office was playing the game with Canada in suggesting to private individuals the release of interned prisoners of war without first consulting the Dominion Government. It all looks to me like a well laid plan."[39]

Blair confided his fears to his minister. Crerar was generally noncommittal on immigration matters. If an individual case might sometimes win his personal attention, he felt hamstrung by the regulations — regulations that Blair wrote — and by the Cabinet's general unwillingness to move on anything concerning immigration. During his presentations to Cabinet, Blair's echo could be heard in Crerar's words: "Since there are probably close to 2,000 of this class of internees now here, most of them I think, Jews, it was felt that if precedents were established whereby we would deal with special cases on our own volition, much difficulty would most certainly follow."[40]

Blair was in charge and he remained an immovable force. Officials who had direct dealings with Blair, Gibson explained, "were thoroughly exasperated. And that isn't an overstatement. And my impression was that a lot of this rolled off him."[41] Yet release became inevitable and Blair was forced to work with External Affairs officials, Norman Robertson in particular.

Under secretary of state for external affairs after Skelton's death in late January 1941, Robertson was described by admirers as a man of "brooding humanity and compassion." Hayes remembered Robertson as a man who "listened with great sympathy."[42] Yet it was difficult for even a sympathetic Robertson to do much for the interned refugees. During the war, recalled Gibson, "so many things were loaded onto External because nobody else wanted to do it or didn't know where else it could be done and some people in External were grossly overworked."[43] Occasionally, however, an individual refugee case would come to the fore. In 1942, for instance, Lester Pearson took an interest in the case of the internee Alfons Rosenberg, once a schoolmaster in Germany. Pearson wrote private school chums on Rosenberg's behalf, while Robertson interceded with Blair. Blair, as usual, was far from helpful.

> There is a rumour current that if employment is offered to any of these internees they will be released to take such employment. As far as I am aware there is absolutely no truth in this rumour and my life is being made miserable

by the amount of correspondence that is coming in here from people ... most of them Jewish people who think it highly unreasonable on my part to refuse the release of any person who has been offered a job.[44]

Although among the most powerful civil servants in Canada, Robertson had little or no influence on Blair and could not override his authority on immigration matters. With Blair in unchallenged control of immigration and no refugee able to be released without his approval, Robertson could only press Blair on a case by case basis while hoping for a change of heart, a change which never came. In February 1942 a Canadian National Committee for Refugees supporter wrote to the editor of the *Globe and Mail* that the Immigration Branch was irresponsibly extending the length of refugee internment. "For some unexplained reason," she protested, "the department prefers to let them stay behind barbed wire and remain useless, frustrated human beings." After investigation a reporter added: "Our information is that the permanent head of the Department of Immigration is a typical bureaucrat, whom it would require strong ministerial pressure to move in the direction desired by those who sympathize with these men." Robertson ordered the clipping filed, but not before he applauded the writer with a "Hurrah" in the margin.[45] In the final analysis, that was all he could do.

Dealing with Blair was harder still for the Canadian Jewish Congress; there was no getting around him. Hayes was always conciliatory in his comments to and about Blair. Courting his favour, Hayes often wrote Blair commending his "wonderful understanding of the plight of these particular refugees," complimenting him on his "assiduity and administrative efficiency" and his "ever present cooperation." This flattery was politically necessary. In fact feelings were strong on both sides. Hayes recalled Blair as:

> a very interesting character. He hated my guts. But that acted to my advantage because I don't think he realized the more he hated my guts, the more ammunition I had to fight him.... He didn't keep secret that if you want to keep up our policy of barring Jewish immigration, you'd better kick Saul Hayes out of the Refugee Board — that strengthened my resolve and it also gave me the ammunition to say it was based, not on merit, but on anti-Semitic policies.[46]

Blair's power was supreme in immigration matters, unchallenged even by his minister, and there was no demand that it be curtailed, at least no demand from Cabinet to which Blair was responsible. Whatever his battles with more progressive public servants like Robertson, Blair was in tune with the anti-immigrant and certainly anti-Jewish spirit of his political masters.

The first releases had come early in 1941 when Cabinet agreed to free refugees with first-degree relatives in Canada. This action would, it was hoped, diffuse criticism while not contravening immigration regulations. Of the total, only three were Jews by religion. But then only eight were freed.[47]

Blair would probably have been happy to stop at eight releases, but he was not to have his way. The next group of refugees to come up for release were skilled technicians required by war industry. The bulk of the most highly skilled men had already been hurried back to Britain and the ever-watchful Blair was not unduly concerned that the release of a few more would be seen as a precedent for more general releases. He would see to that, or so he hoped. In any event, Blair did not have much choice in the matter. The minister of munitions and supply, C.D. Howe, had been alerted that skilled workers needed by the Canadian economy were locked up in camps and he wanted those particular men out. His interest was admittedly pragmatic. But this made his demands for immediate release of selected internees all the more adamant. The release of Anton Fleybeck, a roof prism expert, was requested by Research Enterprises Limited for secret war work. This government-owned operation, created by Howe's department, sent the request for Fleybeck's release directly to National Defence.[48] Four days after the decision to release the first eight refugees, Cabinet authorized the release of Fleybeck "upon being made fully aware of the exceptionally secret nature of the work in which it was proposed that he be employed." The day after Fleybeck's release was approved, Howe discussed the general issue of skilled internees with Blair. Howe had already impressed upon Crerar that he was "very anxious to get some of these skilled men." Now Howe wanted to meet with the British official Alexander Paterson (then still in Canada) because, as the munitions minister told Blair, "he thought that we ought to get these people out of the internment camps and keep them in Canada if they are skilled workers and safe." Paterson and Howe met, and a survey of the skilled workers was undertaken. Between fifty and sixty men were found, machinists, tool-makers and other technicians, whose skills could be put to immediate use in Canada's war industry.[49]

Blair felt trapped. Fifty or sixty men was far more than he had bargained for, and he knew Hayes and the pro-refugee lobby would seize the moment to clamour for more releases. But, except for delaying the process a little, Blair could do nothing to stop the release of skilled workers. Hayes now saw his chance. In a time of war, the pro-refugee lobby argued all the more forcefully, 2,000 educated and skilled men could only be a boon to Canada.

> The key to the whole thing appears to lie in the needs of industry.... I gather that if industry was short of fur-dyers and tailors the Immigration Department would at the request of industry release them, all other things being equal. I therefore must assume that the key note is not generosity towards the internees, but scarcity of labour in the particular industry. A good example arises in connection with the release of several accountants because the Government Department was short of accountants and has asked for several internees to fill the breach.[50]

Meanwhile, public opinion was beginning to turn in the internees' favour. This was reflected in Parliament. In April 1941 one member asked: "What is the possibility of some of these people being permitted to make a contribution in Canada towards defeat of our common enemy?" Another stated: "I think it is desirable if some of these wanted to stay here and it was found convenient that they should be allowed to stay, they would be an asset to our country as I am sure they are to Great Britain."[51]

Although the CJC used every alteration of policy and every shift in opinion to the advantage of the internees, it was not until the prime minister took an active interest in an individual refugee that the gate could be squeezed open and a general policy would emerge. Mackenzie King, wishing to do a favour for a well known American actress, demanded the release of a teenage Italian Jew, and Paterson and Hayes used the issue to force Blair's hand.[52] The way was soon paved for other students and then skilled workers and farmers to be released, temporarily, in Canada.

Working in cooperation with Paterson, the CJC and CNCR used a combination of luck, stubbornness and quiet diplomacy to further the process. It was slow, and it was painstaking, and it left Hayes open to criticism that he was doing little or nothing for the internees. But in the end, it bore fruit. By 1942 significant numbers of refugees had gained release. Of course, other factors forced a change in government policy on special cases. But the CJC and CNCR made use of these openings with remarkable tact and skill to turn the single case into the general rule. Gibson explained:

> The Canadian Jewish Congress would send in discreet representations every so often. The thing to be said about them is that they did not overplay their hand. They kept at it, but they never overdid it so to say. It never became exasperating, as it did with some other people.... I think government institutionally wanted to be careful that it didn't appear to cave in to pressure.[53]

Hayes appreciated this, and he thus played the game and played it well. The Jewish refugee lobby may have seen the gradual opening of a release option in Canada as a victory for quiet diplomacy. But whatever their sense of accomplishment, it was Howe and King, each for different reasons, who pushed open the door to release — a door which, Blair warned, once opened to a few would, through persistent Jewish lobbying, inevitably lead to a mass exodus.

By mid-1943 it was becoming increasingly difficult to ignore the stark truth of the fate of the Jews of Europe. CNCR and CJC workers openly expressed their frustration with Canada's immigration policies. And to demonstrate their case they could easily point to the contributions made by refugees resident in Canada, including the released internees. In a speech to the Senate in May 1943 Cairine Wilson was not adverse to using them as an example of what could be:

> This short speech given in the Senate in explanation of the various efforts of the Canadian National Committee on Refugees to secure admission to Canada of some of the unfortunates driven from their homes through racial or political persecution. Despite 4 1/2 years of consistent work, our efforts have met with little success due to the extremely rigid policy of our Immigration Department which has not been changed despite the appalling nature of Nazi persecution.
>
> The few refugees who have come to Canada are making such a valuable contribution that it is difficult to understand why we refuse to avail ourselves of such an opportunity to show humanity and enrich our own country.[54]

The internee issue was soon raised in the Commons. One French-Canadian Liberal member found it "astounding that these men who feel like we do about the war and want to defeat the Nazis should be kept in an internment camp. I cannot conceive it." On July 9 1943 the subject of Jewish refugees was raised in the House again. This time the pro-refugee advocates outlined in explicit detail the destruction of the Jews of Europe using the figure of six million murdered.[55] The push was on for a new policy to follow the war. With sympathy in the Commons, Hayes and Wilson felt the time was ripe for the total and final release of the remaining interned refugees.

On June 4 Sam Bronfman, the CJC president, led a delegation to meet first with Crerar and then with officials in the Department of Labour. Blair, then on the eve of retirement, was not pleased, and he reacted in his characteristically blunt, colourful and uncharitable way: "Why they went to Labour which has nothing to do with release or with placing refugees in employment, I do not know, unless it indicates that these people are determined by hook or by crook to gain their own ends."[56] Meanwhile Senator Wilson petitioned the prime minister to put an end to refugee internment "in accord with the principle that no refugee whose political record is unassailable continue to be interned. There are now so few refugees in the camp," Wilson wrote King, "we feel that their maintenance involves an unnecessary expense to the Government and also that the mental state of those remaining in the camp is becoming so low that it is likely to create a more serious problem."[57] Blair found this end run to the politicians and labour officials "characteristic of our Jewish friends."[58] And it worked. An order-in-council of 10 December 1943 closed the camps, returned the unreleasable internees to the UK and set out a new status for refugees released in Canada. For these 966 men, freedom in Canada meant temporary residence permits which could be cancelled, reports to the RCMP, restriction to specific jobs without protection from exploitation, and an unsure future. Upon release, refugees were reminded not to make any long-term plans in Canada.

Blair had warned government that the emptying of the refugee camps was a Jewish plot to foist unwanted refugees on Canada. He feared that released internees would set down roots, making it impossible to deport them once the war ended. He therefore made sure that no promise of citizenship was given, leaving their long-term status unclear. As a result, the internees were a group of men in legal limbo. These refugees had entered Canada through the back door and Blair was determined to keep close tabs on them, reinterning any who were troublesome, opposing marriages with Canadians, army enlistment — anything that might eventually lead to naturalization. Until the end of the war the CJC and CNCR, the defence department and other ministries, citizenship judges, employers, and the refugees themselves remained confused about the legal position of released internees. With each step into freedom their status and future in Canada became more cloudy.

Unfortunately for Blair and despite his warnings, the integration of the internees into the larger community progressed more rapidly than he could have imagined. As exemplary workers and outstanding achievers, most internees belied the wisdom of Canada's closed door policy.

In December 1943, just as the final release of internees were completed, the CJC published a pamphlet entitled: "For the Rescue of our Brethren." Illustrated with photographs of released internees busy at war work and on the farms "Producing for Canada, Not for Hitler," this publication was aimed at the Jewish-Canadian pocketbook. Money was needed, Hayes urged, for the future of Jewish immigration to Canada — survivor immigration. The ex-internees deserved help, he stressed, because "the record of the contribution of these men to Canadian life is a credit to the entire refugee movement. We are at present collating all this information and we are certain that when the story becomes well known to Canadians much of the reluctance hampering the proposal to admit refugees will be removed."[59]

A decade of failure to win admission to Canada for any substantial number of European Jewish refugees had left Jewish leaders frustrated and disillusioned but undaunted. The interned refugees, though they arrived accidently, were now an irrefutable presence. Though their future status was uncertain, the example which could be made of their contribution to Canada, both present and future, might be a useful tool in the CJC's larger refugee campaign. Favourable publicity about the activities of the "camp boys"' activities was to be encouraged. Silent diplomacy had outlived its usefulness but stood side by side with public relations and publicity, which had come of age. To what degree the pro-refugee lobby's campaign was important in winning wholesale release of internees may never be known, but at least for the Jewish community it foreshadowed a new activist approach to Canadian political involvement.

In October 1945, with hostilities in Europe at an end, the Immigration Department reviewed the status of the approximately 3,500 refugees resident in Canada, including 966 ex-internees. With the agreement of officials in the Departments of External Affairs, State, Labour and the RCMP, the new director of immigration recommended to Cabinet that the bars to naturalization be lifted.[60] There were clearly many reasons for this long-awaited change in policy. All were self-serving. Evidence of the contributions refugees were making to Canadian industry and trade were plentiful and beyond dispute. Just as important, though seldom admitted, was the growing need to stem criticism of Canada's unbending immigration regulations. The Second World War had created the greatest upheaval of humanity the world had ever witnessed. More than a million displaced people, of whom only a fraction were Jews, would soon press their case for resettlement. Canada was a prime target. To allow the legal admission of some 3,500 refugees already partially integrated in Canada might, some argued, forestall pressure to take more from Europe. Certainly mass deportations of refugees would have caused an outcry. Thus, on October 25, 1945 Cabinet passed an Order in Council allowing first immigrant status then citizenship to refugees who were then living on temporary resident permits.[61] For the interned refugees, five years in limbo were finally over.

Refugees were not a priority issue in wartime Canada. Certainly, Canada put its full weight behind Britain in the war effort, but under no conditions was the acceptance of Jewish refugees considered part of that effort. The interned refugees would have remained incarcerated for the duration of the war if not for a number of factors. Perhaps most important, the British were anxious to wash their hands of the internees. Paterson's mission made this clear. While Britain could not interfere in Canadian internal policy, it would not shield the Dominion from international criticism. Furthermore, the constant pressure brought to bear on government by influential friends of these anti-Nazi prisoners, including Paterson, contributed to the relaxation of treatment and the first releases.

The success of the Canadian Jewish Congress in its efforts to ease the refugees out of internment is somewhat harder to assess. The internees dropped into the CJC's lap unexpectedly. Inexperienced, unsuccessful in the past, the CJC was at first unsure how to handle the problem. Like the government, they hoped that the United States would absorb the refugees and, when all the American immigration schemes failed, they had to scramble for new solutions. The wartime constraints on the Jewish community further complicated the CJC's treatment of the internee dilemma. The fear that by aiding enemy aliens Canadian Jewry could appear unpatriotic was difficult to dispel.

This was the dilemma for all Jews outside Europe during the war against Hitler. No one expressed this predicament more clearly than David Ben Gurion, the leader of Palestinian Jewry during the struggle against the British Mandate. Calling on Jews to join the British armed forces, Ben Gurion declared: "We will fight with the British against Hitler as if there were no White Paper." At the same time, he reminded them, they must remain true to their own national aspirations, and therefore "we will fight the White Paper as if there were no war."[62] Likewise Canadian Jewry joined Canada's war effort wholeheartedly and without reservation, at the same time pressing their particular interests with government. But in Mackenzie King's Liberal Government they confronted the fact that their votes were taken for granted, for the Liberals were the only political party which always could count on a token number of safe seats dominated by Jewish voters. Thus the Jewish leadership was tied to a government sure of its loyalty. Indeed, the abject failure of the Zionist lobby, despite all its public support, only highlighted the determination of government to serve what it perceived as its own best interests. Ultimately, the Jewish community had little power. All these factors came into play in the story of the interned refugees.

Although the CJC set its sights on an aggressive campaign to improve camp conditions and to win release of internees for immigration into Canada, it was not, ironically, their campaign which finally brought results. Clearly the improved public image of the interned refugees, partly attributable to the Congress' public relations campaign, was not lost on high government officials. Yet the real shift in Canadian policy only came when political will, heretofore abdicated to the administrative power of middle-level civil servants like Blair, was asserted forcefully by Cabinet. Once the top level of government took an avid, if late, interest in the refugees, action resulted. And it came quickly. In the end what really counted were not humanitarian issues, not the protests of internees and their supporters, not the quiet diplomatic efforts of Hayes, Wilson, Paterson or even the British Home Office, but the pragmatic economic realism of C.D. Howe and the political calculations of Mackenzie King. It was up to the CJC, CNCR and Paterson to turn Howe and King's different interests in the internees into a generalized issue which ultimately solved the entire internee dilemma. And their success with the internee became a foundation on which the CJC might build. In the struggle to open Canada to the immigration of displaced persons which followed the war, techniques devised during the internee episode were utilized with increasing success.

While the government did its best to cloud the issues when dealing with Jewish leadership during the war, for the interned refugees themselves the issue was crystal clear. One refugee spokesman, writing to his commandant after an attempted suicide in his camp, expressed it for them all:

> Many of the refugees have encountered hardships in Germany ... but they were able to stand all these hardships, because they knew that the treatment they suffered was imposed on them by their deadly enemies.... Many of the men to whom this conviction had given the force not to yield to Nazi oppression, are now, after three years, on the point of being broken in spirit and morale. It may sound strange that men who were able to endure so much, should not be able to stand the friendly treatment we are experiencing here.... But our fate in the last few years and our experiences have made us sensitive. For all of us the thought to be kept detained by Governments and people whom we consider to be our friends, and whom we have assured of our loyalty innumerable times, is unbearable....[63]

Notes

1. Mordecai Richler, *The Street* (London, 1971), 67

2. See Irving Abella and Harold Troper, *None is Too Many* (Toronto, 1982).

3. For discussion of anti-Semitism in Canada during the 1930s, see Lita-Rose Betcherman, *The Swastika and the Maple Leaf* (Toronto, 1975).

4. Abella and Troper, 281

5. For a detailed analysis of the Canadian Zionist lobby, upon which this summary is based, see David J. Bercuson, *Canada and the Birth of Israel* (Toronto, 1985).

6. The 1939 White Paper restricted Jewish immigration to Palestine to 75,000 over five years.

7. *Calgary Herald*, 22 July 1946

8. See Abella and Troper.

9. Gerald Dirks, *Canada's Refugee Policy* (Montreal, 1977), 50

10. For the complete story of the interned refugees, see Paula J. Draper, "The Accidental Immigrants: Canada and the Interned Refugees" (Ph.D. dissertation, University of Toronto, 1983).

11. Public Record Office, Kew, England (PRO), Dominions Office (DO) 35/996/PW19/143, Massey to Caldecote, 22 July 1940

12. Charles Ritchie, *The Siren Years: A Canadian Diplomat Abroad 1937-1945* (Toronto, 1974), 61

13. National Archives of Canada (NA), Department of External Affairs Records (DEA), RG 25, D1, vol. 824, f. 713, Massey to Department of External Affairs, 30 July 1940

14. DEA Records, Central Registry Files (CRF) 621-K-40, pt. 1, memorandum of Coleman, 6 August 1940

15. NA, W.L.M. King Papers, MG 26, J4, vol. 359, f. 3843, "Internees from the United Kingdom," 12 September 1940

16. DEA, CRF 621-B-40, Skelton to Coleman, 21 October 1940

17. PRO, Foreign Office Records (FO) 916/90/KW5/19, Moylan to Satov, 3 July 1941

18. DEA, CRF 621-K-40, pt. 1, Panet to secretary of state, 19 July 1940

19. DEA, CRF 621-K-40, pt. 1, Panet to Skelton, 24 August 1940; *ibid.*, 621-K-40C, memorandum of Coleman, 26 August 1940; NA, Casgrain Papers, MG III, B2, vol. 4, f. 3

20. NA, Immigration Branch Records (IR), RG 76, Internees, pt. 1, memorandum of Blair, 7 August 1940

21. DEA, RG 25, D1, vol. 824, f. 713, memorandum to Skelton, 16 August 1940

22. Canadian Jewish Congress Archives, Montreal (CJC/M), General Files, Rosenberg to Hayes, 26 September 1940 and 19 October 1940

23. *Ibid.*, Rosenberg to Goldner, 10 March 1941

24. The UK representative in Canada later examined the cases of these men and they were cleared of any suspicion. DO 35/996/PW19/1/82 (also PRO, Home Office Records (HO) 45/23515/GEN200/117/163), "Report on Civilian Internees Sent From the United Kingdom to Canada During the Unusually Fine Summer of 1940" (Paterson Report)

25. CJC/M, General Files, United Jewish Refugee Agencies (UJRA), memorandum of Hayes, 10 September 1941; interview with Hayes, Montreal, 11 September 1978

26. HO 45/23515/GEN200/117/163, Morrison to Massey, 24 August 1941

27. Interview with Chaim Raphael, London, England, 18 May 1979

28. CJC/M, General Files, UJRA, memorandum of Hayes, 20 December 1940

29. NA, Canadian National Committee on Refugees, MG 28, V43, vol. 6, f. 27, minutes, CNCR twelfth executive committee meeting, 24 January 1941

30. Paterson report

31. NA, RG 2, ser. 1, PC 4568, PC 5246

32. HO 45/23515/GEN200/117/163, minute of Newsom, 21 August 1941

33. *Ibid.*, Morrison to Paterson, 7 September 1941

34. DEA, CRF 621-K-40, vol. 3, Refugees Report, January 1941

35. Interview with James Gibson, Toronto, 16 October 1978

36. Agudath Israel of America Archives, New York, Michael Tress Collection, F37FF3, UJRA, memorandum of Hayes, 16 October 1940

37. CJC/M and CJC/Toronto, internees files; for example, H. Goldschmidt

38. Interview with Constance Hayward, Toronto, 13, 14 June 1978; IR, RG 76, Internees, pt. 1, Macdonnell to Blair, 7 September 1940, Blair to Macdonnell, 12 September 1940

39. IR, RG 76, Internees, pt. 1, memorandum of Blair for file, 24 September 1940

40. *Ibid.*, Crerar to Blair, 25 September 1940

41. Gibson interview

42. Douglas LePan, "The Spare Deputy, Portrait of Norman Robertson," *International Perspectives* (July/August 1978), 3; interview with Hayes, Montreal, 28 July 1979

43. Gibson interview

44. DEA, CRF 621-AF-40, pt. 1, Pearson to MacDermot, 2 January 1942, Blair to Robertson, 4 January 1942

45. *Ibid.*, "Bureaucratic Mind Acts as Barbed Wire," *Globe and Mail*, 21 February 1942

46. IR, RG 76, Internees, pt. 4, Hayes to Blair, 6 August 1942; Hayes interview

47. RG 2, 7C, reel 1, minutes of Cabinet War Committee, 24 January 1941

48. IR, RG 76, Internees, pt. 1, Sheils to Stethem, 13 January 1941. The need for men with skills like Fleybeck's was underscored in the numerous requests for his release which persisted through April 1941. NA, RG 24, C4, v. 6593, 5-2-12, Sheils to Stethem, 4 February 1941

49. RG 2, 7C, reel 1, minutes of Cabinet War Committee, 29 January 1941; IR, RG 76, Internees, pt. 1, memoranda of Blair for file, 30 January, 12 March 1941

50. CJC/M, General Files, UJRA, memorandum of Hayes, 26 November 1941

51. Canada, House of Commons *Debates*, 1 April 1941, 2058-9

52. See Paula J. Draper, "The Politics of Refugee Immigration: The Pro-Refugee Lobby and the Interned Refugees," *Canadian Historical Society Journal*, VII, 2 (Fall 1983), 81-2.

53. Gibson interview

54. CJC/M, General Files, "Speech of Hon. Cairine Wilson on Nazi Crimes Against Humanity in the Senate of Canada, Ottawa on May 18, 1943"

55. Jean François Pouliot (Temiscouta), Canada, House of Commons *Debates*, 31 May 1943, 3194, 9 July 1943, 4606

56. Blair to Pratt, 18 June 1943; IR, RG 76, Internees, pt. 6, CCIR Petition, 4 June 1943

57. IR, RG 76, Internees, pt. 6, Wilson to King, 11 June 1943

58. Blair to Pratt, 18 June 1943

59. CJC/M, General Files, "For the Rescue of Our Brethren, Paragraphs from a Report by the National Executive Director, UJRWRA," December 1943

60. IR, RG 76, Internees, pt. 7, Jolliffe to Glen, 11 October 1945; Dirks, 124; Abella and Troper, 201

61. Jolliffe to Glen, 11 October 1945; Dirks, 124; Abella and Troper, 202

62. David Ben Gurion, *Israel: A Personal History* (New York, 1971), 54

63. CJC/M, S. Gemicki file, Hintze and Gembicki to CO Camp I, 10 May 1943

Canada's Response to European Refugees, 1939-1945: The Security Dimension

Donald Avery

Canada's response to the victims of nazism and communism has become a matter of intense debate, and most recent studies have been highly critical of the government's insensitivity and lack of vision. For example, Gerard Dirks in his comprehensive study, *Canada's Refugee Policy: Indifference or Opportunism?* declares that humanitarian factors, though present in Canada's policy, were often supplanted by restrictionist considerations.[1] A much more savage indictment comes from Irving Abella and Harold Troper in *None Is Too Many*:

> Like the other western liberal democracies, Canada cared little and did less.... In the pre-war years, as the government cemented barriers to immigration, especially of Jews, immigration authorities barely concealed their contempt for those pleading for rescue. There was no groundswell of opposition, no humanitarian appeal for a more open policy....[2]

These are thoughtful and provocative analyses, but clearly much more research remains to be done about Canada's response to refugees between 1939 and 1945. How, for example, did the Canadian record compare to that of the United States, with particular reference to David Wyman's recent and challenging indictment of the performance of the Roosevelt administration in these years?

> Until the Nazis blocked the exits in the fall of 1941, the oppressed Jews of Europe might have fled to safety. But relatively few got out, mainly because the rest of the world would not take them in. The United States, which had

lowered its barriers a little in 1938, began raising them again in the autumn 1939. Two years later, immigration was even more tightly restricted than before 1938. In fact, starting in July 1941, America's gates nearly shut. The best chance to save the European Jews had passed.

Blame for this callous approach, in Wyman's opinion, is attributable to nativism, anti-Semitism, and widespread fear that many of the refugees were actually nazi infiltrators — a potential fifth column.[3]

Unquestionably, national security considerations also had a powerful impact on Canada's refugee policies during the Second World War. For those refugees who fled from Germany and Austria prior to September 1939, and were fortunate enough to gain entry to Canada, there was the likelihood of being classified as enemy aliens. Although this meant a variety of restrictions on civil rights, most immigrants in this category were left relatively undisturbed. Not as fortunate were the 2,000 enemy alien refugees who were transported from Britain to Canada in June 1940 for safekeeping. At the very least, these men were interned for six months, until either they could qualify for return to Britain or for release in Canada. Those who chose the latter option had no guarantee of permanent sanctuary. A final group, numbering about 2,500, came from a wide assortment of backgrounds: diplomats from Czechoslovakia, engineers and technicians from Poland, and Jewish refugees trying to escape the horrors of Hitler's Final Solution.[4]

Prior to outbreak of war there had been considerable agitation for a more generous Canadian refugee policy, especially after the intensification of Nazi brutality against German Jews in November 1938. One of the most eloquent calls for Canadian assistance came from the newly formed Canadian National Committee on Refugees and Victims of Persecution (later renamed the Canadian National Committee on Refugees, CNCR). In a December 1938 resolution sent to Prime Minister Mackenzie King, the committee claimed,

> that the immigration of carefully selected individuals or groups of refugees to Canada will prove of inestimable value in our national economy by introducing skilled workers and new arts, crafts and industries.... (And) that the assimilation of selected refugees constitutes no serious problems for Canadians since they would come from countries where thrift and frugality have been notable (Germany and Austria), while many would be highly skilled in a variety of techniques and conversant with many languages; further that their devotion to the methods of democracy would be unquestioned.[5]

Indeed, the King government had already recognized that the views expressed by the committee were gaining in popularity. In a memorandum prepared for the Cabinet by officials of the Department of External Affairs and the Immigration Branch, the argument was put forward that "for the time being, at least, public opinion expects the government to make some appropriate contribution toward the solution of the problem which the Christian and civilized countries now find upon their doorstep." The report did, however, indicate a determination to retain existing ethnic ratios. "We do not want to take too many Jews, but in the present circumstances, we do not want to say so. We do not want to legitimize the Aryan mythology by introducing any formal distinction for immigration purposes between Jews and non-Jews."[6] In December 1938, Thomas Crerar, the minister responsible for immigration, briefly broke ranks from the rest of the Cabinet and publicly recommended that Canada accept upwards of 10,000 refugees. This initiative paralleled an Australian announcement that the government was now prepared to admit 15,000 refugees over the next three years. But under intense pressure from his French-Canadian colleagues, and recognizing the political perils, the prime minister chose to repudiate Crerar's proposal. The familiar arguments were put forth: serious unemployment, opposition of provincial governments, and the necessity of restricting Jewish refugees "lest it might foment an anti-Semitic problem."[7]

Jews, however, were not the only group of refugees to have the Canadian immigration gates slammed in their face. In September 1939 the Canadian government received numerous appeals to help 250,000 Spanish refugees, located primarily in France. Most of these appeals emphasized the prospect that these refugees would be forcibly returned to Spain to face "the same terror and persecution ranging from assassination to long term imprisonment the Franco-government is meeting out to thousands of those who supported the Loyalist cause during the Civil War."[8] On this occasion, the Canadian high commissioner, Vincent Massey, gave qualified support to the proposal, arguing that Canada might secure from the Spanish refugee camps "men of eminence in the world of science, education, literature and the arts in whose availability (Canadian) universities might be interested."[9] But, as always, Immigration Branch Director F.C. Blair seemed to have the last word in keeping out refugees who might be a financial burden, a disruptive influence, or a bureaucratic problem. His most convincing argument was directed towards the French-Canadian members of Cabinet: "there would be a tremendous amount of opposition if anything were done to open the door to these penniless refugees who have been opposing Franco."[10]

This bias against left wing refugees and immigrants was longstanding. So too was the view that the Immigration Act could be used to protect the country from communist, nazi, and fascist infiltrators. Naturally, the easiest and most common approach was to exclude suspected subversives at the point of entry, usually on the basis of information provided by British security agencies and the American Federal Bureau of Investigation. Deportation was another way of dealing with foreign agents and alien radicals, at least until most of Europe became the domain of the Axis powers. The Naturalization Act also became an ever more popular weapon to ensure that the foreign born, both alien and naturalized, made loyalty to Canada their overriding consideration. Enforcement of these laws and regulations was generally the responsibility of the Royal Canadian Mounted Police, long an authority in dealing with "dangerous foreigners."[11]

One of the first official expressions of concern that European refugees could pose a serious security threat came from T.A. Crerar. In December 1938, while meeting with the Canadian National Committee of Refugees, Crerar gravely predicted that "certain foreign states would not be above sending certain people to Canada for subversive purposes."[12] The image of the refugee as a destabilizing force had already become a matter of intense debate in various parts of the country. In Quebec, for example, the radical right, as part of their anti-Semitic campaign, charged that recent Jewish refugees had substantially reinforced the Communist movement in the province.[13] In Ontario, even the respectable Toronto *Globe and Mail* encouraged this type of insidious propaganda when it declared, in a November 1937 editorial, that "although it cannot be said that a majority of Jews are Communists, the indications are that a large percentage, and probably the majority of Communists are Jews."[14]

By the end of 1938, the federal government had devised a wide variety of measures to deal with all subversives who threatened national security. In a May 1939 memorandum, Norman Robertson of the Department of External Affairs, acting in his capacity as liaison between the RCMP and the Cabinet, set forth an even more comprehensive list of guidelines to deal with seditious activities. One of these was the recommendation that immigration and naturalization regulations be used against nazis and fascists "in the same way that police now check the records of persons believed to be of radical or Communist sympathies."[15] Not surprisingly, the leadership of the Communist Party of Canada (CPC) were outraged that their movement was "accused of being in a 'sinister combination' with the fascists to weaken the defences of Canada." In February 1939, Tim Buck sent a strongly worded letter to Prime Minister King repudiating charges of disloyalty: "Far from being involved in any plots for sabotage in the event of war we are perturbed at the equanimity which has been shown in official circles towards the penetration, both economically and politically, of this country by fascist agents."[16]

Within the King government, the communists continued to be viewed with intense suspicion, especially by the RCMP. In August 1939, as the international situation became more critical, the commissioner of the force recommended that the CPC be outlawed and its leadership interned. Even though moderates such as Robertson and J.F. MacNeill of the Department of Justice argued that this hard line approach was both undemocratic and inefficient, the RCMP persisted in their war against the communists.[17] Significantly, the ban of the CPC in June 1940 coincided with the growing hysteria in Canada and Britain over internal subversion.

Canadian anarchists were another group of 'leftists' who became the target of Canadian security agencies, and in several cases the deportation weapon was applied. In October 1939 the RCMP and the Immigration Branch attempted to deport Attilio (Arthur) Bortolotti, a member of an Italian anarchist group in Toronto. The Bortolotti case quickly assumed national and international importance for a number of reasons. One was the allegation that the incriminating information used against Bortolotti had been provided by Italian fascists in retaliation for his activities in the 1936 exposure of "fascist attempts to inculcate their ideas in the separate schools of Windsor and Toronto." Bortolotti's lawyer, J.L. Cohen, went even further and charged that within "the police organization in Toronto there has been a good deal of sympathy with both the Italian and French Canadian Fascists." By contrast, Cohen asserted, these police officers seemed when dealing with 'leftists' "to be afflicted with some kind of monomania."[18] There was also the fact that the criminal charges against Bortolotti and his three colleagues, submitted under the Defence of Canada Regulations, had been thrown out of court; the defense claimed, therefore, that the subsequent deportation order, was both unjustified and vindictive. Yet another dimension, which was pointed out in a February 1940 editorial of the

183

Toronto Star, was that to deport Bortolotti to Italy "would be to condemn him to prison for anti-Fascist activities in Canada."[19]

The director of immigration, F.C. Blair, was not swayed by these arguments. Bortolotti was, in his opinion, a menace to national security, "the author of some very dangerous literature," and a man who had a long record of radical activity in both Canada and the United States. Blair made particular reference to an RCMP report that in 1929 Bortolotti had been dismissed from his job at the Ford Motor Company "on account of his arrest by the Detroit Police for the distribution of subversive literature...." Fortunately, there were those within the Canadian government, most notably Norman Robertson and O.D. Skelton of External Affairs, who found Blair's reasoning intolerable, and spoke out in defence of Bortolotti's civil rights.

> Under normal conditions [Robertson wrote] I know that the immigration authorities in both Canada and the United States have been very reluctant to deport persons to the totalitarian countries who are likely to suffer there for their political ideas. This policy, I think, was not only a just and humane one, but I am satisfied that it was the only politically expedient course. Now we are at war it is perhaps more important than ever to maintain these principles.... I do feel that to send a man of his political views back to Italy for an infraction of the immigration laws committed many years ago would do this country more harm, both at home and abroad, than Bortolotti's continued presence in Canada could possibly do.[20]

Skelton echoed these views in a personal note he sent to Blair on 27 March 1940. After complimenting the Immigration Branch for having made "full and careful enquiries before any action (deportation) is taken," Skelton proceeded to lecture the immigration director on political theory and democratic principles:

> There are of course anarchists and anarchists — anarchists who believe in enforcing their opinions by dynamite and others who are naively idealistic in their reliance upon the power of reason to convince people of the sinfulness of control on individuals by State authority. It appears probable that Bortolotti belongs to the latter class though this of course is a matter of fact which we are seeking to determine. If so, I am not at all sure that his presence or preaching would be particularly dangerous in days when the tide is running so strongly in the contrary direction of extending State control over every human relationship.[21]

The combination of public pressure and the intervention of these 'mandarins' resulted in the release of Bortolotti on 29 April, seven months after his arrest. Blair was, however, unrepentant and he informed J.L. Cohen that the only reason why Bortolotti had not been deported was that it had "long been our practice to avoid deportation wherever possible when if carried out would return a person to a country where his life would be in danger." Significantly, the Bortolotti inquiry forced officials of the Immigration Branch and External Affairs to reassess Canadian deportation policies, especially as applied against immigrants and refugees from fascist countries.[22]

Indeed, the status of refugees from German controlled territory had already received considerable attention from Canadian security officials. In late August 1939, the Interdepartmental Committee on the Treatment of Aliens and Alien Property had declared that enemy alien refugees did not constitute a security threat since "their sympathies, in the event of war, by reason of racial considerations or political opinions, would not be with enemy powers." This blanket clearance covered both German and Austrian Jews as well as refugees from Czechoslovakia and Poland.[23] By May 1940, however, the committee had become more security conscious and it instructed all government departments "to make available all information ... relating to enemy aliens, including refugees" to the Royal Canadian Mounted Police.[24] Nor was Canada prepared to accept many new refugees. In part, this was in response to the September 1939 British declaration that "during the war Germany will permit the emigration only of persons whose departure would relieve economic pressure or who would actively further the German cause abroad."[25]

If it was difficult for European refugees to gain entry to Canada after the outbreak of war, it became virtually impossible after the German *blitzkrieg* of May 1940. From Belgium, the Netherlands and France came reports of a sinister German "fifth column" working behind Allied lines. After his flight to Britain, Sir Neville Bland, former ambassador to the Netherlands, warned his countrymen not to trust any German or Austrian "however superficially charming and devoted."[26] This same message was soon conveyed to the House of Commons by Prime Minister Winston Churchill: "After the dark and vile conspiracy which in a few days laid the trustful Dutch people at the mercy of the Nazi aggressors, a wave of alarm passed over this country, and especially in responsible circles, lest the same kind of undermining tactics and treacherous agents of the enemy were at work in our Island."[27] Not surprisingly, these developments profoundly affected Canadians. Public concern and indeed panic was clearly evident in the hundreds of letters and petitions sent to Prime Minister King by a wide variety of organizations.[28] One Toronto resident wondered whether private citizens could "kill at sight enemy agents damaging utilities." Even respectable organizations such as the Canadian Legion indicated that they intended to form protective units which would, if necessary, "take the law into their own hands and act against all aliens in Canada, including naturalized citizens."[29] This threat of vigilante action was taken very seriously by the King government. On 28 June 1940 an important memorandum suggested a number of alternative policies which would reassure the general public that the government was in control of the situation:

> The fact that the German advance since May 10 has been assisted by saboteurs in invaded territories naturally caused concern about aliens in Canada. The success of German efforts resulting in the occupation of half of Europe, even threatening the United Kingdom with invasion, gave Canadians a serious emotional shock. That was natural. What was unnatural was that some interests have exploited people's apprehensions in an effort to embarrass the Government, thus doing Hitler's work.[30]

Part of the government's response was an intense examination of those refugees who attempted to gain entry from western Europe after the fall of France. Much of the information which was utilized by the RCMP and immigration officials came from British and American sources.[31] In June 1940, for example, the RCMP were informed by British intelligence that a Jewish refugee, William Roth, who had been admitted six months previously, might be a Nazi agent. The allegation was based both on Roth's actions while in Europe, and reports that he had been observed "making rather large cash payments to suspicious characters" while travelling between Montreal and New York.[32] At this stage Canadian security authorities were also concerned about Soviet agents. In May 1940, Skelton wrote:

> I am informed by the French Legation that a Miss Sophie Burnstein, who is of Russian birth and has been living in Paris in recent years, has left for the United States on some errand for the Comintern. It is understood that she plans later to apply for entry into Canada as a well-to-do refugee. I have already passed on this information to the Royal Canadian Mounted Police, but thought you might wish to have advance notice of the lady's intentions.[33]

Another type of refugee who caused External Affairs and immigration officials considerable difficulty were those who had the support of powerful religious and political groups within the country. In October 1940, Skelton informed the RCMP and the Immigration Branch that Professor Mordat, a suspected agent from Vichy France, had applied for entry as a political refugee, and that his application had been endorsed by a number of prominent people in Quebec, including Liberal Senator Raoul Dandurand. Under these circumstances Skelton suggested that the application should be approved: "With some misgivings, Mr. Blair and I concluded that Mordat might be a more effective propagandist for the Vichy government as a soldier of France prevented from rejoining his Canadian wife and family by Canadian immigration authorities, than as an active agitator in the Province of Quebec."[34]

Another refugee whose arrival perplexed Canadian immigration authorities was Father Dom Odo, Duke of Wurttemberg. In November 1940 Blair informed Skelton that Dom Odo had sought sanctuary in the Benedictine Monastery at Muenster, Saskatchewan, and that he too had influential contacts who might support his entry: he "is in some way related to the Governor General (Earl of Athlone), and he is on close terms with Cardinal Villeneuve of Quebec." Yet another consideration for the Commonwealth war effort was Dom Odo's potential impact on American Catholics if he sought sanctuary in that country instead of proceeding to Canada:

> The purpose of his coming to Canada was to find shelter in the Monastery of Muenster, Sask. and as he is of enemy citizenship he and his secretary, Kraemer would be compelled to register. I think taking everything into account the best course would be to allow him to come to Canada and see that the Registrar makes his stay at the Monastery one of the first conditions of his being allowed to remain in the country. If we can keep him in the Monastery it will solve all but his own difficulties.

For reasons that remain obscure, Blair was overruled by the RCMP and External Affairs. The influential German cleric was not admitted.[35]

Canadian policies towards European refugees were also strongly influenced by anti-refugee developments in the United States and Great Britain.[36] In both countries the outbreak of war in September 1939 resulted in a drastic change in government policies towards refugees. This was most notable in Great Britain, where friendly enemy aliens and refugees increasingly became suspect. In the United States the hard line approach was somewhat delayed, and immigration policy remained reasonably tolerant through 1939, even toward refugees who had entered the country illegally. In March 1940, for example, Loring Christie, the Canadian chargé d'affaires in Washington, reported that the United States Department of Labour was even "permitting anti-fascist Italians and anti-Franco-Spaniards who are illegally in this country to remain here, since they claim that they are on the blacklist of their respective governments because of their political activities."[37]

Unfortunately, this humanitarian approach would soon end as Americans became increasingly concerned over the possibilities of Nazi and Soviet espionage and sabotage. In some ways this hysteria was a reaction to the belief that Nazi success in Europe had been greatly assisted by the fifth column, and US fears were confirmed by the draconian anti-refugee policies adopted by the British government in June 1940. There is also considerable evidence that various American nativist and racist organizations used the fifth column scare as a means of justifying their long standing views "that foreigners should be kept under close surveillance and that immigration should end."[38] These views found expression both in Congress and in the press. Beginning in August 1940, for example, the *American Magazine* presented six articles on the internal nazi threat under such titles as "Enemies Within Our Gates" and "Hitler's Slave Spies." Not to be outdone, the pro-business journal *Fortune* published a series of articles on fascist and communist activities in the United States.[39]

This agitation had a powerful impact on American immigration policy. In June 1940, the Alien Registration Bill or Smith Act, was passed "virtually without debate and without division," which gave US security authorities greatly expanded powers to deport suspected radicals and subversives, and called for the "registration and finger-printing of aliens."[40] Worse was to follow. In mid-June 1940, the attorney general, Robert Jackson, declared that the idea that a refugee might be admitted to the United States unless he posed a danger to the country "must at least temporarily yield to the policy that none shall be admitted unless it affirmatively appears to be for the American interest." In the summer of 1940 the Roosevelt administration shifted the Immigration and Naturalization Service from the Labor Department to the Justice Department in order "to ensure more effective control over aliens."[41] The authority to issue the all important immigration visa was, however, entrusted to officials of the Visa Division of the State Department. Unfortunately for the refugees, Breckenridge Long and his subordinates often "brought strongly nativist attitudes to the situation," and appeared obsessed with the fear of an alien fifth column.[42]

This negative stereotype was reinforced early in 1941 when there were renewed reports that Germany had established an elaborate network of "unwilling" spies and saboteurs in the United States "by forcing people who had relatives in Nazi territory to serve as German agents under threat of harm to their loved ones." During the May 1941 session of the House Committee on Un-American Activities, one left wing refugee testified that "it was impossible for anyone to be released from a nazi concentration camp unless he signed a pledge that he would help the Gestapo." A similar warning emanated from Laurence Steihardt, American ambassador in Moscow: "Soviet authorities would not issue visas to potential immigrants to the United States unless they had guarantees that these people could be used as espionage agents."[43]

The State Department required little prodding. On 5 June 1941 it began to reduce substantially the number of visas granted to refugees who had "parents, children, husbands, wives, brothers or sisters resident in territory under the control of Germany." These restrictive measures, in the words of David Wyman, "crushed the hopes of thousands who had looked to the United States for asylum."[44]

Not surprisingly, both External Affairs and immigration officials were influenced by American reports that the nazis and Soviets were using refugees as a fifth column. On 31 May 1941, for example, Hume Wrong of the Canadian Legation in Washington forwarded to Ottawa a confidential memorandum which had been prepared by Avra M. Warren, chief of the US State Department Visa Division, on the dangers associated with refugees temporarily located in the Far East:

> There are at present approximately 22,000 European refugees in Shanghai and 2,000 in Japan.... Of the 22,000 in Shanghai, roughly 8,000 are known to be Japanese agents, and of the remaining 14,000, one in four obtained transit through Russia upon the written undertaking that he would become a Russian agent in the Americas should he succeed in reaching this hemisphere. Large numbers have admitted this fact to the American Consuls before whom they applied for United States visas. These admissions have been in many cases corroborated by other means.

The report went on to claim that "of the approximately 2,000 refugees in Japan, more than half are Jewish rabbinical students who escaped from Poland over a period of many years. All refugees in Japan are working in full collaboration with the Japanese against Russia."[45]

Developments in Britain also had important ramifications for Canada's wartime refugee policies. Of greatest significance was the British government's decision in the summer of 1940 to send about 4,500 interned civilian enemy aliens and prisoners of war to Canada for safekeeping. Of these the most tragic groups were the 2,600 civilian refugees in the C category, mostly Jews, who until the dark days of June 1940 were regarded as safe or friendly enemy aliens.[46] The complex reasons why the British government so dramatically reversed its September 1939 policy only to intern "agents, members of foreign organizations and special 'dangerous individuals'" has been thoroughly discussed in a number of British and Canadian studies. What is of central importance for this paper is the role which British security agencies assumed in the fateful decision of June, and the impact which the 2,600 category internees had on the internal and external policies of the Canadian government.[47]

As early as March 1939, British security agencies such as MI 5 warned the home secretary that "the Germans were anxious to inundate this country with Jews with a view of creating a Jewish problem in the United Kingdom." After September 1939, MI 5 and military intelligence intensified their demands for wholesale round-ups of enemy aliens despite the arguments of the home secretary and the Foreign Office that such extreme measures were unnecessary and harmful.[48] Christopher Andrew's study, *Secret Service: The Making of an Intelligence Community*, effectively summarizes the major factors associated with the mass internment:

> The home secretary Sir John Anderson, anxious to avoid the anti-alien hysteria of the First World War, told the cabinet that none of the intelligence services had found any evidence of Nazi plans to infiltrate German and Austrian refugees. Nor, as a group, were the refugees potentially dangerous. He sensibly argued that while wholesale internment would be popular in the short term, the 'inevitably poor treatment' of internees would produce a sympathetic backlash. The chiefs of staff, however, insisted that alien refugees were 'a most dangerous source of subversive activity': 'The most ruthless action should be taken to eliminate any chances of fifth column activities.' Churchill sided with the chiefs of staff rather than with the Home Office.... Most ministers agreed. With the support of MI5, ... the Security Executive energetically supervised the 'round-up.' The result, as the Foreign Office noted, was to raise 'MI5 from their former advisory position to what is in effect an executive function, so that it is in fact their view rather than that of

the Home Office which over matters of internment and detention in the long run prevails.'⁴⁹

The placement and administration of the 2,600 friendly enemy aliens created immense problems for Canadian military and civilian authorities. First of all, they did not fit into the preconceived model of dangerous aliens who had to be guarded, not integrated back into either British or Canadian society. Secondly, the British government, or more specifically the security agencies, had the exclusive authority to screen the internees, and the vetting process was long and laborous. Third, conditions in the eight internment camps were often unsatisfactory from both the point of view of the internees and the officials and staff of Canadian Internment Operations, and later the Commission of Refugee Camps. Certainly the top military officials, General Panet (June 1940 to September 1940), Colonel H. Stethem (September 1940 to 30 June 1941) and Colonel R.W.S. Fordham (1 July 1941 to December 1943), and their camp commandants, had a most difficult task in dealing with such a unique group of prisoners. They were a diverse lot with "hundreds of professionals, mingled with baffled schoolboys and mid-European peasants, all being counted and kept by uniformed soldiers of every rank."⁵⁰

Not surprisingly, there was intense bitterness among the internees over their treatment in both Britain and Canada. "As you will understand," Saul Hayes of the Canadian Jewish Refugee Agency patiently explained to General Panet, "there is a considerable amount of agitation because of the position in which these Jews, themselves first victims of Nazi oppression ... now find themselves." What made this situation even worse was that the screening of internees had not been very thorough: nazis, fascists, social democrats and communists were often placed in the same camp. Author Eric Koch, himself an internee, describes the controversy at the Farnham Camp:

> We had pressed for the removal of the Nazis and nothing had been done, and we realized that unless they were removed there were bound to be more ugly incidents.... As for the majority, this was a highly emotional issue touching on a fundamental principal, namely our status as refugees. To most of us it was irrelevant that a small number of communists were making the most of the confrontation. Jews and gentiles felt equally strong about this principle.⁵¹

Between the fall of 1940, when the British government sent Alexander Paterson to assess the status of the Category C internees, and the end of

1943, when the refugee camps were closed, Canadian authorities had three main responsibilities. One was to facilitate the gradual repatriation of those internees who wished to return to Britain and who passed the security assessment of MI5. The second was to deal with those refugees who wished to remain in Canada, either in wartime jobs, or as university students. A final task was to try to meet the demands of those refugees who had American visas and who wanted to proceed to the United States.

Alexander Paterson's tour of Canadian internment camps, and his subsequent report of April 1941, had a major impact of both British and Canadian policies towards the 'friendly' enemy alien refugees. For the British government, it meant renewed pressure to release not only those who might have legitimate refugee status, but also those who would be an asset in the war effort. The Paterson Report also brought important changes in the operation of the Canadian camps. This was largely associated with his scathing criticism of anti-Semitic guards, insensitive administrators and primitive living conditions. As a result, by Order-in-Council PC 4568, 25 June 1941, the position of Commissioner of Refugee Camps was created and Colonel Fordham was named to the post. He immediately began to improve the conditions in the camps and to expedite the repatriation movement.[52]

In fact, the first contingent of 287 refugees had returned to Britain in December 1940. In making their selections, British authorities were primarily concerned whether the individual could be useful to the war effort. A left wing background was not necessarily a serious disability. For example, physicist Dr. Klaus Fuchs, an inmate at Camp L (Quebec City), was among the first group returned, despite some evidence which suggests that his communist loyalties were not only "well known to the inmates, but also to the army intelligence officers." Obviously Fuchs' greatest asset were his scientific skills. But he also qualified as a friendly alien who had fled from Germany in 1933 for political reasons, and his declaration of loyalty was accepted without reservation: "I have applied for naturalization prior to the outbreak of war. I wish either to take my place in the National Service wherever I may be useful, or to return to my job as Carnegie Research Fellow. If there is any objection to returning to Edinburgh I can continue my work at one of several other Universities."[53]

Canadian security agencies, most notably the RCMP and Military Intelligence, did attempt to monitor attempts on the part of communist, nazi or fascist groups or individuals in Canada to make contact with the internees.[54] For example, in January 1941, a report was submitted to the Director of Internment Operations, about a letter sent to one of the German refugees at Farnham by Kenneth Woodsworth, secretary of the Canadian Youth Congress. In the opinion of the intelligence officer, this represented a dangerous initiative on the part of Canadian communists:

> the letter is a 'feeler' wanting information about others in the camp and offering to give information about others in various camps.... It would seem that the Canadian Youth Congress which in reality has been a 'respectable' front for the operations of the Communist Party, is a dangerous organization to be allowed to communicate with prisoners and to organize on their behalf.[55]

There were also a number of refugee scientists and skilled workers who wanted to become involved in the Canadian war effort, and thereby qualify for permanent residence in Canada. This was not an easy goal to achieve. In September 1940, the Cabinet sub-committee, which had been assembled in June 1940 to deal with the British government's request for internment facilities, declared its opposition to the permanent residence of these men, especially since there was such strong public opposition "to the admission of any large proportion of Jews."[56] Nor did the official position change substantially in 1941. A request sent to Colonel Stethem in May for the utilization of Jewish artisans in Montreal factories brought a curt and negative response from the director of internment operations:

> Up to the present, the Canadian Government has not consented to permit any of these internees to be released in Canada, except those who had first degree relatives, or one or two skilled craftsmen, where their services were urgently required in war work.... There would probably be difficulties if they were given industrial jobs: they are of German nationality, although anti-Nazi, and they would have to be registered as enemy aliens. Whether the other workmen in the factory would object to their presence or not, I do not know.[57]

By the end of 1941, with almost total segregation of the refugee internees from prisoners of war, a much more enlightened policy was adopted about utilizing the diverse skills of these men. In a September 1942 memorandum to officials of the Department of Munitions and Supply, F.C. Blair indicated that of those refugees who chose to remain in Canada, 150 were students, 100 were in farm jobs and another 350 were "in various industries where their services might be useful ... in the war effort." He did emphasize, however, that extensive screening had occurred before these men were released:

in any case the Home Office in London is consulted to obtain their approval, where the record overseas is satisfactory and the camp record here is good, we proceed with release depending of course on the refugees' qualifications. Every refugee is required to register with the police and to report regularly wherever he may be placed. No man is permitted to leave his employer without obtaining our consent and that consent is rarely given because we are determined to prevent these men from drifting about from place to place. We have endeavoured (and I am glad to say with some success) to impress upon these individuals that they ... have an obligation to live up to the conditions under which their release was granted. Those who fail to do it face the possibility of return to the camps and already at least half a dozen have been returned.

In discussing the procedure for security screening, Blair provided an interesting argument, particularly in light of his obvious bias against the entry of Jewish refugees:

I would estimate that at least 90% of those released are of Jewish racial origin, although some of them are of mixed race such as a Jewish father and a German mother. In every case where the race is not Jewish particular care has been taken to check up on the reliability and the attitude of the individual to Nazism. In no case have we yet found any reason to suspect the conduct of persons who have been released.[58]

The task of integrating the refugees into the economy was carried out by immigration officials. They proved to be tough assessors, even in employment situations where refugees complained about "exploitation and oppression ... under-pay and harsh treatment." In case after case, the managerial argument about the importance of maintaining labour stability was accepted rather uncritically. This rigid stance was clearly evident in the case of a Montreal factory where three refugee workers were charged with fomenting unrest "in a manner that indicated they hold and expound the old view of communism that taught that all employers were tyrants and oppressors." As a result, these men were temporarily returned to the internment camps for 'behavior modification.'[59]

Refugee students were much more fortunate in the treatment they received from Canadian authorities.[60] In the summer of 1941, Canadian and British authorities had agreed that it would be better to allow refugee students "to continue with their studies in Canada rather than waste valuable time behind barbed wire." The original plan was that 100 would be admitted to Canadian universities after their records were screened by the Home Office, the commissioner of refugee camps and the director of immigration.⁶¹ In 1942, Colonel Fordham laconically commented that few pre-war immigrants "have had their histories as thoroughly investigated." The programme worked as follows:

> A responsible sponsor, residing in Canada, was found for every student released for the purpose of attending a Canadian university. The sponsor had to be a reputable citizen possessed of assets who would undertake to guarantee the cost of maintenance and the tuition fees of a student. That was to prevent a student from becoming a public charge.... The sponsors were usually found through the agencies of ... the Central Committee for Interned Refugees.... Every sponsor had to meet with the approval of Mr. F.C. Blair, Director of Immigration ... before being accepted.

According to Fordham, the experiment was a great success. "There are released refugees at ten universities in Canada ... and all have given the utmost satisfaction. All have frequently expressed the desire to assist in Canada's war effort in any way possible."⁶² This harmonious situation was, however, soon disrupted by agitation about the military status of 'enemy' refugee students. In December 1942, President H.J. Cody of the University of Toronto wrote to the minister of defence, J.L. Ralston, to clarify whether these men were eligible for military training:

> Last year we admitted about fifteen of these internees. This autumn, however, the application of twenty more have been held up by our Board of Governors.... One group maintains that if we receive these students into the University, we are putting them in a preferred position as compared with Canadian boys of the same age. The latter have to take compulsory military training if they are to remain at the University.... All these lads who are really friendly aliens are anxious to take military service.... Is there any way of taking these young men in some section ... of what is roughly called the COTC?⁶³

Although the problem was temporarily overcome by having the refugee students undertake military training in special units, the issue did not disappear. In March 1943, Tommy Church, the combative member of parliament for Broadview (Toronto), attacked Ralston in the House of Commons for permitting enemy alien students "to wear the King's uniform without taking the test oath. I cannot think of a greater insult to the uniform and to the service generally than to permit this special emblem of the King's service to be used as a camouflage or a masquerade." Church also warned members of the House that it was "unwise to enroll these enemy prisoners in our universities and permit them where so inclined, to get all kinds of information from mingling with the students and staff and ... making use of our science courses and laboratories."[64] This issue was resolved.

The broader question about the loyalty of refugees did, however, remain. This was clearly revealed in January 1943, when Professor J.L. Synge of the Applied Mathematics Department, University of Toronto, sought to overcome the barriers erected by the National Research Council (NRC) against refugee scientists. One of Synge's arguments was that Canada should follow "the lead of Great Britain and the United States, in using all available talent, provided that no risk to national security [was] involved." He was particularly insistent that Alfred Schild, "a gifted mathematician and physicist, who was a student at University College (London) before he was interned," should be employed "in ballistic or radio research with the NRC."[65] This proposal was not well received at the NRC. Colonel F.C. Wallace, director of the Radio Branch, stated that he was "extremely reluctant to consider anyone with an enemy alien background for use in the radio field," while C.J. Mackenzie, the NRC president, indicated that the body had a long standing and unbroken policy "not to employ enemy aliens in any work having contact with secret information." Mackenzie also angrily refuted charges that Canada was more concerned with security precautions than its allies:

> It is true that there are a few aliens of enemy origin working in the United States on secret war projects, but they are very few and most of them have been in the country for some time. Also, they are only allowed to have knowledge of a very partial field of secret projects. As a matter of fact, several distinguished Britishers who have lived for years in the United States had to be formally associated with our Research Council before they could be admitted to certain secret war projects in the United States.[66]

However, during the latter part of 1943 the general status of enemy alien refugees improved substantially. In October 1943, officials of External Affairs suggested that "steps should be taken to remove as far as possible, the restrictions imposed on refugees from the United Kingdom." This proposal reflected growing public pressure for unconditional release.[67] The Canadian National Committee on Refugees (CNCR), for example, called on the War Cabinet to grant these refugees "immigrant status ... for the duration of the war with formal assurances that favourable consideration will be given to an application for permanent residence if at the end of hostilities the record of the individual shows that he has done his best to become adjusted to conditions in this country." In terms of employment, the CNCR recommended that the refugees be removed from the jurisdiction of the Immigration Branch and placed under the authority of the National Selective Service, so that "in the assignment of war jobs in war industries they should not be discriminated against because of their nationality." Senator Cairine Wilson, president of the CNCR, also urged Prime Minister King to relieve refugees from the burden of continual registration on security grounds: "May we suggest that in all cases free from doubt, certificates of exemption be issued by the Royal Canadian Mounted Police permitting the individuals to report as infrequently as is compatible with administrative purposes.... Most of these boys are working for hourly wages and interruption of work with loss of wages should be avoided as far as possible".[68] This representation, combined with the internal arguments of the more enlightened civil servants, had the desired effect. On 10 December 1943, an order-in-council granted the refugees a renewable one year permit to remain in Canada and specified that they would "be released from any restraints or conditions."[69]

Yet many of the interned refugees did not wish to remain in Canada. Instead, they wanted to continue their trek to the United States in order to join relatives and friends. But American authorities had already demonstrated, in the 1940 case of Herman Bondi, that they were not prepared to facilitate the entry of any group of European refugees, especially those who came from Canadian internment camps. In the Bondi case, the justification for exclusion were two-fold: he had not arrived at a US port, and he had not been interviewed and given security clearance by American authorities prior to coming to the United States.[70] In the fall of 1941 British envoy Alexander Paterson sought to circumvent these exclusionist regulations when he visited with officials in Washington. He was, however, thwarted by the Allan Bill, which "stipulated that nobody could be admitted to the USA during the war who had relatives in Germany or German occupied Europe, and no alien could enter the country who had not been a free man for at least a year."

Between 1941 and 1944, Canadian officials on various occasions attempted to carry out Paterson's plan, but with no success.[71] In July 1944, Norman Robertson, under secretary of state for external affairs, informed the Canadian ambassador in Washington, Lester B. Pearson, that he was now convinced that "the continuous difficulties, delays, errors and apologies that have arisen in this matter lead me rather to doubt whether the State Department is actually interested in achieving an arrangement under which entry of refugees is possible." In his reply, Pearson confirmed that the State Department appeared to have no intention of altering its hard-line approach:

> Despite the assurances given us on several occasions it is evident we are up against the ill-will of the Visa Division to deal fairly with these applications. Although it is difficult to assess the reasons for this attitude, it may be attributed, in our opinion, to the resentment caused in the Visa Division by the establishment of the War Refugee Board. As you might recall, the creation of the Board was regarded as an implicit criticism of the work performed in that field by the State Department, eg, the Visa Division. As the Visa Division, however, is responsible for the final decision in each specific case, it can be appreciated that each one is scrutinized with the utmost care and without too great sympathy.[72]

But were Robertson and Pearson justified in criticizing American refugee policies when the Canadian record was so unimpressive? Quite clearly in Robertson's case, he was not only aware of Canada's meagre response to Europe's war victims, but personally embarrassed that his country had not done more. In October 1944, Robertson reluctantly transmitted a report to the British deputy high commissioner on the numbers of refugees admitted into Canada since 1939. "In passing this information which you have requested, I feel I should mention my misgivings about the use to which your Government wish to put it."[73] And well he might have misgivings, for by August 1944 Canada had admitted only about 3,000 temporary refugees. They consisted, Pearson reported, of the following seven groups:

1. Approximately 60 Belgium and Dutch refugees from Spain and Portugal.

2. Approximately 100 Czechoslovak officials and nationals from the United Kingdom and the Iberian Peninsula.

3. The members of the crew of the Norwegian Whaling Fleet brought to Canadian ports when Norway was invaded, this personnel totalling about 300.

4. About 600 Polish engineers and technicians from France and the Iberian Peninsula, following the overthrow of the first mentioned country; some of these were accompanied by their families.

5. About 150 Polish nationals from the Far East.

6. 966 civilian internees brought to Canada from the United Kingdom in 1940 and released for employment or for educational purposes in this country.

7. 447 Jewish refugees from the Iberian Peninsula and Tangier.[74]

Two of these groups merit particular analysis — the 600 Poles and the 447 Jewish refugees. In each case, they reveal important aspects of the economic and security dimensions of Canada's refugee policies.

Between 1940 and 1943 Canadian authorities attempted to bring in hundreds of Polish engineers and technicians who had fled to unoccupied France and Britain after June 1940. The initiative came from the London-based Polish government-in-exile and its representative in Canada. In September 1940, Victor Podoski, the Polish consul general, informed the Canadian government that there were many "chemical and mechanical engineers, technicians of all types and experts in munitions production" in France. His message found a receptive audience in the Department of Munitions and Supply, and in the Department of External Affairs. In November 1940, approval was given for the entry of seventy engineers and their dependents from Vichy France. However, prolonged discussion over which government would assume the transportation costs, and nazi pressure on Vichy, thwarted the repatriation efforts.[75] Gerald Dirks describes the situation:

> The speed with which these arrangements were concluded reflected both the eagerness of the Canadian companies in the manufacturing and munitions industries to acquire skilled labour and the fear of the Polish government-in-exile [that].... Germany would pressure Vichy to hand over the skilled refugees to the Gestapo, which in turn would force the Poles to work in the Reich's own war industries. In January 1942, these fears were shown to be well justified. A Vichy decree prohibited the emigration of all men under the age of forty-five.... By mid-January all attempts to acquire exit permits for these much desired refugees were dropped.[76]

Having lost out on the initial lottery for skilled war workers, the Canadian government was quite responsive to a subsequent Foreign Office suggestion that they accept a few hundred Polish 'experts' who had not yet been absorbed into high priority jobs in the British war economy. During 1941 and 1942, 400 skilled technicians and 265 scientists and engineers came to Canada under the same terms which had been worked out for the Vichy based group. All of these men quickly found employment, and by 1945 had become prime candidates for permanent domicile and Canadian citizenship because of valuable wartime service.[77]

In 1943 and 1944 the debate surrounding the entry of Jewish refugees from Spain, Portugal and Tangier was an even more striking example of the dichotomy in Canada's refugee policy. On one hand, the King government had to respond to the demands of humanitarian groups such as the CNCR, and newspapers such as the *Winnipeg Free Press*, that the time had come "when we have to stop talking about doing something about refugees and get down to action."[78] By contrast, there were strong isolationist and xenophobic forces within the country that resisted the entry of almost all refugees, but especially Jews. There was also the message being sent by Canadian security officials that certain European refugees were a serious security risk.[79]

In the spring of 1943 the Canadian government was pressured by British authorities to grant asylum to greater numbers of European refugees. One major argument was that the few unoccupied countries of Europe such as Sweden, Switzerland, Spain and Portugal were being overwhelmed by the economic and social burdens associated with maintaining the victims of nazism. In April 1943, representatives of Great Britain and the United States met at Bermuda "to discuss proposals aimed at establishing a more adequate multilateral assistance scheme for European refugees."[80] Although the Bermuda Conference, and the subsequent actions of the Intergovernmental Committee on Refugees, produced few solutions for the desperate plight of European Jews, and other victims of nazism, it did force Canadian authorities to open the immigration gates a crack. In particular, arrangements were made to reopen the Lisbon immigration office and to select a limited number of both Jewish and non-Jewish refugees.[81]

Yet even this pathetically small movement caused great agitation in Canada, most notably in Quebec. In the fall of 1943 the leader of the *Union Nationale* party, Maurice Duplessis, publicly charged that there was a conspiracy between various Jewish organizations and the federal government "to place 100,000 Jewish refugees in Quebec."[82] In March 1944 Duplessis went even further, introducing a motion in the Quebec Legislative Assembly which called for a moratorium on large scale immigration because of the dilatory effect it would have on French Canadians. Duplessis' use of the Jewish refugee bogey was quickly endorsed by right wing newspapers such as *Le Bavard*:

> Evidently Mr. Duplessis stirred a hornet's nest when he dared to attack openly a Jewish project to invade our province.... It is enough to know the plan of the Jews and to follow the march of events in order to be convinced that a sinister and powerful organization does not hesitate to take in the dark all the possible means for the entire execution of the plan.[83]

Despite the extensive and persuasive refutations of Duplessis' malicious propaganda, it was an important factor during the 1944 provincial election and a factor in the *Union Nationale* victory.[84]

Criticism of the movement of Jewish refugees emanated from another source — the Royal Canadian Mounted Police. The force was particularly interested in the refugees sponsored by the Montreal Jewish Labor Committee (JLC). Indeed, in March 1943, they requested assistance from the US Federal Bureau of Investigation in checking certain JLC refugees against a "master list of known subversives maintained by the Bureau." The RCMP was also interested in the status of the Jewish Labor Committee of New York City, which was affiliated with the JLC. Although both organizations were given a clean bill of health by the FBI, officials of the RCMP remained convinced that they were dealing with dangerous subversives. This message was quickly conveyed to the Immigration Branch by the assistant commissioner, F.J. Mead, who alleged that many of JLC refugees appeared to have been affiliated with the Jewish Social Democratic Party in Poland "an organization of revolutionaries, and although not connected with the Communist International, its aims are somewhat similar to the latter." The policy was obvious: reject all JLC sponsored refugees.[85]

As usual, F.C. Blair required little convincing. This was most evident when the applications of David Azachs, a JLC referral, crossed his desk. Attached to the Azachs file was the following background information:

> Mr. Azachs was active in trade unions in Latvia and helped to carry on educational work in the labor movement. In 1937 he was imprisoned by the Fascist government of Latvia and subsequently expelled from the country ... Azachs went to France where he became an active worker in the antiFascist press.... Immediately after the occupation of Paris, Gestapo agents sought to arrest Azachs.... He fled to southern France.... Mr. Azachs is said to be in particular danger because the Latvian government under the Soviet Union deprived him of citizenship ... he is being actively sought by the Gestapo.

The accompanying attached 'editorial' comment by Superintendant Duncan of the RCMP, however, indicated that Azachs' resistance to authoritarian regimes did not offset his 'leftist' tendencies:

> David Azachs is only 29 years of age and has engaged in labor activities during most of his adult life. He is persona non grata with the Communists, the Nazis, the Latvians and allegedly everyone in Europe. Information received from various US Government Agencies indicates that his sponsors and references are for the most part affiliated with various organizations

which are either Communistic, Communist front organizations or Communist controlled groups. Further in view of the fact that his mother and sister, as well as his wife's parents and two sisters are in the Soviet Union and apparently are suffering from no difficulties, as appeared on the record, it could hardly be conceivable that he is anti-Communist.[86]

The movement of over 600 Jewish refugees from Lisbon in June 1944, some of whom were sponsored by the Montreal Jewish Labor Committee, caused even more consternation for the RCMP. On 1 June 1944, Commissioner Wood wrote the minister of justice, Louis St. Laurent, expressing concern over the ability of the force to ascertain "the bona fides of refugees entering Canada ... with the object of preventing persons who might be enemy agents from taking up residence here." His complaints were both specific and general. The RCMP had received only a day's notice prior to the arrival of a group of 276 Jewish refugees in Halifax. No background information about the refugees had been forwarded by either British or American security agencies, and the force did not have available "the skilled manpower to do an adequate job of screening." Wood reinforced his warning by pointing out that among the refugees there were at least four possible espionage agents, whom he described as follows:

> Rolf Lohich: "It was learned that he was in the Germany Army as recently as June 1943, and he made unsatisfactory replies to his interrogation."
>
> Eva Kauffman: "Our London correspondent has indicated that this woman and her husband are suspected of being Gestapo agents."
>
> Herbert Kahn and his wife: [were] "... secretly reported to the Federal Bureau of Investigation as being identical in name with Gestapo agents who were sent out of the United States in 1939."
>
> Carlo Randee Perez: "This man was taken from the SS 'Serpa Pinto' by a U-boat commander who stopped the vessel in mid-Atlantic.... The reason he was detained ... is very obscure.... He is being questioned by our officers who are satisfied that he is lying."[87]

The report received St. Laurent's immediate attention. On 7 June he asked Norman Robertson to take this serious matter to the prime minister "because although it is no doubt necessary to do whatever may be compatible with the safety of our State for the relief of persons persecuted in occupied Europe, there seems to be some danger that the admission of these refugees might be used for the purpose of introducing espionage agents in this country."[88] Robertson, however, suggested that the matter could be more effectively handled at the departmental level and recommended that External Affairs, the RCMP and the Immigration Branch coordinate their resources "to ensure that in future the Police had information available which is adequate for them to investigate the background of people who are received and to investigate any grounds for suspicion that may arise." Robertson also suggested that "complete information should be secured from the United Kingdom Security Organization as soon as possible concerning all people who have thus far been brought to this country."[89]

From the Canadian security point of view, the spectre of a refugee fifth column was substantially reduced in the fall of 1944 when the Lisbon screening office was closed, and the movement of Jewish refugees from the Iberian Peninsula was curtailed. Immigration officials had no difficulty justifying this decision:

> with the progress of the war refugees not actually in enemy hands are not now in danger of persecution or loss of life and that as the termination of the war might be expected within a reasonable period, a continuance of the movement of refugees to Canada would not be warranted; they would only reside in this country a comparatively short time before the question of return to Europe would have to be considered.[90]

At this juncture, the main concern of immigration officials and the RCMP was the post-war repatriation of those refugees who had been admitted only for the duration. But their joint investigation soon proved to be a fiasco. In September 1944, a somewhat embarrassed Commissioner Wood informed A.L. Jolliffe, the new director of immigration, that the RCMP could not even locate the majority of the 446 Jewish refugees brought from Lisbon in the spring and summer of 1944:

> It was anticipated that we would be able to keep in touch with these people through the offices of the Canadian Jewish Congress and the Jewish Immigrants' Aid Society but we are now advised that these offices do not maintain contact with refugees who are not in receipt of assistance and, therefore, under the circumstances, it will not be possible for us to keep advised of the whereabouts of those refugees who are not enemy aliens ... the thought occurs that you may have some suggestion to make in this regard and your comments thereon will be greatly appreciated.

Jolliffe was of little assistance, and all he could suggest was that the RCMP contact the Canadian National Committee on Refugees, which might "be able to furnish the addresses to which the individual families were directed."[91]

Repatriation procedures were never implemented. In October 1945, J. Allison Glen, the minister responsible for immigration, recommended that the 3,500 refugees admitted during the war should be granted permanent residence.[92] Glen particularly complimented the 650 Polish engineers and technicians for having "rendered faithful and valuable service connected with the war effort." In 1946 it was another group of Polish refugees — 4,000 officers and men who had fought under General Anders with the British in the Italian campaign — who became the first test case of Canadian post-war intentions.[93]

Canada had no real refugee policy in the Second World War. While about 3,500 so-called refugees were admitted, this action was not in response to any broad international principle or national refugee programme such as evolved after 1945. Instead, those European refugees who slipped under and around the immigration gates did so only after overcoming formidable obstacles, or because of their unique circumstances. Would, for instance, Canada have accepted 966 German and Austrian refugees in 1940 if they had not come as internees? Probably not, for during the war the Government appeared more interested in looking after and using the usually docile POWs than independent and assertive European refugees.[94]

Was the policy restrictive primarily because so many of the refugees were Jews? The answer, on the whole, is yes. Less clear, however, is the extent to which the decisions of 'gatekeepers' such as F.C. Blair, director of the Immigration Branch, and Commissioner S.T. Wood of the RCMP were motivated by anti-Semitism and xenophobia. During the war, Blair, for instance, was opposed to allowing *any* refugees into the country whether they were Spaniards, Jews, Poles, Mennonites or Czechs. In this regard, his position was similar to that of Breckenridge Long of the American State Department's Visa Division. Both saw refugees as creating administrative problems, arousing political controversy, and posing a threat to national security. And both found many powerful allies within the security agencies of their respective countries.[95]

After May 1940, there was widespread concern in Britain, Canada and the United States about European refugees as a potential nazi fifth column. In all these countries, public hysteria, fanned by the 'yellow' press and opportunistic and irresponsible politicians, demanded strong action against enemy aliens, regardless of their anti-nazi credentials. Of even greater significance, however, was the fact that in all three countries the dominant security agencies warned their respective governments against admitting refugees who might either be committed nazi or Soviet agents, or might, through blackmail, be forced to engage in espionage and sabotage. The historical record shows that MI5, the RCMP and the FBI often exaggerated the refugee threat, sometimes because of their own lack of knowledge, and sometimes because of anti-alien and anti-leftist tendencies. It must be remembered, however, that these were desperate times. The men who staffed these agencies believed that they had an awesome responsibility to protect their country from devious and ruthless nazi adversaries. In Canada, the leadership of the RCMP and the Immigration Branch assumed that it would be better in the national interest to reject all refugees, rather than to allow a single nazi or Soviet agent into the country. That this position was both morally wrong and often unnecessary, even from a security standpoint, does not change the fact that the arguments of Blair and Wood carried great weight in the War Committee of Cabinet. Canada was at war, and its government was committed to military goals and not humanitarian considerations. No doubt, the country's refugee policies between 1939 and 1945 were "legalistic and cold," but these policies must be understood within the context of total war, which does not encourage fine distinctions.[96]

Notes

1. Gerald Dirks, *Canada's Refugee Policy: Indifference or Opportunism?* (Montreal, 1974), 255

2. Irving Abella and Harold Troper, *None Is Too Many: Canada and the Jews of Europe, 1933-1948* (Toronto, 1982), 281

3. David Wyman, *Abandonment of the Jews: America and the Holocaust, 1941-1945* (New York, 1984), 5, 11. Although some Canadian ethnic historians have dismissed Wyman's book, the reviews in leading American periodicals and newspapers have in general been laudatory. See, for example, *The New York Times Book Review*, 16 December 1984.

4. Dirks, 44-98. The plight of over 400,000 refugees who fled from Germany between 1933 and 1939 has been discussed in many books and articles. One aspect of this subject which has received particularly good treatment is the movement of Jewish intellectuals to Great Britain and the United States. In Britain, for example, the Society for the Protection of Science and Learning, which included many of the country's leading academics, was able to place 57 refugee scholars in permanent

positions and another 155 in temporary positions between 1933 and 1936. Francis Carsten, "German Refugees in Great Britain 1933-1945," in G. Hirchfeld, ed., *Exile in Great Britain: Refugees from Hitler's Germany* (New Jersey, 1984), 15-16; Lewis Coser, *Refugee Scholars in America: Their Impact and Experiences* (New Haven, 1984). By contrast, no academic organizations were established in Canada to assist refugee intellectuals in their difficult task of gaining Canadian domicile. Lawrence Stokes, "Canada and an Academic Refugee from Nazi Germany: The Case of Gerhard Herzberg", *Canadian Historical Review*, LVII, 2 (June 1976), 150-70; Michael Bliss, *Banting: A Biography* (Toronto, 1984), 252

5. National Archives of Canada (NA), Privy Council Papers (PCO), vol. 779, proceedings of the first meeting of the Canadian National on Refugees (CNCR), 6 December 1938

6. NA, W.L.M. King Papers, memorandum to King prepared jointly by the Departments of External Affairs and Mines and Resources, 29 November 1938; statement to Cabinet by T.A. Crerar, 12 December 1938, cited in Dirks, 57. Australia's more positive response towards Jewish refugees has often been compared to Canada's negative stance. There was, however, strong opposition to the Australian government's offer in 1938 to bring in 15,000 refugees over a period of three years. The American consul general in Sydney reported to his superiors in June 1939 that this plan "faced organized and stubborn resistance" and that there was a distinct possibility "that a serious flare up against the Jew may take place in centres where he is seeking to establish himself." United States National Archives (USNA), State Department, decimal files, 840.48 (Refugees), report of Thomas Wilson, 15 June 1939

7. Abella and Troper, 47. Between January and November 1938 the amount of capital required for a Jewish family to enter Canada increased from $5,000 to $15,000. Moreover, even gifted intellectuals and businessmen who claimed that they had knowledge and inventions which would enhance Canadian industrial performance were usually rejected. In April 1939, A.L. Jolliffe, commissioner of immigration, informed administrators at the National Research Council that his department was "rigidly enforcing the regulations in order to conserve for Canadians any available openings ... if our universities are qualifying men along similar lines." Nor did scientists at the NRC appear concerned with this closed door policy. NA, Records of Immigration Branch (IR), vol. 166, f. 28-2-2, Jolliffe to F.G. Green (NRC), 13 April 1939 and Dr. Boyle to S.J. Cook, 15 April 1939

8. Dirks, 47. The American government was also under considerable pressure to adopt a generous policy towards the 450,000 Spanish Republican refugees who had fled to France. One group, the Non-Sectarian Committee for Political Refugees International Defence, submitted a report on 3 September 1939 urging the immediate admission of these refugees. State Department 840.48; Michael Marrus, *The Unwanted: European Refugees in the Twentieth Century* (New York, 1985), 190-93. The earlier experience of Russian Mennonite refugees desperately seeking entry to Canada in 1929 should be considered when examining Canada's response to Jewish refugees during the 1930s. See Frank Epp, *Mennonite Exodus: The Rescue and Resettlement of the Russian Mennonites Since the Communist Revolution* (Altona, 1962), and Henry Paetkau, "Separation or Integration?: The

Russian Mennonite Immigrant Community in Ontario, 1924-45," (Ph.D. thesis, University of Western Ontario, 1986).

9. King Papers, C-565668, Vincent Massey to O.D. Skelton, 23 February 1939; IR, 665668, memorandum for King, 6 March 1939, and Blair to Skelton, 9 March 1939

10. *Ibid.*, Blair to Skelton, 9 March 1939. The role of F.C. Blair in keeping Jewish refugees out of Canada has been dramatically and extensively discussed in Abella and Troper. In particular they claim that "For Blair the term 'refugee' was a code word for Jew." (8). While they provide abundant evidence to support their contention that the director of the Immigration Branch was "an anti-Semite" (7), perhaps they do not place sufficient emphasis on Blair as "a narrow-minded bureaucrat" who saw his job primarily as one of keeping immigrants out of Canada during the Great Depression.

11. As early as 1936, the Canadian government had made some attempt to deal with the internal threat of fascist and nazi subversive activity. But it was not until the appointment of the Committee on the Treatment of Aliens and Alien Property in the spring of 1938 that sustained planning occurred. NA, Norman Robertson Papers, vol. 12, Skelton to commissioner of the RCMP, 26 March 1936 and file 134, memorandum of 24 May 1939. J.L. Granatstein provides a brief but informative account of these developments in *A Man of Influence: Norman Robertson and Canadian Statecraft, 1929-68* (Toronto, 1981), 80-91. In recent years the threat of nazi and fascist subversion has been the subject of a number of articles and books. Perhaps the best accounts are Robert H. Keyserlingk "'Agents Within the Gates': The Search for Nazi Subversives in Canada during World War II," *Canadian Historical Review*, LXVI, 2 (June 1985), 211-238; Jonathan Wagner, *Brothers Beyond the Seas: National Socialism in Canada* (Waterloo, 1982); J.A. Ciccocelli, "The Innocuous Enemy Alien: Italians in Canada during World War Two," (M.A. thesis, University of Western Ontario, 1977).

12. NA, Canadian National Committee on Refugees Papers, vol. 1, Proceedings of Conference, 6-7 December 1938; summary of interview with the Hon. T.A. Crerar

13. Lita-Rose Betcherman, *The Swastika and the Maple Leaf: Fascist Movements in Canada in the Thirties* (Toronto, 1975), 32-44, 128-35. Early in 1939 the nationalist St. Jean Baptiste Society submitted a petition against Jewish immigration to Canada which was signed by 127,364 people.

14. Toronto *Globe and Mail*, 15 November 1937. This allegation was fiercely repudiated by the Committee on Gentile-Jewish relations which claimed that, of the approximately 15,000 members of the Communist Party of Canada, only about 450 were Jewish. Ivan Avakumovic, *The Communist Party in Canada: A History* (Toronto, 1975), estimated that about 15 percent of the party membership was Jewish during the late 1930s, while Erna Paris, *Jews. An Account of Their Experience in Canada* (Toronto, 1980), put the figure at 20 percent.

15. The report "Nazi-Fascist Activity and the Naturalization Act" was prepared for Cabinet. It outlined in some detail how the Naturalization Act could be utilized as

an effective security device. Robertson Papers, vol. 12. This and subsequent reports indicated that candidates for naturalization were only checked by the RCMP for extreme left wing views. *Ibid.*, memorandum of Robertson to J.F. MacNeill, 20 March 1940

16. *Ibid.*, Tim Buck to King, 23 February 1939. One person who kept Robertson informed about fascist and nazi activities in Canada was Fred Rose, a prominent Montreal communist. According to Robertson, he was "glad to receive any information he [Rose] could furnish." This was passed on to the officer in charge of RCMP intelligence as "information of this kind which was unlikely to reach the RCMP direct." NA, Lester B. Pearson Papers, N1, vol. 13, Robertson to Pearson, 29 October 1946, cited in Granatstein, 85

17. King Papers, C-257904, report, "On a Wartime Intelligence Service"; Robertson Papers, vol. 12, Robertson to Skelton, 28 August 1939; King Papers, C-153968, Walter Turnbull to King, 6 December 1939. Under PC 2667, members of the Communist Party and its affiliates such as the Ukrainian Labor Temple Association were declared illegal and their members subject to arrest. Between 1940 and October 1942, 250 men and women associated with the Canadian communist movement had been incarcerated. Most were placed in internment camps operated by the Canadian armed forces. William and Kathleen Repka, *Dangerous Patriots: Canada's Unknown Prisoners of War* (Vancouver, 1982); William Kolasky, *The Shattered Illusion: The History of Ukrainian Pro-Communist Organizations in Canada* (Toronto, 1979)

18. NA, J.L. Cohen Papers, f. 2761, "Rex vs Arthur Bortolotti," Cohen to J.S. Woodsworth, 29 November 1939, Cohen to Oscar Kitching (President of the Windsor Trades and Labour Council), 1 March 1940, petition of February 1940, Cohen to Crerar, 16 May 1940. On the use of deportation as a weapon against left wing radicals, see Barbara Roberts, "Shovelling Out the 'Mutinous': Political Deportation from Canada Before 1936," *Labour/Le Travail*, XVIII (Fall 1986), 77-110.

19. *Toronto Star*, 26 February 1940. Emma Goldman, the famous anarchist writer and organizer, assumed a major role in the defence of Bortolotti and her other "boys." After three years of trying to raise money for the Loyalist cause in Spain, she had returned to Toronto and become involved in this, her last crusade. Cohen Papers, Goldman to Cohen, 10 November 1939; Candace Falk, *Love, Anarchy and Emma Goldman* (New York, 1984); Donald Avery, *'Dangerous Foreigners': European Immigrant Workers and Labour Radicalism in Canada, 1896-1932* (Toronto, 1979)

20. Robertson Papers, vol. 12, Blair to Skelton, 6 March 1940, Skelton to Blair, 6 March 1939. Significantly, P.J.A. Cardin, acting for the minister of justice, supported the Skelton-Robertson position when he informed Blair that the Canadian government should not "consider deporting individuals from Canada who, if returned to their own country, would be liable to be put to death or incarcerated in a concentration camp for their political or religious beliefs." Cohen Papers, Cardin to Blair, 9 March 1940

21. Robertson Papers, vol. 12, Skelton to Blair, 27 March 1940

22. Cohen Papers, Blair to Cohen, 28 April 1940. Emma Goldman did not long survive the successful defence of her boys. She died in Toronto on 14 May 1940. In March 1940, Loring Christie reported from Washington that "no person has been deported from the United States under the present administration to a totalitarian country if he would suffer there for his political convictions." Robertson Papers, vol. 12, Christie to Robertson, 12 March 1940. Christie also indicated that Blair's suggestion that the FBI should be asked for information on Bortolotti was quite irregular: "my impression is that in the past, when the police authorities in Canada have wanted information from the FBI, they have communicated with them direct."

23. Robertson Papers, vol. 12, report of the Inter-Departmental Committee on Alien Propaganda, 30 July 1939, report of the Committee on the Treatment of Aliens and Alien Property, August 1939, Robertson to Skelton, 24 October 1939, Skelton to Commissioner Wood, 11 December 1939, Robertson to Dr. E. Coleman, undersecretary of state, 1 August 1940

24. At this meeting Commissioner S.T. Wood of the RCMP complained that the force was not receiving the "full cooperation and information in regard to refugees entering Canada." IR, vol. 856, f. 555-4, memorandum of A.L. Jolliffe, May 1940

25. In 1938, at the request of the British government, Canada agreed to accept about 1,200 Sudeten German refugee families. Public opposition to this movement, and the nazi occupation of Czechoslovakia, meant that only about 600 of these refugees actually came to this country. Jonathan Wagner, "British Columbia's Anti-Nazi Germans: The Tupper Creek Refugees," *BC Studies*, XXXIX (Autumn 1978), 3-19; Andrew Amstatter, *Tomslake: History of the Sudeten Germans in Canada* (Saanichton, BC, 1978)

26. Ronald Stent, *A Bespattered Page: The Internment of His Majesty's 'Most Loyal Enemy Aliens'* (London, 1980), 27-29, 47-56; Hirschfeld; A.J. Sherman, *Island Refuge: Britain and Refugees from the Third Reich 1933-1939* (London, 1973); J.P. Fox, "Great Britain and the German Jews 1933," *Wiener Library Bulletin*, XXVI (October 1972), 40-7; Miriam Kochan, *Britain's Internees in the Second World War* (London, 1983)

27. Stent, 70-74; Michael Seyfert, "His Majesty's Most Loyal Internees," in Hirschfeld, 163-91

28. A survey of the King Papers showed that of 228 petitions there were 78 from veterans organizations, 41 from municipal councils, 22 from Boards of Trade, 17 from service clubs, 22 from patriotic organizations, and 11 from various citizen meetings. Significantly, the majority of the petitions came from Ontario (70) and British Columbia (65). King Papers, C-257922-50

29. The federal government made it clear that vigilante action by patriotic organizations would not be tolerated. *Ibid.*, C-257918, memorandum for King, 27 May 1940

30. *Ibid.*, C-239964, memorandum for King, 22 May 1940; *ibid.*, C-239972, memorandum for King, 27 June 1940. These reports not only criticized various private organizations for over-reacting to the situation, but also charged that Premier Hepburn of Ontario had made irresponsible statements. In defending their position, federal authorities emphasized that "no single serious act of sabotage has yet occurred in Canada." *Ibid.*, C-239072

31. Christopher Andrew, *Secret Service: The Making of the British Intelligence Community* (London, 1985), 448-97; Keyserlingk; C.V. Harvison, *The Horsemen* (Toronto, 1967), 86-101; John Sawatsky, *Men In the Shadows* (Toronto, 1980), 60-80; C. Rivett-Carnac, *In Pursuit of Wilderness* (Toronto, 1965), 290-6; Granatstein, 80-91. Federal authorities also utilized the expertise of the Polish and Czechoslovakian consuls in gathering information, especially about communist activities in Canada. Robertson Papers, vol. 13, Skelton to Wood, 21 December 1939

32. Robertson Papers, vol. 13, memorandum of 15 June 1940

33. *Ibid.*, Skelton to Blair, 29 March 1940

34. *Ibid.*, Skelton to Wood, 22 October 1940. A similar case occurred in March 1942 when the Canadian minister in Washington reported that Professor Louis Rougier, "an active Vichy propagandist" in the United States, was trying to get permission to visit Quebec. Pearson also acknowledged that he had received information about Rougier from both the American State Department and the British Security Coordination Office. NA, Department of External Affairs Records (DEA), vol. 2168, Pearson to H.H. Wrong, 13 March 1942

35. Robertson Papers, vol. 13, Blair to Skelton, 8 November 1940; *ibid.*, Skelton to K.M. Mahoney, 2 December 1940

36. See Sheldon Spear, "The United States and the Persecution of the Jews in Germany, 1933-1939," *Jewish Social Studies*, XXX (July 1968), 216-41; David Wyman, *Paper Walls: America and the Refugee Crisis, 1938-1941* (New York, 1968); Leonard Dinnerstein, *America and the Survivors of the Holocaust* (New York, 1982); Henry Feingold, *The Politics of Rescue* (New Brunswick, 1970).

37. Robertson Papers, vol. 12, Christie to Robertson, 12 March 1940

38. Wyman, *Paper Walls*, 184-5

39. *Ibid.*, 186-87; Feingold, 14, 130-5

40. Wyman, *Paper Walls*, 188. In June 1940 Merchant Mahoney, the *chargé d'affaires* in Washington, reported that the Senate had endorsed the Smith Omnibus Anti-Alien Bill "virtually without debate and without division." Robertson Papers, vol. 13, Mahoney to Skelton, 24 June 1940. The Smith Act went further than other American laws in dealing with sedition since it applied in peace as well as in wartime. The act was only used twice during the Second World War. Its notoriety is primarily associated with the successful prosecution of the eleven top leaders of the Communist Party in 1949. The following year, the Supreme

Court of the United States declared that the Smith Act "was a constitutional means for the society to protect itself." Sanford Unger, *FBI* (Boston, 1975), 131

41. Wyman, *Paper Walls*, 187. Ironically, in November 1939, Jackson had chastised the recently created House Committee on Un-American Activities for their irrational "witch hunt" for subversives. This spirited stance attracted favourable comment from officials of the Department of External Affairs. Robertson Papers, vol. 13, Skelton to chief of the General Staff, 30 November 1939

42. Wyman, *Paper Walls*, 193. Breckenridge Long was in many ways similar to F.C. Blair in his determination to keep Jews and other 'troublesome' refugees out of the country. But did that make him an anti-Semite? According to Wyman, "The record does not show him to be overly negative toward Jews simply because they were Jews. He appears to have had good relations with the more conservative Jewish leaders — that is, the ones who did not rankle him or openly criticize him." *Abandonment of the Jews*, 191. According to Feingold, "Long somehow linked Communism and Jewish internationalism." (135)

43. Wyman, *Paper Walls*, 189-205

44. *Ibid.*, 205

45. IR, f. 673931, Wrong to Robertson, 31 May 1941. The security argument was also used by Blair to oppose the entry of some 300 Polish rabbinical students and their teachers (the Yeshiva boys), who had gained temporary sanctuary in Japan. Abella and Troper, 85-95

46. Stent, 70; Seyfert, 163-91

47. Stent, 50-8

48. In July 1936 the British Cabinet had discussed whether they should suppress nazi and fascist organizations in Britain. The following year consideration was given to curtail the propaganda activities of the German and Italian consuls. Fox, 55; Stent, 20-2

49. Andrew, 479-81

50. Stent, 200-60; Paula Jean Draper, "Muses Behind Barbed Wire: Canada and the Interned Refugees," in J. Jackman and C. Borden, *The Muses Flee Hitler* (Washington, 1983), 271-9. See also Dr. Draper's article in this volume.

51. Eric Koch, *Deemed Suspect: A Wartime Blunder* (Toronto, 1980), 222; DEA, 621-BF-40, Hayes to Panet, 9 August 1940

52. Canadian authorities were extremely critical of the British removal policy. On 2 August 1940, for example, Skelton complained about the "indiscriminate shipments of internees to Canada," while on 10 October 1940 Norman Robertson lamented "the difficulties of the Canadian position in trying to cope with a problem it did not create." DEA, 11252, f. 11-1-5, Skelton to Panet; King Papers, C-248518, memorandum of Robertson for King. See also Stent, 217-20; Koch, 190-3.

53. A report by General Panet in September 1940 indicated that there was a large number of professionals among the interned Jewish refugees. King Papers, C-248516, report of the Cabinet sub-committee dealing with internees from Great Britain, 12 September 1940. A complete inventory of "the academic talent" is provided in Koch, 146-73. Among those released in December 1940 were Hans Kahle, former commander of the Eleventh International Brigade during the Spanish Civil War and Dr. Klaus Fuchs, who was part of the British scientific team that had access to the most secret atomic bomb secrets. In 1950 Fuchs was exposed as a Soviet spy. H. Montgomery Hyde, *The Atom Bomb Spies* (London, 1980), 93-116. A second group of 274 internees was returned to Britain in February 1941, and an additional 330 in June. Stent, 75-125

54. Repka; Reg Whitaker, "Official Repression of Communists During World War II," *Labour/Le Travail*, XVII (Spring 1986), 135-66

55. DEA, vol. 6577, f. 1-2-10, memorandum of Military Intelligence, M.D. 3, 15 January 1941. Many of the internees had Canadian contacts. In one case, Hazen Sise, who had been in Spain with Dr. Norman Bethune, corresponded with an internee who had served with the International Brigade. NA, Hazen Sise Papers, Sise to Gerhard Rosenberg, 17 December 1940

56. King Papers, C248516, report of the Cabinet sub-committee, 12 September 1940

57. DEA, vol. 6577, f. 1-2-10, Stethem to W.G. Scully, 21 May 1941

58. Throughout 1941 the Canadian National Committee on Refugees, along with a number of other organizations, pressured the Canadian government to adopt a more flexible approach towards the internees. CNCR Papers, vol. 5, Hayward to Dr. Muriel Roscoe, 6 January 1941; Koch, 149-50. The question of proper documentation for 'stateless' refugees was examined by British and Canadian officials in January 1941. It was decided that the Home Office would issue certificates which would make it possible for the internee to emigrate to the United States, or remain in Canada on a temporary basis. DEA, 6577, f. 1-2-10, Blair to Robertson, 31 January 1941; IR, 673931, #2, Blair to N.H. Vernon, associate director general, Industrial Security Branch, Department of Munitions and Supply, 10 September 1942

59. DEA, 621-AF-40. Joliffe to Robertson, 27 October 1943

60. Koch, 190-1

61. DEA, 621, AF-40, report of Immigration Branch, 13 August 1943

62. King Papers, C292064, report of Colonel Fordham, 11 December 1942. Koch provides a rather negative image of Colonel Fordham: "Like Blair he was a man of his time who reflected prevailing attitudes. No doubt he hated the Nazis in Germany, but the presence of a few Nazis in a refugee camp was not as serious as the far more weighty issue of 'communist trouble-makers'." (227)

63. NA, Department of National Defence Records (DND), vol. 2159, f. 54-27-35-60-1, President Cody to J.L. Ralston, December 1942. Actually, during the fall of

1941 the ever-cautious Norman Robertson had warned the prime minister "of exempting aliens from compulsory training for home defence" since it might "spur the latent xenophobia in this country, and easily take on an anti-Semitic twist because a large proportion of recent immigrants ineligible for naturalization (and therefore for military service), are Jewish refugees from Europe." King Papers, C-239998, memorandum of Robertson, 14 November 1941

64. Canada, House of Commons, *Debates*, 22 February 1943 and 7 April 1943; DND, 2159, 54-27-35-60-1, Church to Ralston, 25 March 1943. King Papers, C-240021, Ralston to Church, 17 March 1943. By March 1944 the government had agreed that "declarant enemy aliens could be enlisted in the Canadian Armed Forces providing that their declaration of intention had been accepted by the Secretary of State ... subject ... to investigation and report by the Intelligence Officers in accordance with military regulations." *Ibid.*, Ralston to Cody, 14 April 1944.

65. As early as August 1940, the National Research Council was considering whether some of the internees might be "absorbed into university laboratories in Canada." NA, National Research Council Papers (NRC), vol. 170, 32-1-54, Mackenzie to Panet, 19 August 1940; *ibid.*, 32-1-97, Synge to Webster, 13 January 1943

66. *Ibid.*, Webster to Synge, 27 January 1943, Synge to Webster, 12 February 1943, Mackenzie to Synge, 18 February 1943. Mackenzie was not being entirely candid about the role that refugee scientists were assuming in either the American or British war effort. According to Margaret Gowing, *Britain and Atomic Energy, 1939-1945* (London, 1965), by October 1940 "enemy alien scientists such as Peierls, Frisch and Simon were already making great contributions to British atomic energy research." (54)

67. DEA, 621, AF-40, memorandum of 13 October 1943. Robertson was quick to assure the director of prisoners of war "that an adequate check from the point of view of security, shall be maintained with respect to refugees released in this country." *Ibid.*, Robertson to Streight, 29 October 1943

68. *Ibid.*, Wilson to King, 2 December 1943. See also Ken Craft, "Canada is Righteous: A History of the Canadian National Committee on Refugees and Victims of Political Persecution," (M.A. Thesis, Carleton University, 1987).

69. On 13 May 1941 the Cabinet had decided to consider individual releases if sponsors could be found who would guarantee the maintenance of the internees. The order-in-council (10 December 1943) only granted them temporary entry permits. Dirks, 90; Draper, "Muses," 276

70. In July 1939 External Affairs had attempted to modify the immigration regulations which specified that refugees who were "registered under the United States quota laws as intending immigrants [were] definitely excluded from temporary admission into Canada". It appeared, however, that neither Canadian nor American immigration officials wanted any changes in this procedure. PCO, file 779, Robertson to Skelton, 3 July 1939. Sir Hermann Bondi was a young scientist who later became scientific adviser to Britain's Department of Energy. Stent, 224-50; Draper, "Canada," 275

71. Paterson's most innovative strategy was to transport those internees who had qualified under the American quota, or who had close relatives in the United States, to Newfoundland where they would be released. In theory, they could then apply for entry to the United States. By the summer of 1941, however, American regulations now excluded refugees who had close relatives in territory under the control of Germany. On 11 January 1942 Blair informed his minister that the American secretary of state had emphatically stated that "American immigration laws do not permit further liberalization." IR, 673931, #1

72. DEA, 621-AC-40, Robertson to Pearson, 28 July 1944, and Pearson to Robertson, 22 August 1944

73. Dirks, 93-95; Abella and Troper, 142-158; IR, 673931, #3, memorandum of Robertson, 15 October 1944

74. King Papers, C-292985, memorandum of Robertson, 10 June 1943; DEA 5127-EA-40, internal memorandum, 28 August 1943; IR, 673931, #9, Jolliffe to minister 17 July 1945

75. IR, 673931, #1, memorandum of Blair, 29 April 1941; proceedings of the Senate Committee on Immigration and Labour, 1946, 82. In June 1941, the Czechoslovakian consul general in Ottawa was able to secure the entry of some skilled technicians who had been stranded in Vichy, France. IR, 673931, #1, Pavasek to Blair, 17 July 1941

76. Dirks, 91

77. IR, 673931, #1, memorandum of Blair, 29 April 1941, and Blair to Robertson, 16 September 1941; proceedings of the Senate Committee on Immigration and Labour, 1946, 77-85

78. Winnipeg *Free Press*, 17 June 1943

79. Abella and Troper, 157-62. IR, 673931, #3, Blair to Rive, 17 February 1943

80. Dirks, 93-5

81. *Ibid.* In October 1943 the Canadian government re-opened its immigration office in Lisbon and once again appointed Odilon Cormier as its representative in Lisbon. According to Abella and Troper, when selecting the 200 Jewish families, "Cormier invoked all the Immigration Branch's restrictions when making his calculations — health standards, racial quotas and family composition" (164). They might also have mentioned the security dimension. In 1942, when examining Polish refugee technicians in Lisbon, Cormier had been instructed that he should pay particular attention to "their technical abilities and their political views." IR, 673931, #3, Blair to Rive, 17 February 1943

82. Montreal *Gazette*, 10 March 1944; Abella and Troper, 162-3

83. IR, 673931, #3, *Le Bavard*, 26 November 1943, translated and summarized by the RCMP. The editor of the paper, Joseph Menard, had been associated with the Quebec fascist movement prior to the war.

84. Herbert Quinn, *The Union Nationale* (Toronto, 1963), 100, 126. Strong opposition to the entry of large numbers of refugees was also evident in Ottawa. On 6 April 1944, Robertson wrote Pearson in Washington "that various members, principally from Quebec, have tabled petitions received from their constituencies expressing opposition to post-war immigration.... In many cases also there is mingled with this an opposition to allowing entry of refugees in which it would not be too unjust to suspect an anti-Semitic bias." DEA, 5127-40

85. IR, 673931, #3, report of Duncan (RCMP), 23 November 1942, and Assistant Commissioner F.J. Mead to Blair, 2 February 1943. The records do not indicate whether Azachs was ever admitted to Canada.

86. *Ibid.*, report of Duncan for Blair, 13 March 1943

87. DEA, 5127-40, Wood to St Laurent, 1 June 1944

88. *Ibid.*, St Laurent to Robertson, 7 June 1944, Robertson to St Laurent, 10 June 1943, Robertson to Jolliffe, 21 July 1944

89. IR, 673931, #9, Robertson to Jolliffe, 13 November 1944

90. *Ibid.*, Jolliffe to Robertson, 23 March 1944, memorandum of Jolliffe, 22 September 1944, Jolliffe to minister, 17 July 1945

91. *Ibid.*, Wood to Jolliffe, 29 December 1944, and Jolliffe to Wood, 7 February 1945

92. As Gerald Dirks and other immigration historians have pointed out, it is not possible to discover exactly how many European refugees entered Canada between 1939 and 1945 since immigration statistics did "not distinguish between regular immigrants and refugees." Dirks, 97. In a 1941 memorandum F.C. Blair provided his own definition of refugee: "In the first place there is no such term as 'refugee' in our statistical compilation.... Our statistics are kept mainly by race. The League of Nations adopted a definition which was not strictly adhered to and the Evian Conference ... adopted an entirely different definition of 'refugee.' The term has come to include pretty much every person who is seeking to change his place of residence, not only because of war, but because of economic, racial and religious difficulties. From this angle, practically all the people who come to Canada, whose homes originally were in Europe, belong to the refugee class." IR, 673931, #1, Blair to Jackson, 21 February 1941

93. PCO, vol. 83, I-50-2, J.A. Glen to Cabinet, 15 October 1945. Donald Avery, "Canadian Immigration Policy Towards Europe 1945-1952: Altruism and Economic Self-Interest," *Zeitschrift der Gesellschaft fur Kanada-Studien* (1986), 37-56

94. Ironically, one of the justifications for the rapid entry of the Polish officers and men was that they would alleviate an immediate labour shortage. Hume Wrong of

External Affairs also pointed out another factor: "The fact that the Polish soldiers would be coming to Canada as agricultural labourers or lumber workers to take the place specifically of German prisoners of war who would be shipped back, would diminish or remove the danger of political controversy". Donald M. Page, ed., *Documents on Canadian External Relations*, 12: *1946* (Ottawa, 1977), 377, Wrong to Humphrey Mitchell, minister of labour, 14 May 1946

95. Abella and Troper, 281. David Wyman, in both *Paper Walls* and *Abandonment of the Jews*, emphasizes the security dimension. See also Richard Powers, *Secrecy and Power: The Life of J. Edgar Hoover* (New York, 1987), 235-40.

96. Andrew, 477-9; Stent, 70-74, 220-225; Wyman, *Abandonment of the Jews*, 7-15, 189-91; Abella and Troper, 284; Granatstein, 84-91

Weird Science: Scientific Refugees and the Montreal Laboratory

Robert Bothwell

The origins of Canada's nuclear programme are usually taken to lie in co-operation between Canada, Great Britain and the United States, a co-operation that was symbolized by the establishment in 1942 of the Montreal Laboratories and, later, by the construction of the first reactor outside the United States, ZEEP, at Chalk River. That this represents one level, and an important one, of Canada's atomic history is not in doubt. Yet it is an incomplete story, for the Montreal laboratory included more than British or Canadian or, in a few cases, American citizens. It was, like its British and American counterparts, a truly multi-national organization. It included refugees from half the countries of Europe, refugees who were not merely incidental in providing valuable technical knowledge, but who were central to its functioning and even to its creation. They were also almost entirely responsible for the laboratory's checkered history, and what might have been its premature demise.

The real beginnings of the Canadian atomic story may be found in the Collège de France in Paris in the late 1930s. There a link between heavy water and uranium was developed, with the idea of building a "boiler" using uranium fuel and a heavy water moderator to start up a sustained but controlled chain reaction. It is not our purpose here to explain the travelling patterns of slow and fast neutrons, merely to observe that the theory of the French "boiler" was plausible, with heavy water serving as a kind of neutron tonic.[1]

The team at the Collège was formidable. Its leader was Frédéric Joliot-Curie, son-in-law of the great Pierre and Marie Curie, the discoverers of radium. He was assisted by, among others, two immigrants to France, Hans von Halban, Austrian in origin, but a refugee since Hitler's annexation of his native country in 1938, and Lew Kowarski, a Russian displaced during the chaos that followed the Bolshevik Revolution of 1917. Halban was distinctly the senior of the two, the child of a scientific family, with a taste for a cosmopolitan atmosphere, for "high society," and for independence. His sense of his own worth was highly developed; it was not unjustified, for Halban was not a negligible physicist. Kowarski, on the other hand, had had to live by his wits, and had made his way late to science. The route he followed, the only one available, made him a laboratory assistant, a disciple to a man, Halban, who was actually, at 31, a year younger than his apprentice. It was an odd relationship but not, at that stage, an unhappy one.[2]

Both men were in full accord about one thing: that deuterium, heavy water, was the key to a successful chain reaction. They and Joliot took out patents on their discoveries, a point that would later be of considerable importance. When war broke out, their experiments continued, with the assistance of the French government, which conveyed 185.5 kilograms of deuterium from Norway to France just before the former was overrun by the Germans. Perhaps the most important effect of this escapade was that the heavy water was denied to the Germans. With it the scientists intended to build a prototype for a power reactor; with it their government intended to have them build a bomb.[3]

The invasion of France in May and June 1940 forced the scientists to take flight, carrying with them their heavy water, at first for central France and then for the port city of Bordeaux, where the French government had taken refuge. The government chose to capitulate, but some individuals preferred to fight on. Joliot was among those who stayed; Halban and Kowarski and their families joined the exodus. They were loaded, with their heavy water, onto a British coaler, under the command of the twentieth earl of Suffolk. After an uneventful voyage, they disembarked at Falmouth and were promptly put on a train for London. There most of the Frenchmen were placed in a railway hotel under official protection. Halban, explaining that he never stayed anywhere but the fashionable Mayfair Hotel, hailed a taxi, and proceeded there with his family in tow and his worldly possessions strapped to the roof.[4]

The Frenchmen had their knowledge, their heavy water and their patents; the rest the British would have to supply. It was natural for the British to integrate their guests into their own atomic research, and that is what happened. Before the end of June, Halban and Kowarski were sent to the university town of Cambridge, where the Cavendish Laboratory had long been a centre of atomic physics. They continued their work on heavy water and uranium reactors, as part of a larger British programme, which drew on the resources of the chemical multinational, Imperial Chemical Industries, or ICI. The association with ICI gave Halban and Kowarski's work an industrial dimension, and even led them, in 1941, to take out a "master patent" on their work. The possibility of a German bomb was a further spur to activity.

The British government concentrated authority over its atomic research under a committee called MAUD, an acronym that stood for nothing in particular. To the committee it seemed that Halban and Kowarski's heavy water-slow neutron research was a sideline, with only the remotest explosive possibilities.[5] But Halban, Kowarski and other continental European refugees helped give Britain an early start in atomic research, earlier than the United States and earlier than Canada, where George Laurence, with the assistance of a summer time associate, was working on a model of an atomic pile.[6]

During 1940 Halban's boiler improved its chances. By December there was "strong evidence" that his experiments would be successful in producing "element 94" — plutonium — and there was reason to hope that the plutonium so produced would "fissure."[7] But while it seemed that there was promise in Halban and Kowarski's work, the result so far as war purposes were concerned was questionable. Even if their reactor produced plutonium, what advantage would plutonium confer on its makers? And where would they get enough heavy water? There the Americans might be helpful, and so might the Canadians, for some heavy water was in prospect at a smelter at Trail, BC.[8]

The MAUD committee did not conclude that the Halban-Kowarski research was likely to have military significance during the likely course of the current war. It did conclude that a nuclear explosion could be produced, that a bomb of feasible size (25 pounds) could be built, but that the most promising avenue was through the construction of a separation plant for Uranium 235. This should get the highest priority. As for Halban and Kowarski's conception of a uranium reactor, or "uranium boiler," it probably could furnish reliable energy, once certain technical problems, such as controlling the reaction, were out of the way. Given the newly stimulated American interest in heavy water, it would be logical to transfer Halban and Kowarski and their work to the United States, so that they could pursue it close to the sources of heavy water and uranium. The report suggested that plutonium derived from the boiler might yet prove attractive, but as yet its fissile capabilities were unproven. As the British official historian has observed, the MAUD committee laboured in ignorance of work simultaneously taking place in the United States that did just that.[9]

Hans von Halban visited the United States early in 1942. The Americans, he reported on 16 March, had completely surpassed the British in resources devoted to atomic research. His team at Cambridge was outnumbered, and to some extent outclassed. Where in Cambridge it was difficult to unearth a mechanic, the Americans had them by platoons. In Cambridge he had not even been able to procure a lathe, while in America it was a matter of going shopping.[10] What should be done? Arthur Compton, the director of the Chicago Metallurgical Laboratory, had two suggestions. Perhaps the British could send over an independent team — Halban's — to work with the Americans, bringing their patents with them. Alternatively, he would welcome Halban and one or two others of his team to Chicago, where they would join the Americans as specialists in heavy water research. "In this case," as Halban noted, "all patents arising would belong to the Americans."

Halban raised the possibility of a trans-Atlantic move with Wallace Akers, an ICI official who had become director of the British "Tube Alloys" (another meaningless title) project. Halban suggested that location in the United States was most desirable, but if that proved unfeasible that he might, just possibly, be situated across the border in Canada.[11] Akers was skeptical but Halban was persistent. "In Canada," Akers protested, "facilities [are] believed practically non-existent and certainly inferior to those in England. Have you any reasons for Canadian suggestion other than advantages of geographical [proximity] British and American workers?"[12]

Akers' harsh assessment of Canada's facilities was not wrong. Why then did Halban persist? The immediate answer is that the American terms were unacceptable. Halban and one or two others could come, and if they did they would no longer be British agents. Akers liked that prospect no more than Halban liked the idea of becoming a subordinate in somebody else's laboratory. From the conjunction of their dislikes there now flowed a commitment to a new idea: Canada. The Americans would go along with a Canadian-based team, so Compton assured Halban. There would be plenty of supplies for all, "something a man of Compton's power can arrange," or so Halban, with an inbred acceptance of hierarchy and influence, believed. There was a basis for Canadian research in the National Research Council (NRC) experiments under Dr. George Laurence, a Cambridge-trained physicist whom Halban found to be "a very likable and brilliant man." Preliminary inquiries at the Council revealed that the Halban team, as Halban increasingly thought of it, would be "very well received."[13]

At the end of July 1942 Sir John Anderson, the minister in charge of Tube Alloys, gave his reluctant consent. Terms were negotiated by Malcolm MacDonald, the British high commissioner in Ottawa, who was told early in August to take up the matter with C.J. Mackenzie, president of the NRC, who was already informed about the subject and had indicated a desire to receive a British laboratory.[14] The British now asked Mackenzie to confirm this. At a meeting with R. Gordon Munro of the British High Commission on 17 August, Mackenzie did that and more, by securing the consent of C.D. Howe, his minister.[15]

This seems unremarkable enough, but in fact what happened in the summer of 1942 is remarkably opaque. The Canadian government agreed in August 1942 to accept and support a lab-full of British scientists. They were to work on atomic research. That much is clear. What is not clear is what the laboratory and its director proposed to do when they got to Canada, how long they expected to stay there, and what the object of their work was to be. The Canadian government for its part — through the agency of Howe and Mackenzie — expected to pay many if not most of the lab's expenses, and to send Canadian staff, both scientific and support, to join the laboratory team.

Speaking in 1961, C.J. Mackenzie argued that his object in welcoming the British project was to get in "on the ground floor of a great technological process for the first time" in Canadian history.[16] This is not surprising. Any administrator, especially in science, was bound to consider the longer term. Mackenzie was anxious to extend Canada's scientific prowess. He was aware that the country was considered to be a scientific backwater. Yet that does not answer the question of what Mackenzie considered the "great technological process" to be. He was not especially expert in atomic physics, though he later claimed to have kept abreast of developments in the field.[17]

Mackenzie understood the difference between the uranium separation project and the heavy water project. He had grasped the MAUD committee's argument that the heavy water method was uncertain even if promising, and he therefore believed that the heavy water project was not for "military application." Plutonium, as he understood it, was a laboratory creation available in only the minutest quantities. This had once been true, but American technology had found a way to larger quantities. And so when he claimed that "Nobody considers using 94 [plutonium] for military purposes," he was doubtless right. The only problem was that his argument was already a few years out of date.[18]

It seems reasonable to conclude that the relevant authorities in Canada had an imperfect understanding of what they were committed to accomplish. This limitation would prove a handicap in the future; in 1942 nobody seems to have suspected that some further explanation might be in order. For good or ill, Canada and Britain were now to conduct a joint atomic energy project which C.J. Mackenzie, the responsible Canadian, does not seem to have believed to be urgent for the war effort. This attitude helps to explain his decision to service the atomic project as an arm of his National Research Council, a body that was still run very much on the principles of peacetime penny-pinching. It was, moreover, wartime government policy to combat inflation by holding salaries and wages to the minimum consistent with survival, a policy that Mackenzie wholeheartedly supported.[19]

This, then, was the organization chosen to hold the purse strings for the Anglo-Canadian atomic project. At the top were a series of committees, political and administrative. Under them, there was never any question that Halban would be director. He had charmed the Canadians he met in the spring of 1942. To Mackenzie he may have brought a whiff of a distant and glamorous world of prize-winning science, the world of the Curies and Lord Rutherford and their renowned laboratories. Below the "directors" came a technical committee (scientific policy committee), chaired by Halban, and consisting of the division heads from his team: chemistry, physics, theoretical and applied, and engineering. All the effective division heads were brought over from England; in addition there was George Laurence, the NRC's senior man in atomic physics, who represented the Canadian interest.[20] The British were to pay the salaries of those they sent, while the Canadians were expected to pick up the tab for the rest. That, the British estimated, would be around $450,000 a year, a figure conveyed to Howe back in August. The British would send some thirty scientists and twenty-five technicians. The rest would have to come from Canada.[21]

The organization of the laboratory was well underway. Halban had his mind made up as to the senior appointments. To head experimental physics, he wanted Pierre Auger of the Sorbonne. For chemistry he chose F.A. Paneth, a German refugee teaching at Durham in the north of England; while Paneth was not himself a nuclear chemist, he was senior and very distinguished, and he knew the junior men in the field. G. Placzek, who would direct nuclear physics, came from Czechoslovakia. Some complications arose from the fact that some of Halban's team were enemy aliens, but by late 1942 the Canadian authorities in London had adjusted to the fact that not all Germans or Italians were "enemies" in the true sense.[22] The only native Englishman in the lot was R.E. Newell, who transferred from ICI. Because of a quarrel between Halban and Kowarski, the latter was omitted. The omission may be attributed to problems in Halban's personal relations with Kowarski, but it may also have to do with the patents which Halban more and more tended to regard as a personal property rather than a collective trust. Kowarski would in any case come later, and under unanticipated circumstances.[23]

The departure was not easy. Canadian immigration formalities had to be gone through, and teams of approved doctors were despatched from London to Cambridge to tap shins and gaze into ear drums. Then families had to pack, and stay packed until appropriate convoy arrangements were ready, for this was the height of the German "wolf pack" submarine campaign. Some saw the dark hand of favouritism in the order of their families' passage, while others were forbidden to travel on the same ship in case all the available talent in a given area was swallowed up in the Atlantic.[24]

Equipment was another headache since most of it could not be had in Canada and had to be transported and reassembled. They had even to find a new laboratory. It was situated in Montreal, Halban's preference, and was first located in a mansion on Simpson Street. In March it moved up the hill to the Université de Montréal's recently-constructed but unoccupied campus. After more than three years of war, Montreal appeared to the British team to be the land of milk and honey, or at least of life without blackout curtains, but with neon, steaks, and well-stocked stores. Dionne's, the fashionable grocery store on St. Catherine Street, became a particular favourite. Better still, the British-paid staff found that they drew not merely their British salaries (the top, Halban's, being equivalent to $7,500 Canadian; the bottom, that of a laboratory assistant, the equivalent of just under $900) but an overseas allowance, untaxed. Their salaries, Halban told them, were to be considered "a war secret," and should be kept from their lesser-paid Canadian colleagues. It followed that evenings and weekends afforded them a style of life which even in peacetime would have been enviable.[25]

A Canadian staff was assembled, and Halban also recruited in the United States. This was difficult since the Manhattan Project had already vacuumed up most of the available supply of physicists and chemists. There were, however, a few left over, mostly of foreign origin and some already in British employ. The most notable of these was Bertrand Goldschmidt. He was a refugee from France, forced to flee the anti-semitic laws of the wartime Vichy regime. Trained in Madame Curie's laboratory, Goldschmidt was one of the world's few qualified radiochemists. In the summer and autumn of 1942 he was working, as a British-paid scientist, in the chemistry division of the Chicago metallurgical project. Goldschmidt was present when, in August 1942, the American chemist Glenn Seaborg announced that he had actually seen a tiny fraction of plutonium — rose-coloured. In Montreal Goldschmidt joined Jules Guéron, another Parisian refugee, and a group of Canadian and British chemists.[26]

To complete the team, Halban and Akers picked among physicists and mathematicians. Bruno Pontecorvo, who had fled from Italy to the United States via Paris in the 1930s, was fed up with teaching in Oklahoma; "the British Security people," Akers told Perrin in December 1942, "give [him] an unusually enthusiastic report." And so Pontecorvo came, to add strength in physics and a gregarious personality to the group. Pontecorvo, however, came at British expense; Mackenzie resisted attempts to place him and other American-recruited staff on Canadian salary. It was probably just as well. The Canadian staff soon came to understand that their salaries were substandard as compared to those of the British-paid refugees, a grievance that Mackenzie steadfastly refused to confront.[27]

The future of the laboratory depended on the impression it could make on the Americans, and that turned on whether the heavy water route would actually be useful during the war. Controlling the supply of American co-operation was General Leslie Groves, an unattractive but undeniably efficient engineer officer. To Groves Halban made his pitch;

in talking with the general, he sketched out sixteen different kinds of reactors, carrying a price tag that must have made Groves shudder. But as Groves knew, in December 1942 the Americans had independently achieved a spontaneous chain reaction. Nuclear fission was an accomplished fact.

Halban's operation therefore became a side-line. The Americans immediately clamped tight restrictions on contacts with the Montreal laboratory, and although some information and, especially, some plutonium slipped through to Canada thanks to Goldschmidt, most real contact ceased. It would not be resumed except on the Americans' own terms, which gave priority to their own experiments and admitted the British only for certain very limited purposes. The British refused to accept the terms and appealed to political authority. The impasse lasted from January 1943 until March 1944, and it conditioned everything that transpired in Montreal with a conviction of ultimate futility.

Adversity did not, in this case, breed camaraderie. C.J. Mackenzie saw the dispute as an Anglo-American problem, to which the solution lay in agreeing to the Americans' terms. C.D. Howe refused to be bothered with it, while the British authorities seemed unable to make any dent on the Americans' conviction that the Montreal experiments were marginal at best and pointless at worst. To Mackenzie the laboratory became a political embarrassment; the embarrassment increased when he learned that the Americans — at least those at the top of the Manhattan Project — disapproved of the way it was composed. "I gathered," Mackenzie wrote after a visit to Washington in January 1943, "that they were particularly apprehensive of discussing all the details and know-how with the Montreal group which is really not an Anglo-Saxon group, and that they felt there was no guarantee that the various nationals — French, Austrian, Russian, Czechoslovakian, German, Italian etc, could be guaranteed for any length of time. I think," Mackenzie added, "that there is a good deal to be said for their point of view." It is unlikely, under the circumstances, that Mackenzie made much of an effort to defend his multi-national laboratory against the charge that its members were unreliable if not disloyal.[28]

The refugees were beginning to have second thoughts about Canada too. It had its blemishes, prominent among them a dependence on the Americans for a large variety of supplies, which it could not make for itself. Its civil service, starved during the 1920s and the Depression, seemed unable to free itself from an obsession with costly and time-consuming economies which demanded that tenders be called for any important scientific supply and even for items in common use, such as safes or desks. Months passed before the Montreal laboratory could procure even material produced in Canada. And if it came from abroad, it would be held up in customs until some higher authority intervened with the right form.

It fell to Halban to cope with these problems, since the administrative staff Mackenzie provided appeared unable to do so. He passed from puzzlement to frustration to irritation to outrage and back. All these emotions were duly conveyed to Mackenzie's subordinates at NRC, and when they appeared to be unable or unwilling to help, to Mackenzie himself.[29] Halban's response was not calculated to improve his standing with his Canadian hosts. But if Halban did not understand the Canadians neither did they understand him, or make much effort in that direction.

Early in January 1943 Halban was approached by a senior administrator attached to his laboratory by NRC. There was a problem, the official reported. It was that a new secretary was Jewish; should she therefore be assigned to work with a Jewish scientist? Halban, who may have been astonished at the question, replied that none of his scientists were of the Jewish faith, whatever their racial origin might be. On reflection, he concluded that "If we succeed in the mixing of people of different origin it can only be to the advantage of the team spirit."[30]

It might have helped if Halban had been able to apply the spirit as well as the formula of tolerance in his own laboratory, but as the spring and summer of 1943 wore on it became obvious that his was not a happy ship. Halban blamed the crew; the crew in turn blamed the captain, whom many of them came to regard as a combination of Bligh and Queeg, if not worse. For the British staff, Halban's connection with ICI did not help, nor did the habit of an ICI-derived division head who liked to encourage the staff by remarking, frequently, "Don't you know there's a war on?" It did not help that Halban's relations with the senior Canadian on staff, George Laurence, descended to the glacial by late March 1943. Laurence, however, was by no means the only object of the laboratory director's wrath, as Halban discovered inadequacies at all levels from the clerical to the scientific.[31]

It would be pointless to reiterate here all the incidents that plagued the first eight months of the Montreal laboratory after it opened its doors on Simpson Street in January 1943. What is important is not the particular incidents, or even their justification or provocation, but their repetition. This meant that by the time Anglo-American atomic relations started to mend, after Churchill and Roosevelt met at Quebec in August 1943, the situation at the Montreal laboratory conspicuously failed to improve. That fact now came to the attention of higher authorities in Britain, for as part of the settlement between the two principal atomic powers, Wallace Akers, the principal ICI representative on the Tube Alloys project, was removed as liaison between Halban and London.

When Sir John Anderson visited the Montreal laboratory on 9 August, he told the scientists that they could proceed with their work.[32] He assumed they would. But when James Chadwick, a Nobel laureate, who had just been appointed to replace Akers, arrived on the 27th, and was shown around the laboratory, he heard a different story. Chadwick was uneasy at what he found. To Mackenzie he commented that the administration was excessive for the size of the laboratory. The NRC director was alert to signs that the Canadians in the laboratory were being excluded from any real understanding of what was afoot, and for that he blamed Halban's "aggressiveness and acquisitiveness." Later, in Ottawa, Chadwick revealed that he did not "hold a high regard for Halban"; with that understanding, Mackenzie decided that he liked the British scientist very much.[33]

Chadwick and Mackenzie understood that Groves would be the man to decide where the Montreal lab fitted in. Unfortunately, Mackenzie could not control or direct Halban to make the best possible impression, and when Groves and his staff visited the Montreal laboratory to discover what the British contemplated its role to be, they were disappointed. As he had done the previous year, Halban outlined a range of possibilities, ranging from homogeneous slurries to a uranium hexafluoride "boiler." Groves was not impressed. Halban conveyed the impression of a man who did not know his own mind, and Groves did not propose to waste time and money on him. After leaving the meeting with Halban, the American delegation resolved to offer little or no help to the Montreal project. Second thoughts were less drastic. Information was exchanged, though not on plutonium separation, and some materials were lent to the Canadians. Taken all in all, however, the Americans had not been convinced that the Anglo-Canadian project

227

should proceed beyond the laboratory stage. After a certain point, in other words, there was no future, and that point was drawing closer and closer. It was a disaster for Halban, whose standing with his Canadian partners sank further: "in relation to Chadwick he is a mere child," Mackenzie wrote, "and a temperamental one at that."[34]

So thought Chadwick, and so thought Halban's staff. The two combined forces, because of Chadwick's custom of dining with junior staff on visits to Montreal, and before long the senior scientist had a large repertoire of Halban stories, all tending to reinforce the impression that the laboratory director was arrogant, uncomprehending and unfeeling. Halban must go, but there was no point in dismissing him unless and until it was known whether his laboratory was to go too.

There was a price attached if the laboratory was to stay. The next stage was a large reactor, similar to the experimental ones the Americans were building. As far as they were concerned, the British and Canadians had to pay, and in the range of $25-50 million, depending on which option was selected. "It seems that either we undertake the fifty million dollar project or we close up Montreal," Mackenzie wrote in December 1943, after a conversation with Chadwick. If only the Americans would give the Canadians the responsibility for the entire heavy water scheme, then it could all be justified. But as Halban learned the next month, on a visit to Chicago, the Americans had designed and were building their own heavy water reactor (known as Chicago Pile 3, or CP-3). They expected to have it operational in six months.[35]

If the Montreal laboratory was not to be overtaken by this event as well, it had to do something, fast. But doing something cost money, which only the Canadians would or could supply. The Canadians would not give money unless they were certain the Americans were cooperating. The Americans would not co-operate unless they thought the laboratory would be useful in the war effort. Every passing month, however, brought the end of the war closer, and made the military argument for contributions less plausible.

To Chadwick it seemed obvious what the solution must include. Halban must go. Difficulties in the laboratory, between the laboratory and NRC, and between the British and the Americans, seemed inextricably bound up with Halban's personality. If the personality could be sacrificed, then just possibly the Americans would take it as a new beginning and abate their refusal to work with the Anglo-Canadian laboratory. After talking to Chadwick in December, Mackenzie expressed the thought to his diary: "if Cockcroft will agree to come to Montreal, Groves will agree to the proposal." In J.D. Cockcroft, Chadwick held a card of unknown value. As a university physicist Cockcroft was unsurpassed. His reputation was high. His acquaintance with the United States was good. The Cambridge physicist had visited Washington only recently, and had been propositioned by Chadwick. Cockcroft was willing to come to Canada, if ordered to do so, provided the laboratory was in a position to benefit from American research and supplies.[36]

Time was running out in more ways than one. Morale in Montreal was plummeting. Halban's reaction was to isolate himself or, if cornered and questioned, to flop back and feel his pulse to see whether disagreement was bringing on heart palpitations. At the beginning of February, George Laurence, irritated by a fresh disagreement with Halban, sent Mackenzie a letter detailing Halban's lapses as a laboratory director and demanding that something be done to resolve the situation before the laboratory collapsed under the weight of accumulated tensions. The other French scientists were restless; one was leaving to join General de Gaulle's headquarters, while the others were showing signs of boredom and preoccupation. Without the Americans they could see no future.[37]

That meant Groves. To Chadwick, Groves seemed a better bet than his civilian masters, who demanded that joint sponsorship be limited to war projects relevant to the current war. And if Halban had not made up his mind as to a proper design for a large reactor (the director was at that moment considering only a pilot plant), Chadwick had: it should be heavy water and natural uranium, and its cost, as he and Mackenzie had discussed it, would be about $50 million.

The other cost, of course, was Halban's departure. With that in train, Chadwick negotiated a final settlement with Groves, giving the Montreal laboratory access to necessary information and heading off the departure of its staff and the dissolution of the laboratory itself. John Cockcroft would come instead, with Lew Kowarski as an additional piece of baggage, and Halban would depart. He did not, at first, go far: merely down the hall to be director of physics. But within seven months he was gone for good as the result of a rash trip to Paris to consult with Joliot-Curé. He only succeeded in undermining what little prestige was left to him in Canada, while ironically failing to impress

Joliot. He lived out his days, after his eventual return to Europe, in Oxford, as a client of a grateful British government.

They had reason to be grateful. Halban's principal contribution to the Montreal project, and hence to British and Canadian atomic energy was a quixotic determination to be his own man, to head a major research team, and to prove the validity of the heavy water line of research that he and his colleagues had undertaken at the Collège de France. A more modest or more realistic man might not have persevered, but Halban's persistence, combined with his business and political connections through ICI with the British government, had made Sir John Anderson, according to a famous story, decide that "That is the horse that I will back." Ever afterwards Hans von Halban was known as "Harry the Horse," at least to his many detractors. Halban was nevertheless the prime mover in establishing the Montreal laboratory, and it is to him that Canada owes the origin of its first nuclear project.[38]

Notes

1. Margaret Gowing, *Britain and Atomic Energy* (London, 1965), 83

2. *Ibid.*, 65-6; B. Goldschmidt interview, Ottawa, 4 June 1986

3. *Ibid.*, 137

4. Ronald W. Clark, *The Birth of the Bomb* (London, 1961), 99-101

5. *Ibid.*, 53-4

6. Public Record Office, Kew (PRO), AB1/30, J. Cockcroft, "Report on a discussion with Dr. G.C. Laurence and Dr. Stedman, 22-11-40," and R.H. Fowler, Central Scientific Office, to C.J. Mackenzie, NRC, 28 January 1941

7. AB1/157, Cockcroft to R.H. Fowler, NRC, 28 December 1940

8. Gowing, 72

9. The MAUD committee report is reproduced in *ibid.*, 394-436.

10. AB1/105, Halban, "Possibilities of the Development of the Boiler in UK and USA," 16 March 1942

11. AB1/34(a), Halban to W. Akers, 27 April 1942

12. *Ibid.*, Akers to Halban, 5 May 1942

13. *Ibid.*, Halban to Akers, 13 and 14 May 1942

14. AB1/207, Anderson to M. MacDonald, 6 August 1942; National Archives of Canada (NA), C.J. Mackenzie Papers, vol. 1, Mackenzie Diary, 9 June 1942, giving the first indication that "S-1" (atomic research) might move to Canada

15. Betty Lee, "The Atom Secrets," *Globe Magazine*, 28 October 1961, quoted in John Porter, *The Vertical Mosaic* (Toronto, 1965), 432

16. Quoted in Porter, 431-2

17. C.J. Mackenzie interview, NRC, 17 August 1977

18. AB1/137, R.E. Newell to Akers, 28 October 1943

19. See W. Eggleston, *National Research in Canada* (Toronto, 1978), for a general account of the Council's history.

20. Mackenzie Diary, 17 August, 2 September 1942; J.F. Hilliker, ed., *Documents on Canadian External Relations*, vol IX: *1942-1943* (Ottawa, 1980), 453-4, M. MacDonald, "Aide-mémoire in Connection with Proposed Transfer of 'Team 94' from United Kingdom to Canada," 2 September 1942. Mackenzie's proposed organization, dated "September," is in AB1/123/80521.

21. *Ibid.*; NA, C.D. Howe Papers, MG 27, III, B10, vol. 14, f. S-8-2 (32), "Record of a Meeting Held in the Lord President's Room," 12 October 1942

22. Halban Diary, 4 January 1943

23. Goldschmidt interview, Paris, 10 June 1985; Spencer R. Weart, *Scientists in Power* (Cambridge, Mass., 1979) 191-2; AB1/123, Akers to Perrin, n.d.; AB1/50, Perrin to Akers, 2 December 1942, and Akers to Perrin, 7 December 1942

24. The relevant correspondence, some of it reflecting little credit on its writers, is in AB1/50.

25. Colin Amphlett interview, Harwell, 29 May 1985; Fred Fenning interview, Reading, June 1985; Halban Diary, 25 January 1943

26. B. Goldschmidt, "Les premiers milligrammes de plutonium," *La Recherche*, 131 (mars 1982), 369; Goldschmidt and Jules Guéron interviews, Paris, 10 June 1985; Leo Yaffe interview, Montreal, 17 July 1985

27. AB1/50, Perrin to Akers, 2 December 1942; AB1/123, Akers to Perrin, 9 December 1942

28. Mackenzie Diary, 18 January 1943

29. See, for example, Halban Diary, 27 January 1943, dealing with the appointment of a switchboard operator, or 25 March in which one of Mackenzie's officials "tries in vain to appease me."

30. Halban Diary, 9 January 1943

31. Amphlett interview; Goldschmidt interview; George Laurence interview, Deep River, 24 July 1985

32. Mackenzie Diary, 9 August 1943

33. Mackenzie Diary, 27 and 29 August 1943

34. US National Archives (USNA), RG 77, Box 60, Entry 5, MED Decimal File, A. Compton to L. Groves, "Exchange of Information with British at Montreal, September 18, 1943," 9 October 1943; Mackenzie Diary, 19 September 1943

35. See AB1/137, Newell to Akers, 28 October 1943, in which Newell described his attempt to persuade Mackenzie of the possibility of building a plant in Canada, at a price somewhere between one and ten million pounds. It was in this conversation that Mackenzie revealed his ignorance of the military purpose of such a plant. For the conversation with Chadwick, see Mackenzie Diary, 8 December 1943; for Halban's visit to Chicago, CRNL Records, 5000 Montreal Labs, Reactor Concepts, vol. 1, "Report on the Visit to Chicago," 8 January 1944.

36. At a meeting in Montreal on 19 December 1943, Mackenzie made it plain that he thought that Canadian money would depend on "what co-operative arrangements could be worked out." Mackenzie Diary. On Cockcroft see Eggleston, 94-5, and G. Hartcup and T. Allibone, *Cockcroft and the Atom* (Bristol, 1984), 126.

37. CRNL Records, 1500 Montreal Labs, File Admin, vol. 2, minutes of 5th meeting of the TCRR, 25 January 1944; this meeting led directly to Laurence's letter, Laurence to Mackenzie, 4 February 1944; Fenning interview; Amphlett interview; Goldschmidt interview.

38. M. Pryce interview; Weart, 206

Commentary

Howard Palmer

The study of ethnic minorities and the Second World War raises a number of questions of concern to students of ethnicity and Canadian society. The war era provides a framework for an in-depth case study of majority-minority relations in crisis. During the war, the Japanese and Doukhobors in British Columbia, Jehovah's Witnesses in Quebec, Hutterites in Alberta, and Germans and Italians in various parts of the country, all found their loyalty questioned and their rights threatened. Hostile majorities demanded government action against these groups.

Under the fluid circumstances of wartime, attitudes were altered, either negatively or positively, toward many different ethnic groups in the country. Wartime hostility was new neither to the Germans nor to the small pacifist religous — Hutterites, Mennonites, and Doukhobors. But the Italians, who had been on the "right" side during the First World War, now found themselves associated with the enemy powers. Similarly, attitudes toward the Japanese shifted significantly; the war years were the most intense period of anti-Japanese sentiment in Canadian history as racist feeling toward the Japanese merged with nationalism and fears of enemy subversion.[1]

The crisis conditions of wartime brought into stark relief some of the broad patterns of ethnic relations in the country. The harsh treatment afforded the Japanese in comparison to either Italians or Germans, the more favorable treatment given the Mennonites in comparison to the Doukhobors, the harshness of the treatment of Jewish refugees — all show the underlying virulence of racism in Canadian society. Minorities such as the Japanese, Jews, and Doukhobors suffered doubly when racism and nationalism fused.

In many ways, wars put democracy on trial since they test the guarantees that governments have promised their citizens. Do the guarantees of individual rights afforded by Canadian citizenship continue to have meaning when loud voices call upon the government to suppress minorities in the name of the public good? Broken government promises to minorities, whether on schools, conscription, or fundamental civil rights, are recurring issues throughout Canadian history. But during the Second World War, the government broke numerous promises and felt justified in doing so — behavior that is still a matter of public interest and debate.

One of the most important issues arising from a discussion of ethnic minorities and the Second World War is that of the contradiction between Canada's stated war aims and the government's treatment of some of its minorities. How do we account for the discrepancy between official beliefs and official policy? The sweeping measures taken against the Japanese Canadians, which included not only uprooting and expulsion from the coast of British Columbia but dispossession and deportation, are actions wildly inconsistent with Canada's stated belief in democracy. In their range and thoroughness, these measures are startlingly similar to those enacted by totalitarian states. This similarity inevitably raises questions concerning the attitude of Canadians toward the war. Did Canadian authorities and the public really believe they were fighting for democracy, or were they just fighting as colonials who had gone to war because Britain had?

One is puzzled by the apparent lack of agonizing among civil servants and politicians concerning, on the one hand, the government's outright racism in their policies toward Jewish refugees and Japanese Canadians, and on the other, their statements about fighting a war for democracy. Were government officials and politicians deluding themselves, or just the Canadian public? Or were democratic principles viewed as applying only to "whites"? Perhaps Watson Kirkconnell's defence of the racial unity of *European* peoples (as cited in the article by William Young), which was intended by the Bureau of Public Information as an effort to promote Canadian unity, is in effect a clear, if unintended, statement of the limits of Canadian unity.

In studying the treatment of ethnic minorities in Canada during the Second World War by the Canadian government, we are left with the disturbing realization that Canada responded to the challenge of war with one of the most magnificent efforts by any of the Allied powers, but also with a wide range of repressive measures, toward German, Italian, and Japanese Canadians and toward some religious and ideological minorities.

The strong revisionist analysis of government policy towards Japanese Canadians written by J. L. Granatstein and G. A. Johnson deserves response. In making the case for the relocation of the Japanese, the authors admit that there was no concrete evidence of subversion. They argue that the Japanese consul hoped to gain the support of Japanese Canadians and attempted to do so, but provide no evidence that he gained their support. Granatstein and Johnson are forced to fall back for evidence of disloyalty either on what might have happened if the government hadn't acted, or on actions taken by Japanese Canadians largely *in response to* the evacuation. The fact that the RCMP immediately interned 38 Japanese Canadians after Pearl Harbor is hardly proof of disloyalty, particularly when the authors have already shown that the RCMP's intelligence work was extremely weak. In order to make their case, they must show that the RCMP had real reason to institute a policy of internment. Keyserlingk and Ramirez show in their articles how flimsy the RCMP's case was against individual Germans and Italians, and that in these cases internments were based primarily on public pressure and in-group vendettas rather than on evidence of disloyalty. Nor is the evidence of disloyal feelings cited by Granatstein and Johnson from the autobiography of Nakano very compelling since the latter's account of positive attitudes among the Issei toward Japan is based largely on those who were in government internment camps. Many of them had been interned for protesting the splitting up of their families by the Canadian authorities.[2] Their resentment against Canadian authorities for this treatment, and the hope of some that Japan might win the war, so they could be freed from internment and united with their families, is hardly surprising under the circumstances. The fact that some Japanese in Hawaii may have wished for a Japanese victory is not evidence of similar sentiments in Canada, when placed against the overwhelming number of accounts by Japanese Canadians which stress their pre-war loyalty to Canada and their outrage (particularly by the Canadian-born majority) at being considered enemy aliens by the country from which they were desperately seeking acceptance.[3]

The Granatstein-Johnson assessment of the military threat also leaves some questions unanswered. Even if local military commanders, reflecting local prejudices, felt the Japanese to be a threat, the key issue is how Ottawa military authorities regarded the Japanese military threat in February of 1942 when the Canadian government decided on the evacuation. Perhaps the perceived military threat from Japan loomed larger later in the year, with the Japanese military victories cited by Granatstein and Johnson, but the Chiefs of Staff military appreciation on 19 February, 1942, five days before the decision to uproot the Japanese Canadians, stated unequivocally that there was no threat of invasion.[4] The authors are right in concluding that stories of Japanese treatment of Canadians in Hong Kong affected Canadian public opinion, but the primary thing that the Hong Kong events and the Japanese Canadian relocation have in common is that the victims in both cases were mainly Canadian citizens.

The "realist critique" treads a thin line between finding the evacuation explainable and finding it excusable. The essence of the argument seems to be that, in wartime, people are guilty until proven innocent. But should Canadian citizens be responsible for the ignorance of their government?

If the evacuation was in fact done because of military necessity, why was it so all-inclusive? Why did it include ninety year olds, the blind, orphans and the mentally ill? If military necessity was the main reason for the evacuation, why was the property of Japanese Canadians confiscated and sold? Why did the government attempt to deport them back to Japan, and why did it refuse to allow Japanese Canadians to return to British Columbia until years after the war ended? Are these government actions simply unrelated measures, or do they show in fact the inner logic of government policy? Granatstein's earlier assessment, in his fine biography of Norman Robertson, of the government's policy toward Japanese Canadians as a "disgrace to a liberal democracy"[5] stands the test of time.

The topic of war, ethnicity, and the Canadian state opens up a range of research questions which suggest possibilities for further study. The question of the interaction between ethnicity and Canadian politics is a topic much neglected by historians and political scientists. How much political power did various minorities have? Obviously some, such as the Mennonites, were able to lobby more successfully than others, such as the Jews. Why did the Canadian government not know more about its ethnic minorities when, in fact, people of non-British, non-French origin made up twenty per cent of the population in 1941 and immigrants of non-British, non-French background made up a substantial portion of the prairie farm population and the industrial work force from Ontario to the west coast? Why was this key aspect of Canadian loyalty and unity such a low priority for the Canadian government? Why did the government have to rely so much on British-born go-betweens with the ethnic groups? It is revealing (as noted by N.F. Dreisziger) that when the government set up the Committee on Cooperation in Canadian Citizenship in the Nationalities Branch, to encourage unity and support for the war effort among non-British ethnic minorities, its members were all of British origin.

Another important policy dimension of the war is the relationship between public opinion and the attitudes of politicians and bureaucrats in the formulation of government policy. Some bureaucrats such as F.C. Blair, as Draper and Avery show in their papers on the Jewish internees, obviously wielded a great deal of power. Were Blair and his colleagues simply enforcing regulations that the public and politicians actually wanted in place? To what extent were bureaucrats simply following orders, or did their own prejudices play an important part in shaping the nature of government policy? This book contains some tantalizing evidence on this topic.

The book also just begins to touch on the key question of the impact of government policy on the groups themselves. Luciuk and Kordan show how the nature of Ukrainian ethnicity in Canada has been shaped by the state; government attempts to influence Ukrainian organizational life have had ramifications that have continued to the present. Ramirez gives a sensitive portrayal of the impact of government policy on Montreal Italians. But most of the authors focus on government policy, and view the topic through the lens of official government records. With regard to the Mennonites, it would be very instructive to follow the debate over alternative service at the local level in Mennonite communities. One wonders how the Mennonite churches responded to individuals who joined the armed forces? How did local Mennonite communities react to news of the deaths of young Mennonite men in the armed forces, or deal with the issue when those accidentally killed before being sent overseas were sent home for burial?

What was the impact of the war on ethnic nationalism and relations with the homeland of eastern European groups whose aspirations for an independent homeland were aroused by changing world politics? Macedonians, Slovak and Armenians, among others, had developed strong organizations in Canada in the inter-war years to support the cause of the liberation of their homelands, and these organizations gained added impetus during the war. The war also had important consequences for both inter-and intra-ethnic relations. The trauma of war helped bring together, at least temporarily, groups such as the left and right wing Hungarians and Croatians, who had been deeply divided during the depression. Tension between the two main rivals in the Chinese community, the Chinese National League and the Chinese Free Masons, was also submerged during the war. Traditional ethnic rivals, the Serbs and Croatians, cooperated in wartime relief for Yugoslavia. The whole question of the relationship of ethnic groups to their homeland, and of the impact of the war on their relations with each other, is one that this book just begins to explore.[6]

Other important issues deserving exploration include the role of different ethnic groups in the Canadian armed forces. Enlistment rates, integration and upward mobility are virtually unstudied. The role of the British and American governments in influencing Canadian government policy toward its minorities is mentioned in several of the papers in this volume, and deserves more systematic discussion. One factor only partially touched on here is the economic dimension of government policy toward minorities. Wartime manpower shortages were important in the evolution of attitudes toward interned Jews and Japanese Canadians and toward the relocated Japanese and the Mennonite conscientious objectors.

From a comparative perspective, the topic of minorities during the war could be expanded further through comparing the treatment of ethnic minorities with that of religious and ideological minorities. Government policy toward Jehovah's Witnesses and communists could be compared with treatment of Japanese Canadians in an attempt to weigh the relative strength of anti-radical, religious, and racial prejudices in determining government policy. Avery's article demonstrates in an intriguing fashion the way some of these prejudices overlapped, as in the case of anti-semitism and anti-communism. The Avery and Granatstein-Johnson articles also touch on an important comparative dimension when they compare Canadian policy to that of the United States. This comparison is particularly important since Canadian officials paid close attention to American policy and often tried to harmonize their policy with American, but it also enables us to isolate uniquely Canadian attitudes and policies. In comparing government policy toward the Japanese in Canada and the United States, we see important similarities and differences. Roger Daniels' work in this area has highlighted significant aspects of political and legal differences between the two countries that led to divergent outcomes.[7]

Finally, while acknowledging the dangers of a presentist approach to this subject, scholars must address the moral dimension of Canadian policy toward minorities during the war. Some would argue that the government's detention of enemy aliens and suspected subversives was reasonable under the circumstances of wartime. It is clear from this study, however, that with only rare exceptions, government policy was riddled with ignorance and uninformed prejudice toward several minorities who were considered security risks. That government policy mirrored widespread public prejudices may be an accurate assessment, but not an adequate response to criticism of government policy. Should government officials not be judged by their own standards? Were many of their actions not directly contrary to the democratic ideals which they presented as the basis of the Canadian war effort?

The tragedy of the war was not only the tremendous loss of human life and resources on the battlefields of Europe. The tragedy was also the tremendous waste of human resources in Canada, brought on by Canadian government policy. There was an immense squandering of the human resources of Jewish internees, of pacifists, and of Japanese Canadians. People's careers and education were interrupted, their possessions robbed, their families broken up. The RCMP spent a tremendous amount of time censoring the letters of husbands and wives who had been separated by government policy, and enforcing petty regulations as Japanese Canadians attempted to cope with one wave after another of restrictions which misguided government officials heaped on them.

The issue of Canada's treatment of ethnic minorities during the Second World War is one with which Canadians still have not fully dealt. The question of redress for Japanese Canadians is not simply a Japanese-Canadian issue, any more than the Holocaust (though of a very different moral magnitude) is a Jewish question. As noted by the National Association of Japanese Canadians in their brief to the Canadian government, "the Government of Canada betrayed not only Canadians of Japanese ancestry, but also the men and women it was sending to Europe and Asia to fight and die in the cause of justice and equality for all."[8]

The papers in this book do an admirable job of illuminating a long-neglected feature of Canadian society during the Second World War. The question of protection of minorities during periods of crisis is one that Canadians, attempting to live together in a pluralistic society, must continue to address.

Notes

1. For a discussion of some of these changing patterns see H. Palmer, "Ethnic Relations in Wartime: Nationalism and European Minorities in Alberta during the Second World War," *Canadian Ethnic Studies*, XIV, 3 (1982), 1-23

2. See Ann Sunahara, *The Politics of Racism* (Toronto, 1981), 66-71

3. The accounts by Sunahara and Kenneth Adachi, *The Enemy That Never Was* (Toronto, 1976) are based on dozens of interviews with Japanese Canadians as well as on the existing documentary sources. For another insightful account which shows the Nisei's outrage at the Canadian government's assumption of their disloyalty, see Roy Miki, ed., *This is my Own: Letters to Wes and Other Writing on Japanese-Canadians, 1941-1948 by Muriel Kitagawa* (Vancouver, 1985)

4. "Under present conditions an invasion on either coast is not considered to be a practicable operation of war. The presence of the British and United States fleets in the Atlantic precludes the possibility of a large scale sea-borne expedition. The immense distances involved and the maintenance of superior United States naval forces in the American Pacific produce a similar situation in the West Coast." NA, Ralston Papers, MG27 III, B11, appreciation of Chiefs of Staff, 19 February 1942, 3

5. J.L. Granatstein, *A Man of Influence* (Toronto, 1981), 167

6. For further discussion of some of these issues, see Jean Burnet with Howard Palmer, *Coming Canadians: An Introduction to a History of Canada's Peoples* (Toronto, McClelland and Stewart, 1988) ch. 8

7. Roger Daniels, *Concentration Camps, North America: Japanese in the United States and Canada during World War II* (Melbourne, Fl., 1981)

8. National Association of Japanese Canadians, *Democracy Betrayed*, a submission to the Government of Canada on the violation of rights and freedoms of Japanese Canadians during and after World War II (1984), 24

Commentary

Harold Troper

In his 1931 book, *A Canadian Child's ABC*, R. K. Gordon offers a rhyming glimpse into the mindset of Canadian parliamentarians of his day.

> To Ottawa from coast to coast
> The chosen come to make the laws
> For weeks they talk about a lot
> Of different things without a pause:
> The railway line to Hudson Bay,
> Taxes and tariffs, and immigration,
> The great St. Lawrence waterway,
> And whether we are yet a nation.[1]

Like parliamentarians of Gordon's day, many Canadian historians today remain preoccupied with "whether we are yet a nation" or, more correctly, with documenting the historical process by which our nation-state has come into being. But, for the most part, one major aspect of Canada's emerging nationhood continues to elude most Canadian historians. Surprisingly, in detailing the historical narrative of a people who come from such a pluralism of origins, Canadian historians have paid scant attention to ethnicity and ethnic groups in Canadian society, at least in as much as they do not fall within the theme of ongoing tensions between the charter anglophone and francophone Canadian communities. As a result, the historical place of tens of thousands of Canadians whose roots reach outside the traditional mother countries has generally remained, as Robert Harney correctly points out, "in limbo between the filio-pietic writings of the ethnic community and the Canadian academic establishment."[2]

That is not to say that discussion of immigration and the consequent emergence of ethnic communities are totally ignored in the writing of

Canadian historians. Far from it. Rather, it is to argue that Canadian historians tend to see immigration and ethnic groups as issues of policy and administration. As a consequence, Canadian historical writing is largely preoccupied with the interests of the gatekeepers, ignoring those who pass through their gates. Immigrant and ethnic experience is too often depicted as little more than an undifferentiated mass infusion of unskilled labour into the national economy, a statistical smudge left by countless immigrant workers brought into Canada to serve the needs of labour intensive industry or agricultural development.

An analysis of why the immigrant and ethnic experience of a nation built by immigrants and alive with ethnic diversity should be so ignored by its historical community requires a study in its own right. Suffice to say that the real life ethnic experience of Canadians, the history of Canadian ethnic communities as they lived it — not as public servants, teachers, social workers and employers observed it — has found precious little expression in the work of the Canadian historical fraternity.

There is an exception. Ethnic communities which do not rate detailed scholarly examination in their own right become the focus of the historian's attention when they run afoul of the state machinery. This is the case in *On Guard For Thee: War, Ethnicity, and the Canadian State*. In spite of the fact that the term "ethnicity" is prominent in the volume's title, the issues examined, with several exceptions, deal not so much with the ethnicity of any particular individuals or group but with the degree of inconvenience the group or a particular set of its members caused the war-time national interest.

In this top-down gatekeepers' history, the ethnic group is seen as little more than an issue to be dealt with, a problem to be resolved. This point of view, it seems, represents not just that of war-time public officials and politicians who are so much the stuff of this volume. It would also seem to represent the views of many Canadian historians who have too readily dismissed ethnicity in Canada as the immigrant's temporary respite on the road to assimilation, a foreign import at best marginal to the development of the modern Canadian nation state. Few regard it as an historical field worthy of their own research time and effort.

Ethnicity in Canada does not depend for its survival on the sanction of Canadian historians. It has remained more resilient and dynamic over time than any wishful assimilationist model allowed. In the process it has helped fashion the Canadian social, political and economic scene far more than most Canadian historians seem yet prepared to believe.

But, what is ethnicity? To begin with, I feel it is most important to emphasize that ethnicity in Canada is not a foreign import. Ethnicity is a product of Canada — of Canadian conditions — and the Canadian ethnic group a creation of this society. True, ethnicity does involve the attempt by people sharing a common ancestral heritage, real or imagined, to preserve important cultural traditions and values over time. But it is far more than this. It is also, as historian Jonathan Sarna has observed, a process of group unification and solidarity in response to conditions and prejudices confronted in the New World. The ethnic group may thus transcend boundaries of the Old World to create a new and distinctively Canadian group consciousness.[3]

Thus, as we seek to understand the ethnic group, we must allow that identity in the New World, perhaps more than cultural preservation of traits from the Old, is crucial. Canadian sociologist Wsevolod Isajiw caps his search for a working definition of the ethnic group and ethnicity in the Canadian context by concluding that ethnicity refers to:

> an involuntary group of people who share the same culture or to descendants of such people who identify themselves and/or are identified by others as belonging to the same involuntary group.[4]

Ethnicity, Isajiw allows, is grounded partly but not exclusively in a base of shared cultural traits. Beyond culture there is one's perception of oneself and how one is perceived by others both inside and outside the ethnic group.

Extending the Isajiw definition, others point out that not only is ethnicity a phenomenon of the society which gives it home, it is also dynamic. Ethnic continuity is not dependent on a museum like preservation of a culture of the past to survive in the New World. It survives because it has an immediacy to its members, including those well beyond the immigrant generation and often those moving up the economic and social ladder. It has been noted of the United States that, in spite of a deeply ingrained civic faith in a melting pot mythology and an educational system dedicated to eradicating it, ethnicity is alive and growing as

> manifestation of the way populations are organized in terms of interaction patterns, institutions, personal values, lifestyles and presumed consciousness of

kind. The assumption of a common heritage as the essential aspect of ethnicity is erroneous.[5]

A corollary of this argument is that ethnicity exhibits itself not just in the public or corporate activities of organizationally active communities. It is also inbedded in the everyday behaviour of the individual. This may prove messy for the historian or sociologist to deal with, but is well worth considering. For example, let us consider the now dated but nonetheless still intriguing and controversial study of Mark Zborowski, *People in Pain*.[6] Zborowski's findings are based on interviews with four groups of hospitalized war veterans — "Old American", Irish, Jews and Italians — dealing with their continuing experience of pain and response to lengthy hospitalization and medical treatment. Among the researcher's key findings was that each of the four groups both understood and responded to the experience of pain differently.

To the "Old American" pain was regarded as an external attack on a basically healthy body. One does not complain; that is pointless. One resists and resists alone. It is a personal failing to give in or lose control. That is to surrender to the invader. Stiff upper lip.

For the Jew, on the other hand, one need not and indeed should not endure pain either in silence or alone. That is unnatural. Pain — physical, emotional, communal, even historical — is for the Jew not the exception the "Old American" believes. It is part of life. Pain is a common experience, one of many which bonds community members together. Therefore, there is no virtue in either anomy or stoicism. What is more, by complaining one is reaching out, signalling one's community to respond with reassuring sympathy and understanding.

According to Zborowski, the Italian sees life as filled with the shared pleasures of family, children, the dinner table, the company of old friends. That is the way life was meant to be. Pain is a spoiler. It denies one the joys of home and family. But if pain denies one pleasure, it does not end the sharing of experience with those who are close. Accordingly, those who previously shared in the pleasures of life now join in bewailing their loss. And should pain recede, this is not celebrated as a personal victory over illness. It is the joyous return of the natural order.

The Irish are different again. For them, Zborowski explains, the issue is not so much pain as it is suffering. What the Irish endure is less a challenge to the body than a test of the depth of one's spirit and the strength of one's faith. Family and friends understand this and their visits are supportive but often without reference to pain or the reasons for hospitalization. A family visit is likely to be abruptly broken off at the first sign of pain.

What does Zborowski's discussion of four ethnic groups' differing understandings of pain have to do with ethnic groups in war-time Canada? While it is obviously difficult to do justice to so detailed a study in just a few paragraphs (and readers should be cautioned to read the original before rendering a final judgement), I believe an important point is made. According to Zborowski, ethnicity and a sense of belonging to an ethnic group helps to pattern individual response to events and frame behaviour and emotions in ways conscious and unconscious. He leaves historians to consider the point that ethnicity runs deeper than the important but still often surface activities of ethnic organizations even when those organizations claim the authority to represent the community. I believe Canadian historians have generally failed to take this into account. If they ever hope to reach beyond gatekeepers' history, I believe it is imperative that they come to grips with the internal history of the ethnic community or communities being examined. To do anything less is to leave mute the voice of the people.

Unfortunately, the essays in this volume rarely look beyond the bureaucracy of state in conflict with the corporate structures of ethnic leadership. Most fail to address the impact of what ethnic identification meant in a Canada at war. The contribution by Bruno Ramirez and to a lesser extent those of David Fransen and Paula Draper stand out as exceptions.

I do not deny the need for historians to assess the state's power in determining such things as immigration policy or the parameters for ethnic group involvement in the civic culture. On the contrary. Much of my own work has explored these very issues. However, for historians to do so without at least understanding or attempting to understand the relationship of state action on the individuals and communities thereby affected seems far too narrow a scholarly exercise. Canadian historiography should be long past the point where the people should be left out of their own national narrative.

War is state enterprise. Ethnicity is not. War commands the dedication of the state's resources, capital and labour to a singular cause — the defeat of an external threat to the survival of the state. In issuing its call to arms, in rationalizing the nation's productive capacities to meet wartime needs, the state reorders the national agenda.

Ethnicity is deeply woven into the fabric of Canadian society. As wartime priorities have an impact on every aspect of the national scene, ethnic groups are not immune. *On Guard for Thee: War, Ethnicity, and the Canadian State, 1939-1945* is a step toward exploring the intricacies of that impact, but only a first step.

Notes

1. R. K. Gordon, *A Canadian Child's ABC* (Toronto, 1931)
2. Robert Harney, "Entwined Fortunes: Multiculturalism and Ethnic Studies in Canada," *Siirtolaisuus-Migration*, 3 (1984), 77
3. Jonathan D. Sarna, "From Immigrants to Ethnics: Toward a New Theory of 'Ethnicization'," *Ethnicity*, 5 (1973), 370-78
4. Wsevolod W. Isajiw, "Definitions of Ethnicity," *ibid.*, 1 (1974), 122
5. W. Yancey, E. Ericksen and R. Juliani, "Emergent Ethnicity: A Review and Reformulation," *American Sociological Review,* 44 (1976), 400
6. Mark Zborowski, *People In Pain* (San Francisco, 1969)

Commentary

John English

In 1945 Lorne Pierce, the writer and publisher, wrote *A Canadian People,* published by the United Church's Ryerson Press. Pierce lamented the divisions which marked Canada's war effort and warned that "Any sector of the nation that refuses to become a full partner in all the nation's work, in war or peace, will atrophy and die." It is, he continued, "written in the stars that people concerned only with their own ailments and wrongs, their own interests and rights, are doomed. Nature spews them out." Canadians must therefore be "willing to leave behind all that can not be readily assimilated into the new Canadian life." That was the path towards "democracy" and national greatness, one which future historians would commend. They would not approve the one urged by "fiddling politicians" who appealed to "secessionists and isolationists, to racialists and anti-war fanatics."[1]

Pierce was a poor prophet and, to many historians, he represents the "racialist" he so strongly condemned. His vision was intolerant of diversity, and he approvingly took as his text Papineau's statement that he would strive to the utmost against any government which had "the barefaced effrontery to call itself the protector of the minority."[2] Pierce wrote in the aftermath of the conscription crisis and just before the allied victory over European fascism. The importance of that victory to what nearly all Canadians understood by freedom and democracy seemed proven by the atrocities the liberators were revealing to the world; the complaint of those who, in Pierce's eyes, had delayed the victory and in some cases even threatened the Canadian contribution to it merited no future consideration. Pierce had lost the regard for minority rights reflected in the peace settlement of 1919. Were not the Sudeten Germans guilty of complicity in the destruction of Czechoslovakia? Had not the *Volksdeutsch* scattered throughout Eastern Europe betrayed their homelands, to serve the *Vaterland* they had left over a century ago? Quislings, Pétainistes, and their ilk elsewhere had immeasurably assisted the Nazi cause and would now receive the punishment they deserved.

Through this lens, the rights and even the existence of minorities appeared most faintly and, occasionally, as a smudge upon the image of Canada. Internationally, Canadian liberals worried little as minority rights disappeared in Estonia, Latvia, Poland, and, as we see in the Kordan-Luciuk paper, Ukraine. In this respect, radical and liberal historians in the 1970s and 1980s have continued the historical interpretations of the 1940s, deploring, for example, the entry of East European "ethnic" problems into the American presidential election of 1944 where political criticism of the Soviet Union damaged the Soviet-American entente.[3] To the eminent historian and self-professed liberal democrat, A.R.M. Lower, the experience of wartime had established the intrinsic value of the western liberal culture of Anglo-American democracies and had shown how alien groups within liberal societies could prove divisive and threaten liberal values themselves.[4] This prescription seemed to reflect what was occurring in North American society. Social scientists in the 1940s and the 1950s assumed that the forces of modern communication, education, and government would break down cultural differences more rapidly than in earlier times, and ethnicity rarely attracted the attention of scholars who seemed to regard the subject as archaic. In the 1960s, a "new ethnicity" was suddenly noticed and its appearance was, if anything, more surprising than the "new radicalism" of those years. As Howard Palmer has pointed out, the two were not without linkages.[5]

This book reflects its times as much as Pierce reflected his. N.F. Dreisziger's opening essay looks to the wartime Nationalities Branch for the foundations of contemporary multiculturalism, but it emphasizes the limits of that effort (a staff of two in 1943) and the difficulty in staffing the branch with competent civil servants who had some understanding of two million ethnic Canadians. The hiring and retention of that peculiar Englishman, Tracy Philipps, reflects the priority which the Canadian government in wartime attached to cultural diversity. The conclusion of W.R. Young's article that the age of multiculturalism lay far in the future seems just: the acceptance, much less the celebration, of cultural diversity contradicted many contemporary assumptions of French and English Canadians about historical change and national character.

The truth is that the Canadian government in wartime lacked the bureaucratic apparatus and the intellectual sympathy to comprehend the attitudes of ethnic Canadians and the effect of the war upon these people. Its overwhelming concern was the struggle in Europe and the Pacific and the prevention of an English-French confrontation on the issue of the war itself. Pierce talked about "civil war"; the public opinion polls with their dramatic split between English and French Canada suggested that such an unthinkable war was not impossible. J. L. Granatstein and Gregory Johnson view the Japanese Canadians from a different vantage point than the one occupied by other authors looking at specific groups. Their sources reflect and create that difference. Rather than looking forward to concepts of cultural diversity, Granatstein and Johnson enter the "mentalité" of the majority in 1941-42 Ottawa: overly-excited, aware of the sudden collapse of European democracies and the role of internal dissidence in that collapse, and resentful of domestic limits upon the defence of Canada. Their perspective explains but certainly does not attempt to justify the panic which led to the evacuation of the Japanese. The article confirms what the other articles argue: that a substantial part of the Canadian population remained *terra incognito*, if not *terra inimica*, for the Canadian bureaucratic, political, and, not least, intellectual elite.

The Canadian state entered the Second World War with a rudimentary structure which expanded haphazardly to embrace the tasks which suddenly were its responsibility. The government grasped at whatever ideas seemed to fit these tasks. Some did so admirably, as was the case with the so-called "new economics." Others were less appropriate, and in this book we can see that liberal individualism, with its tradition of progress through education, modernization, and assimilation, did not meet the requirements imposed upon the state by the existence of two million Canadians of non-English, non-French background. As Fred Dreisziger suggests, however, that same war, by extending the concept of what the state should and could do and by revealing the horrible ends towards which racism led, did more than any preceding event to further the interests of ethnic Canadians.

Notes

1. Lorne Pierce, *A Canadian People* (Toronto, 1945), 46, 61, 66

2. *Ibid.*, 54

3. One finds this view in neo-revisionist as well as the revisionists. See Daniel Yergin, *Shattered Peace: The Origins of the Cold War and the National Security State* (Boston, 1977), 83-6. An earlier revisionist view is Dian Shaaver Clemens, *Yalta* (New York, 1970). Not all agree. See Voytech Mastry, *Russia's Road to the Cold War* (New York, 1979), 247-50, and William Taubman, *Stalin's American Policy: From Entente to Detente to Cold War* (New York, 1982), 55-7.

4. Carl Berger, *The Writing of Canadian History: Aspects of English Canadian Historical Writing Since 1900* (2nd edition; Toronto, 1986), 130; and A.R.M. Lower, *This Most Famous Stream: The Liberal Democratic Way of Life* (Toronto, 1954). See also W. R. Young's paper in this book.

5. Especially in the American civil rights movement. Howard Palmer, "Mosaic or Melting Pot? Immigration and Ethnicity in Canada and the United States," *International Journal*, XXXI (1975-76), 515-8

Sommaire des articles

N.F. Dreisziger, L'apparition d'une bureaucratie du multiculturalisme: les origines de la Branche des nationalités, 1939-1941

Lorsque la Deuxième Guerre mondiale a éclaté, le gouvernement canadien ne disposait pas des rouages bureaucratiques nécessaires pour disséminer de l'information parmi les communautés ethniques et pour amener les membres de ces dernières à participer à l'effort de guerre. Pour traiter avec elles, le gouvernement de Mackenzie King comptait beaucoup sur le principal rouage existant: la police. Un certain nombre de gens se sont alors rendu compte du traitement injuste dont faisaient ainsi l'objet les immigrants et ont porté la situation à l'attention du gouvernement. Durant la seconde moitié de l'année 1940, on a commencé à élaborer des plans en vue de mettre sur pied, à Ottawa, un bureau qui serait chargé de traiter l'information destinée aux groupes ethniques et de servir de lien entre ces derniers et le gouvernement. Les principaux instigateurs de ces plans étaient Thomas C. Davis, un politicien de la Saskatchewan, et Tracy Philipps, une Anglaise en visite au pays. Toutefois, comme on n'arrivait pas à trouver un Canadien qualifié pour diriger ce bureau, la création du Service des groupes ethniques du ministère des Services nationaux de guerre a été retardée jusqu'à la fin de l'année 1941. Après la guerre, les divers organismes qui ont remplacé le service susmentionné ont poursuivi le travail qui avait été entrepris. On peut donc dire que la Deuxième Guerre mondiale a donné aux groupes ethniques l'occasion d'exercer une plus grande influence dans les affaires nationales du Canada.

William R. Young, Chauvinisme et nationalisme: les groupes ethniques canadiens face à l'échec de l'information gouvernementale durant la guerre

Peu après le déclenchement de la guerre, le gouvernement s'est efforcé de dissiper les soupçons des immigrants arrivés depuis peu au pays, particulièrement ceux qui étaient originaires de pays ennemis. Il y a toutefois eu une exception à cette règle, à savoir les Japonais qui, après le mois de décembre 1941, ont tous été littéralement "rayés" de la carte du pays. Le gouvernement, et plus spécialement ses organismes d'information, a essayé de convaincre les membres des communautés ethniques qu'ils étaient promis au plus bel avenir au Canada et que le fait d'y vivre avait fait d'eux des citoyens à part entière, qui partageaient leur destinée avec tous les autres Canadiens. Bien que ces objectifs admirables aient été poursuivis durant toute la guerre, le gouvernement n'est pas parvenu à vaincre la xénophobie latente des Canadiens anglais ou français, ni à éviter les difficultés engendrées par la rivalité de groupes ethniques peu disposés à oublier les querelles qui avaient déchiré leurs patries respectives en Europe. En conséquence, le gouvernement évoqua des raisons banales pour battre en retraite ou essaya tout simplement d'ignorer le problème.

Robert H. Keyserlingk, Briser le complot nazi: l'attitude du gouvernement canadien vis-à-vis ses citoyens d'origine germanique, 1939-1945

Durant la Deuxième Guerre mondiale, le gouvernement canadien a mieux traité les Canadiens d'origine allemande que lors de la guerre précédente et ce, même si le régime nazi d'Hitler présentait une menace beaucoup plus sérieuse que celle qu'avait posée le régime du Kaiser en 1914, si un plus grand nombre de Canadiens d'origine allemande vivaient alors au pays et si la crainte de la présence d'une cinquième colonne au Canada était très répandue. Pourtant, plus de 800 Canadiens d'origine allemande ont été internés, car, aux yeux des autorités, ils constituaient un danger pour l'effort de guerre canadien. Grâce à la Loi sur les mesures de guerre et au Règlement sur la défense militaire du Canada, qui conféraient au Cabinet des pouvoirs illimités pour s'ingérer dans la vie des gens durant la guerre, le gouvernement, bien à l'abri des yeux du public, a pris des mesures coercitives contre certains Canadiens d'origine allemande, tant citoyens qu'immigrants reçus, en invoquant l'existence d'un complot nazi au Canada. Toutefois, aucun complot de ce genre n'a été découvert. La police obéissait aux ordres des politiciens qui, eux, réagissaient aux pressions du public, désireux de voir échouer un complot nazi imaginaire et ce, aux dépens des membres de la communauté canadienne d'origine allemande. C'est pourquoi des centaines de ces personnes ont été internées. Néanmoins, comme les preuves à l'appui de ces internements étaient peu convaincantes et qu'on ne pouvait prouver l'existence de sabotage et d'espionnage, la plupart des Canadiens d'origine allemande ont été rapidement libérés. D'ailleurs, dès 1943, même les ressortissants allemands purent s'enrôler dans les Forces armées canadiennes.

Bruno Ramirez, Les Italiens de Montréal et la Deuxième Guerre mondiale

Après que l'Italie eut déclaré la guerre aux Alliés, le 10 juin 1940, les autorités canadiennes ont déclenché une vaste opération d'urgence afin d'exercer une surveillance et un contrôle plus étroits des communautés italiennes se trouvant au Canada. Pour faciliter cette opération, les autorités ont décidé de conférer le statut "d'étrangers ennemis" à tous les Canadiens d'origine italienne qui n'avaient pas encore été naturalisés, ainsi qu'à tous ceux qui avaient été naturalisés après le 1er septembre 1929. Ces mesures d'urgence furent instituées parce qu'on craignait que des gens ou des groupes d'origine italienne, fidèles au régime fasciste, ne posent des actes qui auraient pu mettre en danger la sécurité de l'État canadien. En conséquence, plusieurs centaines de personnes ont été internées dans des camps militaires, et la police a constamment surveillé ces communautés.

Dans son article, l'auteur analyse les répercussions sociales et psychologiques de ces mesures sur la communauté canadienne italienne de Montréal. Pour ce faire, il décrit cette communauté dans le contexte social et culturel de l'entre-deux-guerres, et examine les formes les plus répandues de conscience ethnique qui avaient surgi parmi les Canadiens d'origine italienne de la première et de la deuxième génération. Il insiste particulièrement sur le fait que le sentiment de fierté, dont les Canadiens d'origine italienne faisaient preuve à l'égard des progrès faits par l'Italie et dont le régime fasciste italien faisait état dans ses campagnes de propagande, était plus une manifestation d'auto-identification ethnique que l'expression d'une allégeance politique à un pays étranger. Ce sentiment était très présent dans les associations de la communauté et constituait un des signes les plus visibles d'appartenance ethnique affiché par les Canadiens d'origine italienne. Même les gens et les membres des associations qui se disaient anti-fascistes croyaient en une forme "d'italianité" qui révélait un sentiment d'attachement à leur ancienne patrie aussi fort que celui exprimé par leurs adversaires. En fin de compte, le fait que les autorités canadiennes aient été déterminées à partager les Canadiens d'origine italienne en deux groupes, à savoir ceux qui étaient loyaux et ceux qui ne l'étaient pas, indique que l'État canadien faisait preuve de peu de considération pour les immigrants et qu'il ne comprenait pas du tout la nature du phénomène ethnique mis en branle par l'immigration.

Bohdan S. Kordan et Lubomyr Y. Luciuk, Les Ukraino-Canadiens, la construction de l'esprit national et l'État canadien, 1939-1945

En raison des circonstances particulières et des exigences créées par la guerre, la sécurité intérieure du pays constituait une question d'importance vitale pour les autorités canadiennes. Comme certains très hauts fonctionnaires s'étaient mépris sur la loyauté des Canadiens d'origine ukrainienne, il y eut d'importants débats et de nombreuses consultations pour déterminer si ce groupe ethnique représentait une menace pour l'État et pour trouver les meilleurs moyens de faire face à une telle menace s'il y avait lieu. Pour répondre à une menace perçue, les hauts fonctionnaires de L'État avaient donc décidé de faire surveiller cette communauté organisée et d'en contrôler les affaires en y intervenant. Les auteurs affirment que ces mesures, et les conséquences très fâcheuses qui en ont résulté, auraient pu être évitées si les hauts fonctionnaires canadiens s'étaient montrés sensibles à la tâche d'envergure à laquelle l'État canadien a dû historiquement faire face, à savoir l'édification de la nation. L'expérience vécue par les Canadiens d'origine ukrainienne, et par ceux qui ont appuyé leurs revendications, montre bien que les autorités ne sont pas parvenues à comprendre et à solutionner les problèmes qui ont surgi ni à saisir les occasions d'édifier la nation et d'établir une solidarité et une sécurité entre les groupes ethniques du Canada qui se sont présentés à elles. Les auteurs terminent en affirmant que, paradoxalement, les actions entreprises par ceux qui étaient chargés d'édifier la nation et d'assurer la sécurité de l'État ont peut-être eu l'effet contraire. En fin de compte, on n'est pas parvenu à assurer la sécurité, tant recherchée, et on a aussi perdu la chance de jeter les bases politiques de l'intégration des immigrants à la société canadienne.

J.L. Granatstein et Gregory A. Johnson, L'évacuation des Nippo-Canadiens en 1942: une critique réaliste de la version reçue

Dans leur article, les auteurs tentent de jeter un regard neuf sur les circonstances qui ont entouré l'évacuation des Canadiens d'origine japonaise en 1942. Ils examinent certains des points de la version admise de l'évacuation, points qui, dans certains cas, peuvent être mis en doute et, dans d'autres, ne peuvent l'être. Ils ne sont pas tendres à l'égard des services canadiens du renseignement, du rôle du consulat du Japon, des attitudes des Canadiens d'origine japonaise, avant et après le bombardement de Pearl Harbor (le 7 décembre 1941), et du rôle des militaires durant l'évacuation; de plus, ils se demandent s'il existait vraiment une menace militaire sur la côte Ouest du Canada à ce moment-là.

En se servant de nouvelles et d'anciennes preuves, les auteurs démontrent que la GRC et les services du renseignement militaire n'étaient vraiment pas très au fait de la situation des Canadiens d'origine japonaise à cette époque. Ils soulignent que le consul japonais en poste à Vancouver avait reçu l'ordre, du ministère des Affaires étrangères à Tokyo, d'utiliser un Canadien né d'immigrants japonais pour recueillir des renseignements ou pour espionner. Ils montrent que les Canadiens, plus particulièrement ceux de la Colombie-Britannique, se sont inquiétés lorsque, avait le déclenchement de la guerre du Pacifique, certains Canadiens d'origine japonaise ont donné leur appui à l'invasion de la Chine par le Japon. Ils soulèvent également des questions au sujet des conseils prodigués par les planificateurs militaires d'Ottawa, et ils expliquent que des officers supérieurs des trois éléments des Forces armées en Colombie-Britannique avaient exprimé leurs inquiétudes relativement aux Canadiens d'origine japonaise et à une attaque possible des Forces impériales japonaises. Les auteurs indiquent qu'entre 1942 et 1943 l'Amérique du Nord aurait pu être attaquée; à l'appui de leur thèse, ils précisent que les chefs de l'état-major conjoint, la plus haute autorité militaire chez les alliés, soutenaient ce point de vue. Les auteurs partagent l'avis que les Japonais d'origine canadienne ont été victimes d'une société raciste et d'un gouvernement indifférent qui n'a pas eu le courage de défendre les idéaux qu'il prétendait défendre. Néanmoins, les auteurs croient qu'étant donné les inquiétudes qu'éprouvaient les militaires et les membres des services du renseignement relativement à la tournure soudaine et désastreuse des événements après Pearl Harbor, le gouvernement fédéral avait des raisons suffisantes pour évacuer de la côte les Canadiens d'origine japonaise.

David Fransen, Les Mennonites du Canada devant la Deuxième Guerre mondiale

Les 100 000 Mennonites qui vivaient au Canada en 1939 n'étaient vraiment pas prêts à faire face aux événements au moment de la déclaration de guerre. Étant des pacifistes convaincus, les chefs mennonites étaient absolument persuadés que les jeunes en âge d'aller au combat ne devaient pas prendre les armes; toutefois, ils étaient profondément divisés quant à la participation des membres de leur communauté à l'effort de guerre. Certains croyaient que le service au sein d'une unité non combattante, tel le Corps médical de l'armée, constituait une solution de rechange acceptable et même souhaitable au service militaire. D'autres, au contraire, pensaient qu'il ne fallait avoir aucun contact avec le monde militaire, même dans une unité non combattante. De nombreux efforts pour concilier les divergences d'opinions entre les chefs mennonites échouèrent. Néanmoins, un programme de service de rechange vit le jour, principalement en raison des recommandations émises par les Mennonites. Au départ, ce programme n'était qu'un réseau de camps isolés; il devint toutefois graduellement un système plus complexe qui servait à répondre aux besoins urgents de main-d'oeuvre du pays en fournissant les gens qui possédaient les compétences et l'expérience requises. La diversification du programme ne représentait pas seulement un moyen adopté par le gouvernement pour régler le problème de la pénurie de main-d'oeuvre. Elle illustrait également l'influence que les chefs mennonites exerçaient sur la politique officielle du gouvernement. Dans une certaine mesure, cette influence était due à l'indéniable sincérité des chefs mennonites et au travail acharné accompli par les plus jeunes d'entre eux. Cependant, il y a d'autres raisons importantes, bien que moins positives, qui ont contribué à permettre au gouvernement d'ajouter foi aux actions des Mennonites. Tout d'abord, d'autres groupes de pacifistes moins coopératifs, notamment les Doukhobors et les Témoins de Jéhovah, avaient créé une impression très désagréable à Ottawa. Ensuite, et c'est là une suprême ironie du sort, le fait que plusieurs jeunes Mennonites renièrent leur foi pour s'enrôler dans les forces armées permit aux leaders de cette communauté de voir leur point de vue mieux accepté par les autorités. Comme les Mennonites se sont montrés conciliants avec l'État, notamment en proposant un programme de service de rechange et en s'enrôlant en grand nombre, ils ont produit à Ottawa une impression beaucoup plus favorable que ceux qui se sont montrés inflexibles dans leurs convictions traditionnelles de non ingérence dans les affaires de l'État.

Paula Jean Draper, Loyauté fragmentée: les Juifs canadiens, le gouvernement de King et le dilemme des réfugiés

Lors de la Deuxième Guerre mondiale, les Canadiens d'origine juive se sont retrouvés dans une position précaire face à leur gouvernement. En effet, ils espéraient qu'en faisant appel à la conscience des chefs de leur pays, ils parviendraient à faire modifier la politique étrangère du Canada et à faciliter ainsi l'entrée de leurs frères en Palestine. Ils exhortaient également le gouvernement à changer sa politique en matière d'immigration de façon à ce que le Canada puisse accueillir ceux qui avaient besoin de secours. En accordant la priorité aux questions juives, la communauté juive du Canada prêtait le flanc aux accusations de manque de loyauté à l'égard de son pays d'accueil, une situation dans laquelle elle ne pouvait se permettre de se retrouver si elle désirait parvenir à ses fins. En effet, pour que le public appuie les causes juives, il devait percevoir la communauté juive comme entièrement loyale au Canada et aux politiques du gouvernement en matière de guerre. Lorsqu'en 1940 les Britanniques transférèrent 2 000 réfugiés allemands et autrichiens d'origine juive dans des camps de prisonniers canadiens, la loyauté des juifs du Canada fut mise à rude épreuve. Le gouvernement, aux prises avec cette situation et conscient du fait qu'il existait au sein du monde politique des sentiments anti-immigrants et anti-juifs, a tenté d'attacher à ces réfugiés l'étiquette "ennemi". Toutefois, en 1942, suite aux pressions de Britanniques et de Juifs et à l'intervention du premier ministre, 966 réfugiés ont été libérés; le fait qu'ils constituaient une main-d'oeuvre qualifiée avait également joué en faveur de leur libération. Comme la communauté juive n'avait pas réussi à faire libérer beaucoup de réfugiés, elle resserra les rangs pour faire éventuellement face au gouvernement. En conséquence, elle mit sur pied des stratégies plus efficaces qui ont été utilisées dans les luttes qu'elle a menées après l'Holocauste.

Donald Avery, La réponse canadienne aux réfugiés européens, 1939-1945: le point de vue de la sécurité

Durant la Deuxième Guerre mondiale, le Canada n'avait pas de politique établie en ce qui a trait aux réfugiés. Même si 3 500 réfugiés ont été admis au pays durant cette période, cette pratique ne répondait pas à un grand principe international et n'entrait pas non plus dans le cadre d'un programme national à l'intention des réfugiés, comme on en a établi un après 1945. En effet, ce n'est qu'en surmontant de formidables obstacles et en profitant de circonstances extraordinaires que ces réfugiés en provenance d'Europe étaient parvenus à se glisser entre les mailles du filet de l'immigration. C'est en invoquant la sécurité du pays que le gouvernement canadien parvenait à justifier ses politiques de contrôle serré de l'immigration. Après mai 1940, de nombreuses personnes en Grande-Bretagne, au Canada et aux États-Unis se sont inquiétées du fait que les réfugiés en provenance d'Europe pouvaient constituer une "cinquième colonne" nazie. Au Canada, les chefs de la Gendarmerie royale du Canada et de la Direction de l'immigration croyaient qu'il était préférable, dans l'intérêt national, de refuser tous les réfugiés, plutôt que de permettre à un seul agent nazi ou soviétique d'entrer au pays. Bien que ces politiques aient été immorales et souvent inutiles, même du point de vue de la sécurité, les arguments avancés par les "gardiens de la sécurité" avaient beaucoup de poids au sein du Comité de guerre du cabinet. Le Canada était en guerre et son gouvernement se préoccupait d'objectifs militaires et non de considérations humanitaires. Il ne fait aucun doute que les politiques applicables aux réfugiés, qui furent en vigueur au pays entre 1939 et 1945, étaient "formalistes et froides"; toutefois, pour les comprendre, il faut les replacer dans le contexte de la guerre totale, période qui laissait peu de place aux distinctions subtiles.

Robert Bothwell, Les réfugiés scientifiques et le laboratoire de Montréal

C'est habituellement à la coopération entre le Canada, la Grande-Bretagne et les États-Unis, coopération qui fut symbolisée par la création des laboratoires de Montréal, en 1942 et, plus tard, par la construction, à Chalk River, du premier réacteur (ZEEP) à l'extérieur des États-Unis, qu'on fait remonter les origines du programme nucléaire canadien. Bien qu'il ne fasse aucun doute que cette coopération tripartite constitue une étape importante de l'histoire de l'énergie atomique au pays, il ne faut pas oublier que ce n'est qu'une étape. En effet, le laboratoire de Montréal n'employait pas que des Britanniques, des Canadiens et quelques Américains. C'était, tout comme les laboratoires du même genre situés en Grande-Bretagne et aux États-Unis, un véritable organisme multinational. Dirigé par l'Autrichien Hans von Halban, de 1942 jusqu'au début de 1944, ce laboratoire comptait des réfugiés provenant de la moitié des pays d'Europe. Ces réfugiés n'étaient pas seulement des éléments secondaires qui apportaient des connaissances techniques précieuses, mais bien des gens dont dépendaient le fonctionnement du laboratoire et même la création de celui-ci. Ils ont été presque entièrement responsables des hauts et des bas qu'a connus le laboratoire et des événements qui ont mené à sa fermeture peut-être prématurée.

Contributors

Donald Avery is an associate professor of history at the University of Western Ontario. He is the author of a study of European immigrant workers and labour radicalism in Canada from 1896 to 1932, and a number of articles on Canadian immigration, ethnic and labour history.

Robert Bothwell is professor of history at the University of Toronto. He has recently written two major studies of the atomic energy industry in Canada and is now collaborating with J.L. Granatstein in an examination of Trudeau foreign and defence policies.

Paula J. Draper received her Ph.D. from the University of Toronto in 1983. She is a research fellow at the Multicultural History Society of Ontario, director of the Holocaust Documentation Project of Toronto Jewish Congress, and the author of a monograph on the holocaust.

N.F. Dreisziger has been teaching history at the Royal Military College of Canada since 1970. He is the writer or editor of several books and articles on such diverse subjects as Canadian-American relations, Hungarian diplomatic and political history, and the Hungarian community in Canada.

John English is professor of history at the University of Waterloo and the author of several books on Canadian political history in the twentieth century. A former editor of the *Canadian Historical Review*, he is writing the official biography of L.B. Pearson.

David Fransen, formerly an official historian at the Departments of Finance and Defence, works at the Intelligence Advisory Committee of the Privy Council Office in Ottawa. The subject of his University of Toronto doctoral thesis was the Rowell-Sirois Royal Commission.

J.L. Granatstein, a professor of history at York University since 1966, is the author of books on Canadian political history, Canadian-

American relations, conscription, and the Second World War. He is completing a study of Canadian-Japanese relations.

Norman Hillmer is senior historian at the Department of National Defence, visiting professor of history at Carleton University, and president of the Canadian Committee for the History of the Second World War. His publications centre upon the history of Canadian foreign and defence policies, 1919-1945.

Gregory Johnson, a graduate of the University of British Columbia, is writing a York University doctoral dissertation on the impact of the far east on Canadian-American-British relations from 1937 to 1950.

Robert Keyserlingk worked for many years in the Department of External Affairs before migration to the University of Ottawa, where he is professor of history. He has written a number of works on the Second World War in Canada, the United States, Great Britain and Europe.

Bohdan Kordan teaches politics at Grant MacEwan College in Edmonton, Alberta. With Lubomyr Luciuk, he is finishing an historical atlas dealing with the Ukrainian experience in Canada.

Lubomyr Luciuk is a Canada research fellow and assistant professor in the Department of Geography at Queen's University, Kingston, Ontario. His specialty is the twentieth century Ukraine and Ukrainians in Canada.

Howard Palmer is a professor in the Department of History at the University of Calgary. Former research director of the multiculturalism program, Department of the Secretary of State, and former editor of *Canadian Ethnic Studies*, he is the author of many books and articles on ethnic studies and Alberta's politics.

Bruno Ramirez is a professor of history at the Université de Montréal and a well-published authority on labour and immigration history in North America, the Italians of Montreal in particular.

Harold Troper, professor of history at the Ontario Institute for Studies in Education, has written widely on the history of immigration and inter-group relations in Canada. He recently completed a study with Morton Weinfeld on Ukrainian-Jewish relations in Canada since 1945.

William R. Young, currently a senior research officer at the Library of Parliament, has taught at McGill, Simon Fraser and York Universities. His publications include several about Canadian domestic propaganda during the Second World War.

Index

ASB, *see* Alternative Service Branch

ASW, *see* Alternative Service Work

Abbott, D.C., 17

Abella, Irving, 152, 179

Adachi, Ken, 102, 111

Adachi, Nobuhiro, 111

Adamson, Justice, 143-4

Aeltestenkomitee, 135, 136

Akers, Wallace, 220, 224, 227

Alaska, 108, 118

Aleutian Islands, 108, 118, 119

Alexander, Major-General R.O., 115

Alien Registration Bill, 188

Allan Bill, 197

Allied relations, Canada, 37, 42, 91-7, 114, 153-4, 160-1, 172, 196-200

Alternative Service Branch [ASB], 142, 145

Alternative Service Work [ASW], 140-3

American Magazine, 188

anarchists, Canadian, 183-4

    see also Bortolotti, A.

Anderson, Sir John, 190, 221, 227, 230

Andrew, Christopher, 190

Anglo-Canadians, 5, 32, 33-4, 36, 39, 46, 155, 248, 249

Angus, H F., 3, 109-10

anti-semitism, 41, 46, 151-2, 155, 163-4, 166-7, 170, 180, 181, 182, 192, 193, 200, 204, 224, 226, 238

arrests, 55, 58-9, 73, 74, 80, 111

    see also internment

Association of Canadian Clubs, *see* Canadian Clubs, Association of

Atlantic Charter, 93

Auger, Pierre, 223

Australia—admission of refugees, 181

Austria, 180

Azachs, David, 201-2

Banting, Dr. Frederick, 164

Barrie, W.C, 12

[Le] Bavard, 200

Bayley, Charles, 80

Beech, Commodore W.J.R., 115

Belgium, 7, 185

Ben Gurion, David, 172-3

Bender, Harold S., 133-4

Bermuda Conference, 200

Bevin, Ernest, 4

Blackmore, J.H., 153

Blair, Frederick Charles, 158, 163, 164-8, 169, 170-1, 173, 181, 184-5, 187, 193-4, 195, 201, 204, 237

Bland, Sir Neville, 185

Bondi, Herman, 197

Bortolotti, Attilio [Arthur], 183-5

    see also anarchists, Canadian

Brais, Philippe, 41

Brethren in Christ, 134, 139

Breton, Raymond, 76

British Columbia Provincial Police, 103

British Columbia Security Commission, 105

British Security Coordination, 103, 105, 116

Brockington, L.W., 6

Bronfman, Sam, 170

Bruti-Liberati, Luigi, 80

Buck, Tim, 183

Bund, 3, 34, 57, 58, 59

Bureau of Public Information, *see* Public Information, Bureau of

Burnstein, Sophie, 186

CCCC, *see* National War Services, Department of — Committee on Cooperation in Canadian Citizenship

CHPC, *see* Conference of Historic Peace Churches

CJC, *see* Canadian Jewish Congress

CNCR, *see* Canadian National Committee for Refugees

CPC, *see* Communist Party of Canada

Cabinet Committee on Public Information, 5

Cabinet Sub-Committee on Internment, 156

Cabinet War Committee, 3, 8, 18, 119, 205

Calgary Herald, 154

Cameron, Donald, 43

Camp L, 192

Camp R, 158-9

Campanilismo, 76

Camps, *see also* Camp L; Camp R
    —internment, 155, 157, 158, 162, 167, 170, 181, 191-4, 197
    —labour, 136-7, 139-45

Canadian Broadcasting Corporation, 34

Canadian Clubs, Association of, 6, 11, 15, 16

[The] Canadian Column, 40, 41

Canadian Congress of Labour, 153

Canadian Corps Association, 34

Canadian Dental Corps, 143

Canadian Fellowship Service, 136

Canadian Internment Operations, 191

Canadian Japanese Association, 109

Canadian Jewish Congress [CJC], 41, 155, 158, 159, 161, 163, 166, 168-9, 171, 172, 173, 203

Canadian Jewish Refugee Agency, 191

Canadian Legion, 33, 186

Canadian National Committee on Refugees [CNCR], 161, 163-4, 166, 168-9, 170, 173, 180, 182, 196-7, 200, 203

Canadian National Committee on Refugees and Victims of Persecution, *see* Canadian National Committee on Refugees

Canadian Palestine Committee, 153

Canadian Society for German Culture, *see* Bund

Canadian Unity Council, 43

Canadian Youth Congress, 193

Canadianization, 85-6, 89, 93

"Canadians All" (pamphlet and radio series), 6, 34-5, 36-7, 40

Carpatho-Ukrainian Republic, 87

Casa d'Italia, 74

Cavendish Laboratory, 219

censorship, 33, 44, 92

see also National Revenue, Department of

Central Committee for Interned Refugees, 195

Chadwick, James, 227, 228-9

Chicago Metallurgical Laboratory, 220

China, 108-9

Christie, Loring, 188

Church, Tommy, 195

Churchill, Winston, 185, 190

Citizenship and Immigration, Department of, 21

Claxton, Brooke, 17

Cockcroft, J.D., 229

Cody, H.J., 195

Coffman, Bishop Samuel F., 133-4

Cohen, J.L., 183, 185

Coldwell, M.J., 117, 153

Coleman, E.H., 8, 9, 10, 14, 22, 157, 160, 162

Collège de France, 217, 230

Colton, T.L. (Mr. and Mrs.), 105

Commission of Refugee Camps, 191

Committee of Elders, *see Aeltestenkomitee*

Committee on Cooperation in Canadian Citizenship, *see* National War Services, Department of — Committee on Cooperation in Canadian Citizenship

Committee on Enemy Aliens and Enemy Alien Property, 4, 8

Commonwealth Prime Ministers' Conference, 1944, 153

communism, 37

Communist International, 201

Communist Party of Canada [CPC], 3, 90, 93, 94, 183, 193

communists in Canada, 36-7, 38-9, 58, 60, 94, 183, 191, 192-3

Compton, Arthur, 220, 221

Conference of Historic Peace Churches [CHPC], 134, 136, 141

Conference on the Japanese Problem in British Columbia, 112

conscientious objectors, *see* Jehovah's Witnesses and Mennonites

conscription, 31, 39

Cook, Ramsay, 2

Crerar, Thomas A., 3, 15, 163, 165, 167, 170, 181, 182

Croil, Air Vice Marshal G.M., 117

Custodian of Alien Property, Office of, 93

DAF, *see* German Workers Party

DOCR, *see* Defence of Canada Regulations

Dafoe, J.W., 12

269

D'Amico, Costanzo, 73, 74

Dandurand, Raoul, 187

Daniels, Roger, 238

Davis, Thomas C., 3, 10, 12-14, 15, 17-18, 19, 20, 23, 40, 137

Defence of Canada Regulations [DOCR], 2-4, 53, 55, 58-60, 183

defence policy, 112-6, 118-9

denaturalization, 61

deportation, 102, 121, 157, 158, 172, 182, 183-5, 188

Deutscher Bund, see Bund

Dirks, Gerard, 179, 199

Dom Odo, Father, Duke of Württemberg, 187

Doukhobors, 144-5, 146, 233

Dower, John, 110

Dunton, Davidson, 40

Duplessis, Maurice, 200-1

Embury, J.F.L., 141

England, Robert, 3, 9, 14, 15, 20, 21, 23

espionage, 53-4, 107-8, 120, 189, 202

  see also fifth column

Examination Unit, 105

External Affairs, Department of, 6, 16, 19, 21, 91, 92, 93, 95, 96, 97, 105, 114, 153-4, 163, 165, 171, 181, 185, 187, 189, 196, 199

FBI, *see* Federal Bureau of Investigation

Farnham Camp, 191

fascism, 37, 77

fascists in Canada, 36-7, 58, 60, 78-9, 81, 152, 182-3, 191, 193

Federal Bureau of Investigation [FBI], 182, 201, 202, 205

Ferguson, George, 39

fifth column, 7, 34, 54-5, 60, 104, 106-8, 116, 120, 180, 182, 185, 186, 188-90, 203, 204

Finland, 88

Fleybeck, Anton, 167

Fordham, Colonel R.W.S., 191, 192, 195

Foreign Office, Great Britain, 190, 199

Fortune, 188

France, 60, 185, 186, 199, 218

French Canadians, 5, 11, 31, 34, 39, 40, 46, 77-8, 181, 200, 248, 249

Fuchs, Klaus, 192

gambariya, 111-2

Gardiner, James G., 3, 7-9, 10, 13, 17, 22, 33, 139, 140

Gardiner, Robert, 141

George VI, 56

German Canadians, 7, 8, 34, 36, 42, 53-70, 110, 233, 235

German Labour Front, 3

German Workers Party [DAF], 57, 59

Germany, 31, 87, 90, 180, 185, 189, 199, 247

Gestapo, 189, 199, 201, 202

Gibbon, Murray, 3

Gibson, James, 163, 165, 169

Glazebrook, G.P., 40

Gleason, Philip, 79

Glen, J. Allison, 204

Globe and Mail (Toronto), 39, 53, 166, 182

Goldmann, Nahum, 153

Goldschmidt, Bertrand, 224, 225

Gordon, R.K., 241

Government Code & Cypher School, 107

Great Britain, 155-6, 187, 219

Grierson, John, 21, 42-3, 44, 45

Groves, General Leslie, 224-5, 227, 229

Gueron, Jules, 224

Halban, Hans von, 218-30

Harney, Robert, 241

Harvison, C.V., 54

Hayes, Saul, 158-60, 161, 162, 163, 165, 166, 168, 170, 171, 173, 191

Heeney, Arnold, 3, 5

Hickerson, John, 114

Hitler, Adolf, 36, 55, 60, 132

Hlynka, Anthony, 90-1

Home Office, Great Britain, 164, 191, 194

Hong Kong, 116-7, 236

House Committee on Un-American Activities, United States, 189

Howe, C.D., 167, 169, 173, 221, 222, 225

Hutterites, 146, 233

ICI, *see* Imperial Chemical Industries

Immigration Act, 182

Immigration and Naturalization Service, United States, 188

Immigration Branch, *see* Mines and Resources, Department of — Immigration Branch

Immigration, Department of, 164, 169, 171, 189

Imperial Chemical Industries [ICI], 219, 223, 226, 230

intelligence, 56, 61-2, 81, 103-5, 107-8, 120, 190, 192

    see also MI5; British Security Co-ordination; Royal Canadian Mounted Police; Federal Bureau of Investigation

Interdepartmental Committee on the Treatment of Aliens and Alien Property, 185

Intergovernmental Committee on Refugees, 200

internment, 2, 4, 34, 45, 55, 58-9, 60-3, 71, 72, 73, 74, 75, 80-1, 94, 110, 112, 114, 115, 155-74, 180, 183, 190-8, 204, 235

Isajiw, Wsevolod, 243

Issei, 109, 111, 112

Italian Canadians, 8, 36, 58, 60, 71-84, 109, 110, 233, 235, 237

italianità, 77, 79

Italy, 72, 78, 80

JLC, *see* Jewish Labour Committee

Jackson, Robert, 188

Janz, B.B., 134, 135, 138, 139, 142

Janzen, Jacob H., 134, 138, 139

Japan, 31, 106-9, 117-9, 189-90

Japanese Canadian Citizens' League, 109

Japanese Canadians, 32, 45-6, 58, 101-30, 233, 234-6, 238, 239, 249

Japanese Hawaiians, 111, 112, 116, 235

Japanese in Hong Kong, 116

Japanese in Malaya, 116

Jehovah's Witnesses, 34, 144-5, 146, 233, 238

Jewish Immigrants' Aid Society, 203

Jewish Labor Committee [JLC], 201, 202

Jewish Social Democratic Party, Poland, 201

Jews, Canadian, 109, 151-78, 233, 234, 235, 236, 238, 239

Joint Intelligence Committee, 103

Joint Services Committee, 113, 114, 115, 119

Joliot-Curie, Frédéric, 218, 229

Jolliffe, A.L., 203

Justice, Department of, 59, 93

Kahn, Herbert, 202

Kanadier Mennonites, *see* Mennonites

Kauffman, Eva, 202

Kaye (Kisilevsky), Vladimir J., 11-12, 15, 20, 23

Keenleyside, Hugh, 3, 102, 104, 110, 115

King, W.L. Mackenzie, 3, 5, 17, 31-2, 36, 39, 46, 111, 119, 131, 153, 168-9, 173, 181

Kirkconnell, Watson, 3, 6, 9, 13, 14, 15, 18, 20, 21, 23, 34-5, 37, 38, 43, 44, 233

Kisilevsky, Vladimir J., *see* Kaye, Vladimir J.

Klassen, C.F., 138, 141

Knowles, Stanley, 154

Koch, Eric, 191

Kowarski, Lew, 218-20, 223, 229

Labour, Department of, 142, 170, 171

LaFlèche, Major-General L.R., 40, 44, 45, 137, 138, 139, 140, 144

Lapointe, Ernest, 8, 10

Lash, G.H., 14, 15, 17, 19, 33

Latvia, 201, 248

Laurence, George, 219, 221, 222, 226, 229

Lohich, Rolf, 202

Long, Breckenridge, 188, 204

Lower, A.R.M., 45, 120, 248

MAUD, 219-20, 222

MCRC, *see* Mennonite Central Relief Committee

MI5, 190, 192, 205

MacDonald, Malcolm, 221

MacInnis, Angus, 110

Mackenzie, C.J., 196, 221-2, 224, 225, 226, 227, 228, 229

Mackenzie, Ian, 102

MacNamara, Arthur, 142

MacNeill, J.F., 4-6, 14, 22, 183

Madonna della Difesa, 74

"Magic," 107, 108, 118

Malania, L., 96-7

Manhattan Project, 224, 225

Manuilsky, M., 96

Martin, J.B., 138

Massey, Vincent, 107, 108, 155-6, 157, 158, 181

Mead, Frederick J., 105, 201

Melançon, Claude, 17

Mendel, Dr., 164

Mennonite Central Relief Committee [MCRC], 135, 136, 138, 141

Mennonites, 57, 131-50, 233, 236, 237, 238
　—*Kanadier*, 133-4, 135
　—*Russlaender*, 132-4, 135, 138, 139, 140
　—Swiss, 133-4, 138

Mess, James E., 15

military preparedness, Canada, 1, 117-9

Mines and Resources, Department of, 140, 144, 145
　Immigration Branch, 16, 163-4, 166, 181, 183, 185, 197, 205

Moffat, Pierrepont, 110

Monaco, Vicenzo, 73

Mordat, Professor, 187

Morii, Etsuji, 105

Mowat, Herbert, 153

multiculturalism, Canada, 1, 2, 21-2, 243, 248

Multiculturalism Canada, 2

Munitions and Supply, Department of, 199

Munro, R. Gordon, 221

Mussolini, Benito, 36, 77

NRC, *see* National Research Council

Nakano, Takeo, 111-2, 120, 235

National Association of Japanese Canadians, 102, 239

National Council of Education of Canada, 10

National Defence, Department of, 9, 105, 157

National Film Board, 45

National Research Council [NRC], 105, 196, 221, 222, 226, 228

National Resources Mobilization Act, 7, 136

National Revenue, Department of, 33, 44

national security, 57, 81, 94, 102, 119, 180, 182-3, 185-7, 192-3, 200, 203, 204

National Selective Service, 197

National Socialist Workers' Party, 3

National War Services, Department of, 7, 9, 11, 12, 17, 21, 32, 33, 37, 39, 93, 136

    Committee on Co-operation in Canadian Citizenship [CCCC], 1, 20-2, 37, 38, 39, 40, 43, 237

    Nationalities Branch, 1, 6, 20-2, 23, 37, 39, 40, 43-4, 91, 95, 248

Nationalities Branch, *see* National War Services, Department of

naturalization, 55, 170-1, 182

Naturalization Act, 182

naturalized Canadians, 2-3, 34, 72-3, 102, 111, 186

naziism, 36

nazis in Canada, 34, 53-4, 57, 58, 59, 60-1, 158-9, 182, 191, 193

New Canadian, 109

New Republic, 39

Newell, R.E., 223

Nisei, 105, 106, 107, 108, 109, 111, 120

Norway, 60

Norwegian Whaling Fleet, 198

Oastler, James, 34

Office of the Custodian of Alien Property, *see* [The] Custodian of Alien Property, Office of

Ouchi, Edward, 109

pacifism, 146
   see also Jehovah's Witnesses and Mennonites

Palestine, 153-4, 173

Panet, General E. de B., 157, 160, 191

Paneth, F.A., 223

Paterson, Alexander, 161-3, 167, 168, 172, 173, 191-2, 197

Payne, Chester, 94

Pearson, Lester B., 165, 197-8

Perez, Carlo Randee, 202

Perin, Roberto, 78

Permanent Joint Board on Defence, *see* defence policy

Perrault, René, 39

Petawawa, Camp, 72, 74

Philipps, Tracy, 10-12, 14-16, 17, 18, 19, 20, 21, 23, 38, 39, 40, 42, 43-4, 45, 85-6, 89-90, 93-4, 97, 248

Pickersgill, J.W., 3, 37-8, 104

Pierce, Lorne, 247, 248, 249

Placzek, G., 223

Podoski, Victor, 199

Poland, 87, 248

Polish Canadians, 11, 42

Pontecorvo, Bruno, 224

Pope, General Maurice, 112-3, 115

Port Alice, 113

Portugal, 200

Power, Charles G., 17, 117

press, 3, 32-3, 41, 74, 188, 204

see also *Calgary Herald, Globe and Mail* (Toronto), *Toronto Star, Vancouver Sun, Winnipeg Free Press*

—English language, 35, 36, 37, 42

—French language, 35, 37, 42

—"foreign language," 5, 18, 33, 35, 36, 37, 39, 41-2, 44, 74, 81, 106

Prince Rupert, B.C., 113

prisoners of war, 157, 162-3, 204

propaganda

—Canadian, 5-6, 9, 34, 36-7

see also Public Information, Bureau of

—foreign, 5, 78, 106, 108-9

Provisional War Book, 58

Public Information, Bureau of, 6, 8-9, 13, 17, 18, 20, 32, 33, 34, 36, 38, 40, 234

see also Wartime Information Board

"Purple," 107

Queen Charlotte Islands, 115

RCMP, see Royal Canadian Mounted Police

RCN, *see* Royal Canadian Navy

racism, 34-5, 45-6, 101, 120, 145, 188, 233, 238

Rae, Saul, 40

Ralston, J.L., 113, 195

refugee policy, Canada, 179-81, 199-200

refugees

—Austrian, 180, 185, 204

—Belgian, 198

—Czechoslovakian, 180, 185, 198

—Dutch, 198

—French, 198

278

—German, 180, 185, 192-3, 204

—Jewish, 179-80, 185, 189-90, 191, 194, 198-9, 200-1, 202, 203, 204

—Norwegian, *see* Norwegian Whaling Fleet

—Polish, 180, 185, 198-9, 204

—Portuguese, 198-9

—Spanish, 181, 198-9

Reid, H.G., 14

Reimer, D.P., 135

Research Enterprises Limited, 167

Ritchie, Charles, 156

Rive, A., 158

Rivett-Carnac, Charles, 56

Robertson, Norman, 3, 4, 8, 10, 12, 13-14, 15, 19, 20, 22, 40, 44, 58, 59, 78, 86, 90, 92, 95, 110, 154, 165, 166, 167, 182, 183, 184, 197-8, 202-3, 236

Roebuck, Arthur, 153

Roosevelt, President Franklin D., 119

Rosenberg, Alfons, 165

Rosenberg, Louis, 158-9

Rossow, Robert, Jr., 117

Roth, William, 186

Royal Canadian Air Force, 103

Royal Canadian Army Medical Corps, 142

Royal Canadian Mounted Police [RCMP], 4, 16, 33, 37-8, 53-5, 56-9, 60-1, 72, 73, 74-5, 87, 90, 93, 102, 103, 104, 106, 108, 112, 120, 171, 182, 183, 185, 186, 187, 192, 197, 201-2, 203, 205, 235, 239

Royal Canadian Navy [RCN], 103, 108, 112, 113-4

Russia, *see* Soviet Union

St. Laurent, Louis, 202

sabotage, 53-4, 108, 116, 186, 188, 205

see also fifth column

Sarna, Jonathan, 243

Schild, Alfred, 196

Schultz, Bishop David, 135

Seaborg, Glenn, 224

Secretary of State, Department of, 21

security measures, *see* national security

Shanghai, 189

Simpson, George, 3, 18, 19, 20, 21, 40

Skelton, O.D., 3, 9-10, 12, 14, 15, 19, 87, 97, 156, 184, 186-7

Smith Act, *see* Alien Registration Bill

Sommerfelder, 132

Soviet Union, 42, 87, 88, 91, 92-3, 189-90, 248

Spain, 181-2, 200

Special Committee on Measures to be Taken in the Event of War With Japan, 113

State, Department of, 171

State Department, United States — Visa Division, 197-8, 204

Steinhardt, Laurence, 189

Stephan, John J., 111, 112, 120

Stethem, Colonel H., 191, 193

Stevenson, Air Commodore L.F., 115

subversive activities, *see* fifth column

Sunahara, Ann Gomer, 102, 111

Swalm, Ernie, 139

Sweden, 200

Swiss Mennonites, *see* Mennonites

Switzerland, 200

Synge, J.L., 196

Thorson, J.T., 3, 17-19, 20, 22

Toews, Bishop David, 132, 135-6, 138, 139, 144

Toronto Board of Trade, 153

Toronto Star, 184

Trades and Labour Congress, 153

Troper, Harold, 152, 179

"Tube Alloys", 220, 221

Turnbull, Walter J., 4, 5, 38

UCC, *see* Ukrainian Canadian Committee

ULFTA, *see* Ukrainian Labour Farmer Temple Association

UN Special Committee on Palestine, 154

UZC, *see* United Zionist Council

Ucluelet, B.C., 113

Ukrainian Canadian Committee [UCC], 12, 88-9, 92, 95

Ukrainian Canadians, 11-12, 14, 18, 38, 42, 85-100

Ukrainian Labour Farmer Temple Association [ULFTA], 93

Ukrainian National Federation, 88

Ukrainian Press Bureau, 11

Union Nationale party, 200-1

United Kingdom Security Organization, 203

United States, 9, 160, 179-80, 187-9, 196, 220, 238, 243, 244, 248

United Zionist Council [UZC], 153-4

Université de Montréal, 223

Ushijima, Hidehiko, 111

Vancouver Sun, 116

Vangelisti, Father, 74-5

vigilantism, 7, 34, 186

Vining, Charles, 39, 41, 42

WIB, *see* Wartime Information Board

Wallace, F.C., Colonel, 196

War Measures Act, 2, 53

War Refugee Board, United States, 198

Warren, Avra M., 189

Wartime Information Board [WIB], 6, 38-9, 41, 42-3, 44-6
  see also Public Information, Bureau of

Wartime Prices and Trade Board, 39

Westman, L.E., 142, 144, 146

Wilgress, Dana, 92-3

Wilmott, H.P., 118

Wilson, Cairine, 153, 161, 162, 163, 169, 170, 173, 197

Winkler Conference, 132-4

Winnipeg Free Press, 12, 39, 44, 200

Wood, S.T., 14, 16, 18, 19, 87, 90, 105, 202, 203, 204

Woodsworth, Kenneth, 193

Wrong, Hume, 93, 189

Wyman, David, 179-80, 189

xenophobia, 7, 32, 33, 45-6, 185-6, 200, 204
  see also vigilantism

ZEEP, 217

Zborowski, Mark, 244-5

Zionism, 153, 154, 173